*Katharine
Hepburn*

Also by Michael Freedland

Al Jolson
Irving Berlin
James Cagney
Fred Astaire
Jerome Kern
Sophie – The Story of Sophie Tucker
Errol Flynn (In the United States, *The Two*
Lives of Errol Flynn)
Gregory Peck
Maurice Chevalier
Peter O'Toole
The Warner Brothers

And with Morecambe and Wise
There's No Answer to That

Katharine Hepburn

Michael Freedland

W.H. ALLEN · LONDON

1984

Copyright © 1984 by Michael Freedland

Phototypeset by Phoenix Typesetting
Printed and bound in Great Britain by
Mackays of Chatham Ltd, Kent
for the Publishers W.H. Allen & Co. Ltd,
44 Hill Street, London W1X 8LB

Reprinted July 1984, September 1984

ISBN 0 491 03421 0 (W.H. Allen hardcover edition)

FOR DANI

Her Declaration of
Independence – and my
love

Acknowledgements

Katharine Hepburn is in anyone's eyes an outstanding personality. Not everyone unreservedly admires her, but no one will deny the excitement she has brought to the screen and to the very small percentage of the world's population who have been privileged to see her on stage. She is a name that will ring out in theatre history long after the notion of seeing a *new* Hepburn film will no longer be in living memory.

Katharine Hepburn is a complex personality. For that reason, the number of people who have co-operated with me in producing this book is a matter that gives me great satisfaction and invites my deep appreciation. Not all of them necessarily wanted that co-operation to be in the public awareness. For that reason, to them my thanks are summed up simply in this sentence. To others, I am happy to couple their names with my profound gratitude. They include:

Eve Arden, Pandro S. Berman, Betsy Blair, Frank Capra, Cyd Charisse, Joseph Cotten, the late George Cukor, Douglas Fairbanks Jnr, Nina Foch, Bill Fraser, Samuel Goldwyn Jnr, Neil Hartley, Patricia Hayes, Paul Henreid, Jack Hildyard, Wilfrid Hyde White, David Kossoff, Leigh Lawson, Fred MacMurray, Rouben Mamoulian, Lord Olivier, Gregory Peck, Richard Quine, Mark Rydell, Ginette Spanier, Nigel Stock, Milton Sperling, Dean Stockwell, Ralph Thomas, Toyah Willcox, Hal B. Wallis, Jack Warner Jnr, Billy Wilder and Loretta Young.

Others helped in numerous ways. Particular thanks go, therefore, to Martin Pedrick, Carol Epstein, the other librarians of the Academy of Motion Picture Arts and Sciences in Beverly Hills and those of the British Film Institute and the British Library. Also I must thank my daughter Fiona for her help in researching this book and my son Jonathan for preparing the index. Special thanks, too, to my editor Amanda Girling with whom this is for me a pleasant reunion.

Above all my greatest thanks to my wife Sara without whom, there would be nothing.

Michael Freedland
London, 1983

[vi]

Morning Glory

*P*RESIDENT WOODROW WILSON, architect of the League of Nations, hope of American peace lovers and disappointment of so many others, was perhaps one of the first people to see a performance by Katharine Houghton Hepburn. As he glanced out of a window at the White House, horses were bridling while their owners and drivers pulled heavily on the reins. The few noisy, smelly automobiles that were choking their way along Pennsylvania Avenue were braking jerkily.

A crowd of women gathering there was causing havoc in the street where the destiny of America was being decided every hour of the working day. 'Votes for women,' they cried, and in their midst a four-year-old red-headed girl, spindly and tall for her age, was handing out pamphlets to every passer-by she could find as she peeked out from the mass of ground-sweeping skirts that engulfed her.

It was 1913 and little Kate was enjoying the experience immensely. If Katharine senior, known to her intimates as Kit, had time to notice her daughter's enjoyment she would have been gratified indeed: she could have asked no more of any daughter. Mrs Hepburn, a New England Houghton whose cousin had once been Ambassador to the Court of St James's, had strong beliefs and enormous self-confidence.

Women had rights to their own minds and their own bodies. That was why she so keenly divided her time between organising suffragette meetings and birth-control campaigns. Both ideas had elements of paradox about them. Unlike many other feminists of her day – or any other time for that matter –

her attitude did not imply a sense of superiority of the female sex, a despising of men. She was not only happily married – her husband was a man of immense physical and moral strength – but she had also been happy to give him six children.

Thomas Norval Hepburn was viewed by those who knew him – and even by those who resented it – as an aristocrat. You could tell that from his tall, lean authoritative bearing, and from his accent. Even when young, there was an air of the patrician about him, a vocal twang that told you he was a Southerner from Virginia. Legend has it that he was of Scottish aristocratic descent – and that the lover of Mary Queen of Scots, the Earl of Bothwell who was a Hepburn, was a direct ancestor.

Possibly to the disappointment of some of his family who may have believed their position in life decreed that theirs was not to toil, he studied medicine at the famous Johns Hopkins Hospital and proved to be brilliant. While still young he was appointed to the staff of the hospital at Hartford, Connecticut – where he met the beautiful Kit Houghton.

It was not difficult to see why they went together so well: they were the handsome couple personified, he with his wide shoulders, chiselled face and striking red hair; she with her soft face and superb figure. Both had immensely strong wills, neither had any respect for what in the milieus in which they were raised would have been considered convention.

Dr Hepburn was a urologist, involved in a form of medicine polite people did not talk about at their dinner parties. When they did, they referred to it in smirking asides behind cupped hands or fans. Doubtless some found it difficult to suppress blushes born out of personal experience and perhaps unpublicised gratitude. For Dr Hepburn was a specialist in venereal disease.

Two events in his life had persuaded him to take this course. The first was simply seeing a play, a strange influence for such a sophisticated man of the world. It was Brieux's *Damaged Goods*, itself a crusade to find a cure for syphilis. The other influence was more direct. A beautiful young woman patient

[2]

came to see him with the tell-tale sores and discharges around her sexual organs. She was seriously ill with fever. Between fits of delirium she revealed that the man she had very recently married had been to bed with a prostitute. The girl had had syphilis and infected the customer who had now transmitted the disease to his bride. He was so moved by this story that he decided on his speciality. It did not please the people of Hartford, especially when with Dr Charles Eliot he founded the American Social Hygiene Association.

Kit was even less favourably accepted in Hartford society. Not only was she a keen suffragette and advocate of birth control, but she was a member of the Peace Party, which made her in local eyes a socialist. That was, of course, what both Hepburns were – if only because their idol was George Bernard Shaw and whatever he wrote seemed to have some relevance for the world in which they lived.

It was, the people in what served as the local social register decided, a strange way for a girl of her breeding to behave – almost a betrayal; certainly a throwback to some dark period in her past, perhaps to the time when she was orphaned as a thirteen year old. Kit and her younger sisters were given a home by their uncle Amory Houghton, the one whose son Alanson would before long head the Grosvenor Square embassy and in turn the one in Berlin, too.

Kit didn't much like the idea of living with family. 'We love uncle very much,' she told her sisters. 'But there's no point in letting him alter the course of our lives.' She decided to make him change his mind about their upbringing by making a tremendous noise around the house. Uncle got the hint and Kit was sent off to boarding school and then to Bryn Mawr, the exclusive ladies college in Philadelphia.

But Katharine Hepburn would later admit that the family even at that early time had its share of 'nuts' – like her paternal grandfather. 'He never even owned a toothbrush. He'd say he didn't want to become dependent on anything. So he cleaned his teeth with the same washcloth and soap he used for the rest of his toilet.' That could explain his granddaughter's fetish, as an adult, with bathing. In recent

[3]

years she has been known to take an average of five baths a day.

The Hepburn children came along rapidly. First Tom, then Katharine, followed by Dick, Bob, Marion and Peggy. (In adult years, Kate was to destroy her birth certificate. For documents that required a date of birth to be revealed, she used her father's day and month. She said that it was no one's business. However, she never made any secret of the year – 1909.)

Thomas and Kit had children because both decided they wanted them. If Kit ever felt she had to justify the frequent use of her reproductive process to the women she was trying to persuade to subdue theirs, she would say that she was both strong and wealthy enough to enjoy having babies. There was someone at home to look after them all when she went on her crusades. Sometimes, of course, she took them with her – like the time when she introduced her second child, little Kate (as Katharine inevitably and forever after became), to the White House. And not just Kate. Kit was in an advanced state of pregnancy at the time. It saved her being arrested – and, much to young Kate's disgust, prevented her having a badge to wear that showed prison bars with the legend 'Votes for Women' printed all over it.

Kit's son, Richard, was born soon afterwards.

Once a baby was six months old she would take it with her on her demonstrations, leaving the child in an anteroom with a nurse when convenient to do so, while she carried out the important tasks of preparing leaflets, addressing envelopes or speaking to enthusiastic crowds of militant women or to State legislators who were rapidly growing less tolerant of her demands.

The Hepburns' first child Tom was very much the apple of their eyes. Tall and strong like his father, he became Kate's idol: what he did, she wanted to do. She wasn't interested in playing with dolls or the other feminine things little girls were supposed to enjoy. She persuaded her mother to allow her to wear boys' clothes when she played and had her hair cut so short it looked as though her head had been shaved. She even wanted people to call her Jimmy.

[4]

But the pretence didn't convince everyone. Once when a woman happened to mention that she seemed, for all her bravado, a fragile child, Kate rounded on her. 'Who's stronger, me or that tree?' And then attempted to demonstrate the fact by charging directly at the nearby trunk with her head, like a bull going for the matador. She survived, slightly dazed, bruised and considerably blooded but proud that she had proved that she was at least the tree's equal.

Tom, who had taken it upon himself to be his sister's guardian in such matters, was more than slightly impressed.

'Who's that goofy girl?' a boy asked him on one occasion. His response was a sharp right hook to the jaw of the unfortunate boy, who crashed to the floor, Kate's honour remaining intact.

The Hepburns were, as a family, very conscious of the way they believed life had to be lived. When there were subjects that children wanted to talk about – and of course there always were – then talk about them they did. No nonsense in their household about storks bringing babies from behind gooseberry bushes. The Hepburn kids were told in plain terms about sexual intercourse. When the doctor discussed the intimate details of his work – although naturally never mentioning names or even hinting as to identity – the children were not told to leave the room.

Kate's own independent outlook – and the way she expresses it – can be traced directly back to that time. As an actress she would say: 'I like to know, if I can, more than anyone else about what's going to happen because I was trained by my parents that if a silence occurs, then speak up and everyone will accept what you say, because no one else is speaking.' There are a score of directors and other actors for whom that will sound familiar.

'I had the most marvellous childhood,' Kate has said in old age.

Her father was the one to whom Kate looked for solace, understanding and leadership. For all his wife's suffragette activity, he was the head of the home, no one disputed that. Not that he disapproved of his wife. When Kit wanted to bring the British women's-rights leader Mrs Emmeline Pankhurst to

America, he wholeheartedly agreed that she should stay at the Hartford house.

At first, however, Kit *had* worried about joining the movement. 'I'm afraid it might handicap you,' she told Thomas, bravely deciding that the best form of attack on this issue was the defence of meeting the opposition head on at the first opportunity.

Her husband looked her in the eye and said: 'No "might" about it. It would be a definite handicap. But go ahead. Life isn't worth while unless you do things you believe in. If I haven't enough brains to succeed in spite of it, why, I'll take the penalty.'

He was a man to whom the family went naturally for advice. He not only had a wealth of medical knowledge at his command, but was a dab hand at manipulating the New York stock exchange. As far as his children were concerned, however, there were more important things that had to be learned.

Kate, for instance, thought she was cursed by her freckles and red hair. Her father said that the only thing she had to worry about was exposing herself too much to the blazing sun at their Connecticut summer home at Fenwick. It was advice she would one day rue for not taking to heart, but as a young child she would never be allowed to expose her shoulders when she went swimming. Instead, every time she entered the water she had to be sure to wear a blouse under her bathing costume.

Other children were subjected to similar strictures, usually for modesty's sake. That wasn't a concern of the Hepburns. The parents would talk about nudism, not because they wanted to practise it themselves, but because it existed and therefore had to be discussed. Years later, Kate would say: 'I remember listening and thinking to myself: "Some day, nobody's going to wear any clothes." The only thing that bothered me was I would be totally freckled from head to foot and nobody would want me.'

Thomas knew about his daughter's worries on this score. 'I want to tell you something, Kate, and you must never forget

[6]

it,' he said. 'Jesus Christ, Alexander the Great and Leonardo da Vinci all had red hair and freckles and they all did all right.'

In spite of this indulgence, her early life was not totally idyllic. 'I had a spanking upbringing,' Kate recalled. She was spanked regularly until she was nine years old and when she wasn't spanked, she was made to have cold baths – a habit she continued for the rest of her life and when no obvious punishment was called for. 'The baths were responsible for my later perversity,' she said. 'They gave me the impression that the more bitter the medicine, the better it was for you. That may be the reason I came to think that the more insulting the press was, the more it stimulated me.'

The children were not allowed to have the run of the house as though they had it under their own personal control, a young person's fiefdom. The doctor was once so annoyed by how they had taken everything over, that he called all six of them into his study to proclaim: 'I'm thoroughly tired of having my bottom drawer used as a warehouse. Just because you can reach it, is no reason why I should find everything from knives to turtles among my clothes.'

His children – and particularly Kate – gave him plenty of cause for more serious aggravation from time to time. When she was five years old Kate got lost, and solved the problem in a manner that later generations would find not at all out of character.

She had been out shopping with her mother when they were separated. Kate wasn't unduly concerned. She knew that grownups found their way home whenever they needed to, so there could be no great mystery involved. She simply went up to a woman getting into one of the open cars that were gradually making their presence felt on American streets, gave her address and requested to be taken home.

The woman asked no more than the standard rudimentary questions and agreed to the child's plea, marvelling, no doubt, at her quiet confidence. When the car drew near the Hepburn residence, Kate told her politely but firmly: 'You needn't go any further. You wouldn't understand. Everyone at the house speaks French.' In fact, only the cook Fanny Ciarrier spoke French regularly.

'It's all right, Fanny,' Kate told her when she had rung the bell and been admitted to the house. 'A lady brought me home. I'll put myself to bed.'

The cook took no notice. And at first nor did anyone else – until the phone calls started to come. First Kit rang, then Thomas – with neither wanting to tell the other that he or she was worried about the child's non-appearance, or even bothering to tell the cook why they were each ringing. The doctor wanted to talk to his wife, Mrs Hepburn to her husband. Finally, after about half a dozen calls, the doctor rang again and at last asked the cook if his wife had called and if she had, was there any message about when she would return?

'No,' said the cook. 'There's nobody here but Tom, me and Kate.'

'Kate . . .?'

'Yes. She's been here fast asleep for more than an hour.'

When Katharine Hepburn needed solutions to problems, she simply went out to find them. And was usually allowed to take the consequences. There was the morning, for instance, when a policeman called at the door. 'Your little girl is at the top of that tall tree,' he told the doctor. 'I can see her red hair sticking out above the green.'

'For heaven's sake,' said Thomas, 'don't call her. You might make her fall.'

The policeman went away, lifting his helmet so that he could scratch his head. Dr Thomas Hepburn went back to his paper.

The wonder of a perfect childhood in which nothing ever seemed to go seriously wrong was violently exploded the Easter when Kate was ten years old. She and Tom had gone for the holiday to stay with friends in New York. On Saturday night there had been a party at which the sixteen-year-old Tom had tried hard not to allow people to tell him how handsome he was growing and had got a little nauseous from eating too much cake.

On Easter Sunday, Kate looked for her brother so that they could play together. She couldn't find him in his bedroom – or anywhere else in the strange house, for that matter. Eventually, she found her way to the attic. What happened next was like a scene from a horror movie. There was a long shadow on the floor and, suspended from one of the beams in the roof, Tom's body – swinging. He had hanged himself.

Shocked, but seemingly in full control of herself, the ten-year-old child vainly tried to find someone else in the house. But she knew that a doctor lived nearby. She calmly walked to his house and knocked on the door. A maid answered. 'Would you get help please?' she asked. 'My brother's dead.'

'If he's dead,' said the maid, 'nobody can help him,' – and she shut the door in Kate's face.

When the doctor did eventually come, he estimated that the boy had been dead since three o'clock that morning. It was never to be established whether Tom had actually committed suicide or had simply been playing a game that had gone terribly wrong. The incident was to be used for years afterwards as an example to children not to mess with ropes around their necks.

Was it the play they had seen just a few days earlier? In Mark Twain's *A Connecticut Yankee at King Arthur's Court*, which had impressed Kate and Tom so much, they had seen a man contract his neck muscles so much that he avoided death when he was hanged. Or was it the similar story their father had told him a little time before that, about a black man living near his home who had avoided a lynching by using just that same technique? Could Tom have been testing the theory for himself in the early hours of the morning when there was no one around to disturb him? It was possible, perhaps even probable, because nobody imagined Tom had any problems other than those of teasing girls and elders. But they couldn't be sure either, and that uncertainty was perhaps the hardest pain of all.

Without Tom at her side, Kate retreated into a shell which only her apparent over-confidence could crack. It was, of course, a defence mechanism. She became at times painfully shy.

Her father used to joke: 'All my children are shy. They're afraid to go to parties for fear they'll be neither the bride nor the corpse,' by which he meant that Kate was frightened nobody was going to ask her to dance. She also interpreted it as meaning that she was afraid nobody was 'going to think I was wonderful – and I was never willing to watch any other girl being wonderful'.

Always wanting to analyse the things she had either said about herself or others had said about her, she thought the matter over, years later. She said: 'So shyness is really a form of egomania, isn't it? The fear you aren't going to be the bride or the corpse. Actors are all egocentrics. They aren't shy. They're self-conscious in the strict sense. They always see themselves in a situation. I'm very aware at the moment I come in the door, sit down and sort of ask: "How am I doing Joe?" And then, after I got seated, I have to get out of there, too.'

But she didn't appear to be shy when it came to proving herself in competition with other children of her own age. She used to swing from trapezes and do other kinds of acrobatics. At the Oxford School in Hartford, she was a champion swimmer and shone at figure skating. As she would often say, if there was a race the only place she wanted was first. And for all the anxiety of her mother to involve the whole Hepburn family in what she did, Kate believed that the way she behaved at school would be a forerunner of everything that followed.

Everything that was good seemed to happen at home at Hartford or in the summer house at Fenwick. The finest compliment the Hepburns could pay a departing guest was to say 'It's been fun having you.' For fun, she believed, was what life was all about. Fun and equality.

'I really was not brought up to feel that women were underdogs. I was totally unaware that we were the second-rate sex.'

She demonstrated that determination, in spite of her shyness, on the stage, too – without anyone realising that they were in at the pre-dawn chorus of a great actress's career. Kate, her brothers and a friend named Robinson Smith, who was to grow up to become a theatrical producer, established their own summer stock company in the family dining room at Fenwick. They used all the props they could get – the Hepburn furniture,

Kit's powder and lipstick, old teachests . . . And it was not all simply for the glory of appearing on stage.

The talk of the neighbourhood was the lecture given a short time before by Bishop Howden of New Mexico. The cleric had told a terrible story about the condition of the Navajo Indians. The Hepburn Repertory Company decided to put on a play in their aid – charging 50 cents a seat, which a number of the mothers round about thought was much too expensive. When Kate heard their objections she called a meeting of her company and, as a result, the mothers and their children were told to take their half-dollars elsewhere. That too would strike chords in people's minds years later.

The play was *Beauty and the Beast,* in which the thirteen-year-old Kate wore a blue velvet Lord Fauntleroy suit with silver stripes. She completed the ensemble with a donkey's head that looked as if it might have last been used in a production of *A Midsummer Night's Dream.* The performance raised 60 dollars for the Navajo children – who bought a gramophone with the proceeds. Kate also wore a dyed beard for a production of *Bluebeard* – Mr Smith played the leading lady.

There was little cause for discord in the Hepburn house. The only rows were political ones – with the doctor taking a more radical stand than his wife in support of the Soviet revolution or debating just how far either of them was prepared to go in accepting some of Bernard Shaw's more outlandish theories.

The Hepburns' socialism didn't prevent their maintaining family tradition. When she was sixteen years old, Kate followed her mother's example and took her place behind a desk at Bryn Mawr. Her fellow students at the Philadelphia college were not quite sure how to take the haughty-looking redhead when she made her first appearance at the dining table.

She was determined to look her best and wore a sweater that she thought showed herself off to perfect advantage – until one of the girls, in a studied remark which she thought terribly clever at the time and probably immediately forgot (but which Kate never has), said: 'Ah, self-conscious beauty!' It could have been meant as a compliment. To the young terribly unsure

[11]

Katharine Hepburn it was an experience as deflating as a let-down car tyre. She ran from the room in tears.

Women who are now great-grandmothers remember Katharine Hepburn as hardly being a fashion trendsetter. In fact, her favourite item of dress appeared to be an old green coat fastened with a large safety pin – it was a coat she would wear a few years later in the film *Morning Glory*.

Bryn Mawr wasn't a total success for Kate. She learned to play golf brilliantly – and to study rather less successfully. She played tennis to the admiration of almost everyone who saw her. But the college did teach her one thing. There were the stirrings in her mind that she wanted to be an actress.

Her father had hoped that she might want to be a doctor, which would have also satisfied her mother and her suffragette friends. But after Kate had taken part in one college play she wanted to do another. When she heard that to qualify for the drama section she needed to get a certain number of high grades in her academic studies, she pressed ahead with doing just that. As a result, she improved immensely. In history, she studied under Dr Howard Levi Gray and gained a 'high merit' grading of about 78 per cent. But theatricals were more the activities she prized.

In this she was helped by a leading Shakespearean scholar of the day, Dr Horace Furness Jnr. He was the one who selected her to take part in the college's May Day celebrations. She was given the lead in the play *The Woman in the Moon*, and later in *The Cradle Song* and *The Truth about Blayds*.

The Woman in the Moon was significant: dressed in the free robes of a woman of ancient Greece, she played Pandora. She used the costume again in the May Day procession and adamantly insisted that she wasn't going to wear sandals. 'Pandora was barefoot,' was all she said and walked on the gravel without anything on her feet.

Not all her contemporaries were willing to admit she had any noticeable talent. One said to her: 'You're a freak of nature. You'll never last.' But others thought differently. A decade later, a Bryn Mawr teacher, Mrs Hortense Flexner King, was to write: 'We could still see the girl with the tight bun of reddish hair, screwed up on the top of her head, scurrying into the library with an armful of books. (Miss Hepburn playing Miss Hepburn, under the direction of Dr Gray, was the title of that drama.) Or we could see her on that one occasion when she gave a hint of things to come dressed in the Greek costume of *The Woman in the Moon.'*

The theory that she 'would never last' was, however, reinforced every time she had to try out for team games. She so hated the idea of competing with others of her age for places in college teams her only aim was to show how awful she was in them all. It was plain that the only thing she really wanted to do was to go on the stage.

2

Stage Door

DR HEPBURN RELUCTANTLY accepted his daughter's decision and gave her fifty dollars which he said was a once-and-for-all stake. If she didn't make it as an actress by the time the fifty had been spent, she would have to change her mind or, at least, go it alone.

Her first step was a trip to Baltimore, where Edwin Knopf had his own production company. It was a secret visit. Kate feared the reaction of a self-righteous father if the success she so desperately wanted didn't materialise. She had previously tried to phone Knopf but he wasn't interested in talking to her – or allowing anyone else in his organisation to do so either. So she decided to storm his office in person, and once there refused to leave until he offered her a part, no matter how small.

It was a formidable picture that Kate presented that day to Mr Knopf. Her hair was unkempt. Her nose was shiny and she wore a sloppy sweater and a pair of blue jeans. Knopf looked straight at her as she demanded that she be given a chance. It was a daunting prospect and one that Mr Knopf wasn't sure he was strong enough to resist, although he did tell her that her voice was too high and shrill.

Her first role was in *The Czarina*. Another small part in *The Cradle Snatchers* followed. It was a comparatively small company, but it did attract the occasional 'guest' performer such as the celebrated New York actor of the day Kenneth McKenna who took to Kate and suggested that she would benefit by taking elocution lessons. She accepted the advice: her teacher was Frances Robinson-Duff in New York, who must partly take the blame for one of the most famous voices in the world.

It was 1928. Before the year was out, Katharine Hepburn was in New York, all ready to play a secretary in Knopf's production of *The Big Pond*. There was to be a week of rehearsals before the opening at Great Neck. At the end of that week a huge row broke out between the producer and his leading lady whom he peremptorily fired and he offered the job to Kate.

As she was to tell writer Charles Higham, she was always very good at reading parts until it came to actually performing them. The night of her opening performance she came to the theatre late – after vanishing to a nearby railway station where she ate a great many blueberries. When she got back to the theatre she decided that her lace panties were too irritating to wear so she cast them off before going on stage. The rest was not a happy experience. She forgot her lines, her cues and the things she was supposed to do in the part – which she lost the next day.

She would continue to get fired – mainly because she was terrified in front of an audience. Her face would grow red and she would lose her voice. It happened in *Death Takes a Holiday*. She was ready to star in the play in 1928. Out-of-town bookings were arranged. There were plans to take the play to Broadway – except that she was sacked before it could reach New York. Eventually, the part went to a young lady who would before long do fairly well for herself in Hollywood. Her name was Claudette Colbert.

Kate was due to play opposite Leslie Howard in *The Woman in his House*. Again, she was fired just before opening night. One veteran actress who was with Kate at one of these early attempts at stardom insists she heard her tell the director: 'I can't play it that way – because I don't feel it that way.' What she was now beginning to feel was that she was never going to make it on the stage. That being so, she was going to break with all that she had previously promised herself – and get married.

Not long before, sculptor Robert McKnight had taken her out

to the country for an afternoon with the intention of popping the question. But, he confessed long afterwards, she spent the whole time talking – about love, life, art and Katharine Hepburn. He didn't have the chance to make his proposal – or decided after that barrage that he had changed his mind. But now she was determined to say 'yes' to someone.

It was an impulsive gesture, one that came before any serious thought as to the consequences of the act – and certainly before she had a specific man in mind. There had always been men in her set and many of them suggested marriage. When a wealthy insurance agent named Ludlow Ogden Smith proposed, she accepted – as much to his surprise as hers. They had met at a dance during her junior years at Bryn Mawr. They married at the Hepburn family home in Hartford without any of his social register friends knowing about it.

It was a stupid act for which she was practically immediately sorry. She felt she wasn't ready for domesticity and hated every aspect of being a wife – her mother told her she probably would. She also hated the name Smith – as a result of which he agreed to change it to Ogden Ludlow. Kate called him 'Luddy'. The marriage lasted all of three weeks. But the separation was kept as secret as the wedding ceremony. She and 'Luddy' remained platonic friends, and it was a long time before the arrangement was officially declared as dead as it always had been.

For a time Kate returned to her family in Hartford. She still adored her parents, and her father in particular for whose broad shoulders she now had a specific use. Before long, however, she decided that what she had to do was to get back to work. So she returned to Frances Robinson-Duff for help. Her teacher was sympathetic. She arranged for her to do summer stock with the Berkshire Playhouse in Stockbridge, Massachusetts – where once more her own sense of what was right led to further problems. The company stayed at the home of a clergyman, his wife and two daughters. When the conversation at dinner turned to the work of a certain now-forgotten poet, Kate bought the man's work just to argue the point that he was a lousy writer. Over a long succession of meals, she pressed on with her argument while most of the others shouted or yawned in their soup.

Kate was pretty good at getting bored herself. In *The Hound of Heaven*, she was required to call the name of one of the play's characters from the wings. She found that terribly tiresome. So instead of the name she was supposed to shout, she called out that of her best friend, Laura Harding. The director hated her for it. He warned that if she did that too often, she might do it on opening night. 'Miss Hepburn,' he demanded. 'You just can't do that.'

'No,' she replied. 'Who's going to stop me?'

For the run of three plays, no one did – except that she continually protested that she was being given mediocre parts in which she herself was strictly mediocre too. She needed to do better things.

Kate thought there might be some hope when the offer came to understudy Hope Williams in Philip Barry's play *Holiday*, a piece that was to have considerable impact on her career a few years later on, but after six months she hadn't gone on stage for a single performance.

Hers was the typical young actress's story, haunting the offices of every management and agency who would let her through their front doors and into a seat in their waiting rooms. Later she would recall: 'By the time I had visited one or two offices, my face would be moist with perspiration, my hair disarranged and my clothes in disarray. But I was too bashful to ask anyone where the ladies' room was.'

She decided that the answer to her problems was the prestigious Theatre Guild. Founded in New York in 1918 to present high-quality dramatic productions, it was a theatrical society in which its managers were the arbiters of policy and were not excessively concerned with the necessity of making money above everything else (although for years they acted as George Bernard Shaw's American theatrical agents).

It was to them that the young Katharine Hepburn came seeking work. The Guild was presenting Turgenev's *A Month in the Country*. What she did not know at the time was that she very nearly got the second lead, a young girl supporting the star Alla Nazimova.

The man who considered her for the part of the girl was the play's young director Rouben Mamoulian, who had written the English version of the play and was on the threshold of a brilliant Broadway and Hollywood career (in which he ran the gamut from the classics to Fred Astaire musicals like *Silk Stockings*). He saw Kate and thought she might be the answer to a problem posed by the fifty girls who had already read for the juvenile lead – and been discarded. None of them had seemed to fit his requirements. He thought, however, that Katharine Hepburn might be the one who did.

Generations later, an eighty-four-year-old Rouben Mamoulian recalled for me what had happened that day in 1928: 'The part of the young girl is almost as important as the lead and certainly for a director the more exciting one to cast. A director is always trying to get the best performance out of an actor or actress. The other great pleasure is to try to discover a new talent. I've always been anxious to discover a new person and after a few times you get to trust your intuitive judgment on that person.

'I thought I'd look for unknowns, and I asked Cheryl Crawford, the casting manager of the Guild, to try to find me one. Then one day this young girl walked in. Red haired, freckled, tennis shoes on and shaking with excitement and nervousness. I tried to put her at ease and asked her to sit down.'

'What have you done?' he asked the still quaking redhead.

'Not very much,' she said.

'You know what I have in mind for you could be a very long and important part. The vital thing for you is to be ready when a break comes – but I think this one is going to be very difficult.'

Nevertheless, he gave her a scene to read, told her which part to work on and to disappear into an adjoining room while she cast an eye over it. She came back and read it, still very nervous. 'It wasn't any good,' Mamoulian recalled for me. 'She was too nervous, very young. I told her again that she had to be ready for a part like this and she wasn't ready yet. If I ever had a small part, I said I would let her know.

[18]

'What struck me about this young girl was that there was a certain luminosity in the face. That's the only way I can put it. There are some faces that seem to create light rather than be lighted. Hers was like that. Garbo's was like that.

'I went out and told Cheryl Crawford to take this girl's name down. "She's got something," I said, "and next time we have a small part available, remind me to get her."

'She put her name down. The play opened in New York. After two weeks, the actress who played the maid – a part with about four lines to say – got sick and we had to find a replacement. I said, "Get that girl who read for us a few weeks ago. What was her name?"

'Cheryl said, "Katharine Hepburn." Well, she did the whole season in New York and then a whole season on the road.'

I asked him if Kate showed any reluctance at taking such a small part. 'Are you kidding?' he said. 'She jumped at it. It was, after all, her very first Broadway run.'

He has never worked with her since. But he knows that the part of the maid in *A Month in the Country* was an important milestone in Kate's life. 'There are certain accidents that make you wonder whether they are really accidents or are controlled by fate.'

The red-haired, freckle-faced girl coming to audition for a part she didn't know existed may have been one of those fates. Like the time he spotted a young extra voraciously taking notes and then offered him a lead role in the play in which he already had a small part – his name: Charlton Heston. Or when he gave an opportunity to another shy and inarticulate, awkward youngster he thought 'had something' and might be good as a boxer in *Golden Boy*. That was William Holden.

'Casting,' as he told me, 'is intuitive. Sometimes, you have to make decisions that are against all reason. It was like when Michelangelo used to look and look at a piece of marble. Eventually the figure he wanted, came to him.'

After two seasons as the maid in *A Month in the Country*, the figure inside the marble called Katharine Hepburn was ready for more important things.

Finally, Kate managed to persuade a Broadway management

[19]

to give her a chance with a part of some substance – playing the daughter of one of the most respected Broadway actresses of her day, Jane Cowl. The play was *Art and Mrs Bottle*, by Benn Levy – who wanted to discard Kate the moment he saw her arrive at the theatre wearing faded silk pyjamas and an old Chinese-style coat. What particularly irked him was her glowing nose. 'Where does she get that shine?' he demanded within Hepburn's earshot. 'Cold water and yellow soap?' The answer was that Kate was carrying a flask of pure alcohol in her pocket – which she would douse over her face at every possible opportunity.

Levy finally got his way and Kate was fired. 'She looks a fright, her manner is objectionable and she has no talent,' he said. Jane Cowl tried to persuade her to use makeup but the combination of cosmetics and alcohol made her face look even worse. With the part lost, there wasn't any point in trying. For once, though, things were working in her favour. Fourteen actresses were auditioned and still no suitable girl could be found. In the end, Miss Cowl said: 'Remember the Hepburn child?' and Kate was hired again.

Not that she now did things the way people wanted her to do them. Jane Cowl was particularly embarrassed by the way Kate kissed her in the first act. That was in the script. What she was not expected to do was to leave a huge lipstick impression on Jane's cheek – which the audience spotted and laughed at throughout the remainder of the act. Jane gave her a blot-proof lipstick to use the next night – but when she went on stage, Kate left the same cupid's bow imprint on the star's face.

'Did you forget to use that lipstick?' Miss Cowl asked her.

'No,' said Kate. 'I just thought I might not like it.' It all fitted into the Hepburn personality, all part of the education of a young New England girl brought up to express herself. She didn't yet have the sense to know that there were nicer ways to behave.

From then on, the star kept the younger actress at arm's length whenever the script said 'kiss'. Years later when reminded of this by the *Saturday Evening Post*, Kate said: 'Could I possibly have been so rude to so lovely a person? It seems incredible, doesn't it? And unforgivable.'

[20]

She went back into repertory after *Art and Mrs Bottle*. Her father saw her in *The Man Who Came Back* at Ivorytown, Connecticut and was surprisingly impressed. He told her: 'This is the first time I've ever thought you might have some talent.' But it was difficult to persuade her that that was so. She played more roles – and was sacked some more times.

After five performances opposite Leslie Howard in *The Male Animal*, she was fired again, although never told why. Was it because she was taller than Howard? Possibly. It might also have been because of what some people called her 'vicious temper'. Plainly she and Mr Howard were not destined to work together. She took her disgust to the play's writer, Philip Barry, a man who not very long afterwards would play an important part in her life.

Her language vibrated the walls of Barry's apartment when the writer came out of the bath to greet her. 'You can't let them do this to me,' she shouted. 'You've always said I was ideal for the role. I am! I am! They're ruining your play! They're gypping me (she has always loved using words that sound right for her; if they don't exist, she makes them up and this is typical) and I won't stand for it.'

That was when Barry had heard enough. 'You know,' he replied 'they're right about you. Nobody with your vicious disposition could possibly play light comedy. You're totally unsuited for the part and I'm glad they threw you out.'

It didn't take any great stretch of anyone's imagination to conclude that Katharine Houghton Hepburn was not exactly destined to have a hugely successful theatrical career. But she was not her father's daughter for nothing. The man who had once ordered that she be left at the top of the garden tree and that she remain in college when her teachers wanted to send her home was not going to let her give up that easily.

And in 1931 she was back at work on Broadway in the Moroscow Theatre production of *The Warrior's Husband*. The untidy, pristine-clean Miss Hepburn of Hartford stunned everyone who came to see her as she pranced around the stage in a leopard's skin playing the queen of the amazons. But what really got people excited was seeing her run down a staircase

[21]

carrying a toy deer. The tunic she wore emphasised the slimness of her legs. 'I never made a hit until I was in a leg show,' she was to joke.

But a hit she did make now; both with the audiences and her leading man Colin Keith Johnson. She was called on to bang him over the head – sometimes she did it so hard that his nose bled. A doctor was constantly in attendance should her enthusiasm for her craft run away with her. The critics for once shared Kate's enthusiasm. After a respectable run, the play was ready to move to London, and the Hepburn psyche was all geared up to cross the Atlantic with it. Except that, at the last minute, the play's producers decided not to risk an investment that was anything but gilt-edged. The life of the play was over.

That was precisely how Katharine Hepburn now viewed her professional existence. It hadn't exactly been easy and there was nothing on the horizon to give her any hope that things were going to get any better.

She could not have been more wrong. Laura Harding had introduced her to the agent Leland Hayward who in turn had an idea. He thought that the wayward actress might do very well 3,000 miles away in the other direction. There was a starring role in a new movie that he believed would do her very nicely.

Katharine Hepburn was on her way to Hollywood.

3

Spitfire

*T*HE FILM THAT Hayward had in mind was a new play which RKO had bought called *A Bill of Divorcement*. It had been a huge smash on Broadway with Katharine Cornell, but the film company now wanted a new face for their production. Clemence Dane's moving story of the relationship between a shell-shocked World War One veteran and his young daughter would be virtually untouched.

Hayward had suggested Hepburn to Myron Selznick, brother of David – the man who had recently taken over RKO, and who was rapidly pulling what had been one of the poorer Hollywood studios into the big time. Agents were paid to know what was happening in the studios, and Hayward had heard that Jill Esmond, wife of Laurence Olivier, had already turned down the part.

Everything hinged on the results of the screen test at a small New York studio hired for the purpose by RKO. Kate herself was not optimistic about the outcome. After all those unflattering things said about her face for so long, who could possibly like her enough to agree to pay good money for her services in front of a camera? She, of course, had not heard what Rouben Mamoulian had said about the 'luminosity' of that face.

The test – a scene from the Philip Barry play *Holiday* in which Kate had been the never-called understudy – was directed by Lillie Messenger, the RKO woman who spent all her waking moments searching for new talent. Miss Messenger thought she had made a find. Hayward's hunch had paid off. David Selznick saw the test and he too liked what he saw. But by the time the film arrived from New York, he was in a position in which he was almost forced to like it. John Barrymore, his star, playing the father, was only available on loan from MGM for a fortnight and his bright young director George Cukor was daily pressing to be allowed to start work.

Cukor, in fact, was more enthusiastic about the find than was Selznick. He saw the test, noted Kate's gauche movements – and wasn't quite sure whether he liked or hated her unusual voice. But what she did, he decided, was accomplished 'with enormous feeling'. She was very, very interesting to him. 'Yes,' he told his boss. 'Let's have her.'

But Kate hadn't really wanted to go to Hollywood. And that was why she was being difficult again and demanding what she was later to call 'an impossible price' which any studio would be crazy to meet. When they met that 'impossible price' and offered her $1,500 a week, she went.

The film was very much Selznick's baby. He had wanted to make it for years, but until now any picture about insanity had been as likely to get an OK from a studio mogul as one that condemned motherhood, the Stars and Stripes and apple pie. Once he had been appointed as production head at RKO, however, the way was clear to indulge his fancy.

He announced that not only was he going to make *A Bill of Divorcement*, but he was going to star an unknown called Katharine Hepburn, which was not such a strange decision as it first seemed. If RKO was going to succeed at the top of the Hollywood tree it would have to do it by creating new stars along with using established names. It was the policy that brought Fred Astaire, a top name on Broadway and in London but a virtual unknown to 90 per cent of the world's film audiences, to their studios.

Nevertheless the announcement was not a recipe for perfect peace and harmony on the RKO lot. 'Everyone was shocked silly,' Selznick later wrote. None more than Selznick himself who, when he realised what he was paying this girl, wondered whether he ought not to have a long session with the RKO psychiatrists. The people who said they were shocked were to be even more so before long.

[24]

Kate persuaded Laura Harding to go with her on the journey to California, an exciting one for them both – Kate because she felt that she was at the start of a new career, and one that would give her a chance to forget all the unfortunate hiccups that had punctured her stage life; Laura, who was heiress to the American Express company fortune, because she was seeing a new part of the country and watching the way America's most exciting industry worked with all its glamorous personalities.

They chatted on the long train journey like schoolgirls on a mystery outing. During their first night on the train, Kate pointed to the new moon shining through the trees as their train whizzed along. 'Don't look at it through the window,' said Laura. 'Never look at a new moon through glass. It's unlucky.'

The window was pulled up and the two girls, the wind rushing through their hair, peered out and admired the beauty of what was before them. Just when everything seemed so perfect a hot cinder hit Kate in an eye. It was a small one and she managed to force it out quickly enough, but it smarted and as she rubbed the eye, so the stinging sensation got worse. The eye ran, started to feel increasingly heavy and grew more and more red. By the time the train drew into Pasadena station, it was not a pleasant sight that greeted Pandro S. Berman, the young man who was being groomed by Selznick as a producer and who was now acting as his assistant. 'I was terribly shocked and disappointed,' he told me, remembering that moment more than forty years later.

Hollywood was at the dawn of its most glamorous era. Just five years before, Al Jolson and Warner Brothers had shown that the cinema had a voice. Kate was part of a large army of New York actors and actresses who had been welcomed to the Los Angeles suburb as much because they knew how to use their vocal chords as for their other talents. The film colony had recovered from the shock of the talkies and was once again the Mount Olympus to which lesser mortals would come in search of their gods. The giant palm trees, the incessant sunshine, the large, low Spanish-style houses with their swimming pools symbolised everyone's idea of perfection and comfort in the midst of the Great Depression.

In truth, it was a good time for the studios. On Wall Street, bankers might be throwing themselves out of skyscraper windows but lesser men, used to the idea of going out at eight o'clock every morning, still left home at that time – to wait in parks and breadlines until the cinemas opened. For five or ten cents, they could escape from the cruelties of reality and at the same time maintain the dignity of feeling they had somewhere to go, to say nothing of not always revealing to their wives and families that they were without work. On the other hand, husbands, wives and children were at the toughest of times prepared to scrape together pennies so that they could spend an evening away from the pressures of life.

Exhibitors realised how much they benefited from what the show-biz 'Bible', *Variety* had dubbed Wall Street's 'egg' and decided it was worth their while to change programmes twice a week. Twice as many films to show meant twice as many films for the studios to make. It was into this environment of prosperity amid the gloom of the last days of Herbert Hoover's administration and on the eve of Franklin D. Roosevelt's sweep to power with his promises of a 'New Deal', that Katharine Houghton Hepburn took her place among the stars.

She was brought to the studio almost immediately after her arrival. And it was Berman who was given charge by David Selznick of introducing her to all the people she had to get to know. Together they went to the makeup and hairdressing departments. 'You won't be able to do anything at all with my hair,' she told the woman in charge. 'I always have it a-la concierge,' she said, pointing to the tight knot. She was given a knowing look that said, 'We'll see about that.'

Berman took her to the wardrobe people who doubtless had some serious qualms about making this trouser-wearing young woman into the kind of lady Selznick wanted to see in his films. It was, after all, the age when girls were supposed to look frilly and frivolous on the screen. 'She was so bedraggled and her eye was so swollen at the time, it was impossible to make a fair judgment about her,' Berman told me.

Before long the two became fast friends and played tennis together. This did not at first seem to be the relationship that was going to develop with her director George Cukor, or for that matter with John Barrymore, to both of whom she was introduced by Berman.

Barrymore seemed to think that any young lady on the lot was fair game and demonstrated the fact in what he considered to be a suitable manner. He called her into his dressing room and proceeded to take his clothes off as an eye-rubbing, mouth-gaping Katharine Hepburn looked on. But she was sufficiently in charge of her senses to make clear, doubtless using the kind of invective others who knew her better had already got to appreciate, that she wasn't that sort of a girl. 'There must be some mistake,' she blurted, not really knowing how it could have happened and certain it was a reflection on her own morals, which must have been considered extremely loose.

Her relationship with Cukor was without that kind of dimension but was strained nevertheless. The director didn't quite know what to make of her. He, too, took her round various parts of the RKO lot and into the studio commissary, always the place where the most scandalous tales spread the quickest.

The Hollywood writer Adela Rogers St John described the scene that day: 'When she walked in with Mr Cukor, several executives nearly fainted. Mr Selznick swallowed a chicken wing whole. We beheld a tall skinny girl entirely covered with freckles and wearing the most appalling and incredible clothes I have ever seen in my life. They looked like something Lee Tracy would design for the Mexican Army to go ski jumping in. Yet, you can tell they were supposed to be the last word.'

Cukor's reluctance was based on purely professional reasons. For years he was quoted as saying that she came out to Hollywood and proceeded to act like a 'sub-collegiate idiot'.

'I have never said that – or felt it,' Cukor told me shortly before his death. 'What I said was that she had some somewhat irritating qualities. She was highbrow and very self-assured.'

Whatever words he used at the time, they seemed to be on a

[27]

collision course at that early stage of their relationship. Despite her appearance, she was making a great deal of fuss about her clothes. All the evidence was that she wasn't exactly an expert on such matters, yet she had the apparent audacity to say that the wardrobe prepared for her wasn't quite right and she wouldn't wear it. She told him that her outfits had to be designed by Chanel – a delightful irony as things would turn out forty years later.

'Do you really like that rig you've got on?' Cukor asked her. 'I certainly do,' she said. 'It was created specially for me by one of the finest houses in Paris.'

'Well,' said the director. 'I think it stinks. I think it's the worst looking thing I ever saw on any woman in my life. I think anyone who would wear it outside the bathroom doesn't know what clothes are. Now what do you think of that?'

'You win,' she said. Had the fight gone the other way, all the authority that Cukor intended to exercise in the weeks that followed would have been nullified. Her relationship with Cukor improved as filming progressed – to the point where before long they seemed to have a definite respect for each other.

Despite everything, twenty years later, she said she felt much the same towards John Barrymore. 'He never criticised me,' she said. 'He just shoved me into what I ought to do before the camera. He taught me all that could be poured into one greenhorn in that short time.'

There *had* been moments of criticism from her film 'father', however, and Barrymore, who had to have cue cards to help him know his lines (he once explained: 'My mind is filled by the poetry of Shakespeare; you don't want me to sully it with all this shit, do you?') still tried to give the impression that he was more interested in trying to find ways of getting Kate into bed. He pinched her behind. 'Do that once more,' said Miss Hepburn 'and I'll stop acting.'

'I wasn't aware that you'd started,' he replied.

She had not much better an opinion of him. Years later, she recalled: 'I remember watching Jack's first scene and thinking, "You're not much good . . . hmmmm."' But as work on the film progressed, she revised her ideas.

There was one scene they had together in which Barrymore's

[28]

role took on an exciting reality for her. She told him: 'I think you are my father.' Then, she remembered, he 'took my face in his hands. He looked long at me and he was absolutely shattering, simple . . . I never realised then that Jack was such a disturbed human being. He always tried to help me.' It was a sudden bridging of the generation gap.

Others, too, shared the confidence that Barrymore suddenly discovered he had in her. Cukor and Selznick decided that she had been well worth the $1,500 they had invested and the critics seemed to agree. Cukor was particularly grateful at the ease with which she did her work in front of the camera. 'Those are the naturals,' he told me, 'the women who see a camera professionally for the very first time and yet you know are as comfortable in front of it as they would be in their own living room. This was Katharine Hepburn. She laughed a lot, too – which was another good sign. There was something impishly mischievous about her.'

Cukor had been right in his assessment of her feelings in front of the camera. 'I was never frightened of the movies,' she said. 'I can remember thinking, "Oh, this is great. Oh, that camera! That's a friend. This is very easy." Warm! Cozy! Ummm! Never embarrassed me.'

Not that she took her work as seriously as the amount of effort which she put into it seemed to indicate. 'My sister is going to be a farmer,' she said. 'Her job is much more important than mine. Acting is just waiting for the custard pie.' Her screen test had confirmed this judgment. As she said long afterwards: 'You never saw anyone who looks so young and absolutely ludicrous and madly anxious to succeed. It absolutely exhausts me just to look at it.' *A Bill of Divorcement* gave a very different impression.

She wasn't so happy, however, with the trappings of Hollywood life. Although she became even more addicted to tennis than ever before and was now a regular fixture at the smart Beverly Hills Hotel courts, the hot sun was irritating to her. She also refused to obey most of the Hollywood conventions.

A star, for instance, was expected to be seen by her public

in diamonds and mink – and then only at arm's length at premieres and other engagements which the studios decided were right for her. When it was politic to make her seem like the girl next door, there were carefully cultivated magazine spreads organised by the studios themselves, and fairly guaranteed of publication because it suited the newspapers to play the Hollywood game. They got both heavy advertising and all the stories they wanted in exchange for the ones that the studios wanted pushing.

But Kate was not going to go along with any of this. She sat herself down by the kerb with traffic rushing past her and scribbled personal letters and replies to fan mail. Much more difficult was her reaction to reporters.

'Are you married, Miss Hepburn?' asked one.

'No, never have been,' she lied.

'Any children?' asked another pretending to be oblivious to her answer. 'Yes,' she said. 'Five. Two white, three coloured.' That wasn't the sort of thing calculated to please the publicity department and certainly not Mr Selznick, the mogul who employed them.

As Cukor once told a BBC interviewer: 'She was rather smart-assed and very hoyty-toyty and acted as if we were all ignoramuses.'

Kate never underestimated what she had done in that first film. Nor was she ever modest enough to deny that she stole the show from Barrymore. But she explained: 'I knew that when I signed for it. It's an ingenue playing against a star who must carry the burden of the play. The carrying of the whole movie was an ordeal for Barrymore. A girl who hasn't been seen before with a wonderful part playing against the star always has a chance to steal it. It's rigged, you know. Lots of girls' parts are written that way. That's why you have so many girls who are not known winning Academy Awards in their first picture.'

Despite the success of *A Bill of Divorcement* in 1932, Kate made up her mind that she wasn't going to stay married to Hollywood – even if she wouldn't go so far as to file for the sort of arrangement indicated by the title of the film. At the first

[30]

opportunity after some additional scenes had been shot, she left for New York and sailed for Europe. With her was the man who was still legally her husband. 'I like him,' she explained to some curious friends. 'It is very important to like the man with whom you are in love.' Saying she was in love was probably taking things too far.

The couple booked steerage passages, 'because I always throw up on sea voyages and I don't see why I should do it on a first-class ticket'. They got as far as the Austrian Tyrol, where there was a cable awaiting Kate from Selznick. He had a new picture in mind for her.

This new idea didn't work out and Selznick left RKO, but Pandro Berman was all ready to produce another picture. And this time with Kate in the starring role. It was to be called *Christopher Strong*, about a female flyer, and was to be directed by one of Hollywood's few women directors Dorothy Arzner with whom Kate didn't get on at all well. The result showed in the film. It was no disaster, but no great triumph either. 'She wasn't at all easy to work with,' Berman told me. 'She was a very sweet and fine girl. But she had a little bit of a chip on her shoulder about Hollywood – until she became part of it.'

I wondered whether there was perhaps an element of a superiority complex about her. 'I guess you could call it that,' said Berman. 'But I think that it was more a case of her being scared. She was, in fact, frightened to death.' It continued even beyond *Christopher Strong*. 'She was nervous about the choice of material, about her beauty – or as she saw it, the lack of it. I don't think she thought she was any better than anyone else, but she felt she was not going to be photogenic enough.'

Her voice was the thing that stopped audiences short as they sat in theatres listening to her. If they had never seen anyone like Kate before, certainly they had never heard anyone like her. 'Those New England tones were shrill at times,' Berman recalls. 'To the average listener, she sounded a little affected – although I don't think she was. I think she spoke naturally. It wasn't a great asset to her unless she was in a picture in which she needed to get great sympathy.'

Despite the success of her first film, there were 'great

doubts', said Berman, about the material they were ready to offer her. Looking back now, he would not have chosen Kate for *Christopher Strong*.

One thing about working with her was that you knew where you were. 'Katharine was the most definite person. She was very quick off the trigger. There was no stalling around with her and she was very intelligent – more so than most of the women stars of her time. She either liked a script or she didn't – and I was careful when I got to know her a little better to approach things from a point of view when I knew I would have a little working for me.'

Meanwhile, the gossip columnists were trying to see how much Kate had working for herself. What would her work in the film town do to her marriage? Adela Rogers St John, one of the few Hollywood scribes who knew of the existence of Mr Smith wanted to know. Writing in *Liberty* magazine she said: 'Whether this marriage can survive their long separations, whether it will weather the new problems that must come from Katharine Hepburn's success no one can tell. Certainly, it's not easy to conduct a marriage at 3,000 miles apart to keep a close union when two people are both vitally absorbed and keenly ambitious . . . This much is certain: Katharine Hepburn is today interested in her work above everything else.'

Before Pandro Berman offered Kate her third role, in Zoe Atkins's *Morning Glory*, he travelled almost daily to the writer's Pasadena home to discuss the script in the minutest detail. That done, he asked Laura Harding to read it first. If *she* liked the idea of Kate playing a young ambitious and determined actress let loose in New York, the director knew she could persuade her friend to do it.

'I wanted her to read it without saying anything about it to Katharine. If she didn't like it, *then* I'd see what Katharine would say about it. But Laura was crazy about it and she gave it to Katharine to read even before I could give it to her. On that film, Laura acted as a sounding board for me and it worked beautifully. But I never did it again. I didn't have to. I knew Katharine better myself.'

The film co-starred Adolphe Menjou and Douglas Fairbanks

Jnr, with whom Kate at first seemed to have a somewhat stormy relationship. At one stage, he had gone on record denouncing 'her masculine mind and her compulsion to go out of her way to be insulting'. That is not at all how he remembers it now.

'I think *Morning Glory* was the first time I met her,' he told me, 'although neither of us can be sure that we didn't first meet when she was doing *Warrior's Husband* in New York.' The big question for the rest of the cast was 'how she would go as a romantic leading lady', he remembered. 'But the studio had this great confidence that she could do it. And she had great confidence that she could do anything – and she can. In fact, she did it so well that people now forget that Adolphe Menjou and I were in it at all.' He was aware of the sense of insecurity which she must have felt. 'But there isn't one of us who isn't insecure at some time or other.'

His abiding memory of the film is that 'I was crazy about her when I saw her on the set. I don't think I was the only one. Other people who worked with her went head-over-heels for Kate and I had a particularly big crush on her. Of course, I'd have been a dead fool if I hadn't. I'd have had to have had my head examined and my heart examined too. But I think I had a couple of other rivals at the same time – and we didn't dare compare notes with each other. We quite deliberately hardly spoke! Yet I don't know how aware of it *she* was at the time. We've joked about it a great deal since.'

There was one night when Fairbanks thought he had their relationship firmly sewn up. She agreed to have dinner with him. 'Everybody worked very early in the morning, so after dinner that night, instead of going out somewhere after eating, she said something about getting up early the next morning. So I dropped her home. After doing so I just pulled up at the roadside. I don't know why. Maybe just to moon – to think, "Oh dear me – isn't she grand?" And the next thing I saw out of the corner of my eye, at the back of the house, running through to another street was the little figure of Kate dashing out – and going off somewhere into someone else's car. I never knew who it was.' (People have theorised that it was probably Leland

[33]

Hayward who was top of the Hepburn romantic charts at the time. It was not the sort of thing that happened often to the handsome and dashing young Fairbanks.)

This first venture into a romantic movie has been one of the well-documented moments of the Hepburn movie career. People remember her scenes with Fairbanks and Menjou. What few know about are the parts of the picture which could well have heralded a future for Kate and Douglas Fairbanks together in the Shakespearean theatre. For a dream sequence in the film, they re-enacted the balcony scene from *Romeo and Juliet*. It went so well that more scenes from the play were shot – all the ones in which the young lovers were either alone on stage or solely in the company of the nurse.

'They invited hundreds of people to the set to watch us all dressed up as Romeo and Juliet – and we thought, and still think that we were pretty good,' Fairbanks recalled for me. It went so well that there was talk of their starring in a new film version of the play. But it never happened. 'We both got busy on other things.'

In fact, even the dream sequence was excised. It was thought to be too long to fit into a movie of that kind without distracting audiences' minds from the main plot. 'All that remains of it,' Douglas told me, 'are some stills. When I asked what had happened to the negative of the scenes that we shot, I was told it had been destroyed. We thought it would have been nice for "historical purposes" to have had that bit of film in which I looked rather like a decadent string bean of sorts. And she's pulling her head away from me, looking as though I needed a bath. It's a pity it has been lost – *nobody* even knows about it ever having been shot.'

Douglas Fairbanks today recalls that making those Shakespearean extracts seemed the most natural thing in the world to them both. 'It's like if you can play the piano at all, sitting down and performing beautiful music. We enjoyed the beauty of it all – which is just what it was. The beautiful music of Shakespearean verse. We had both had some training and some professionalism and it was a joy to play this music, as it were. But we probably worked harder on that segment than anything else in that picture.'

It was nevertheless the start of a lifelong friendship. If giving each other pet names has any significance in the romantic view of things, then there was great affection indeed. 'We took to calling each other Pete – and I've never quite known why. She signs her letters to me, "Pete" and addresses them to "Dear Pete".'

Morning Glory was a sensational success. Suddenly the awkward red-haired freckled girl whom David Selznick had always regretted having on his contract list was the favourite of the studio. And with good cause. For her third film and after only two years in Hollywood, she was honoured by the Academy of Motion Picture Arts and Sciences and given an Oscar for being the best actress of 1933. The young actress playing a young actress who had gone to New York to succeed had gone to Hollywood – and succeeded.

Next came *Little Women*, with Kate as Jo. It sent audiences into ecstasies, broke all records at the world's largest cinema, the Radio City Music Hall in New York and, *Vanity Fair* magazine reported, 'brought out from their lairs elderly ladies who all but drove up in fringed surreys to see their first movie since *Birth of a Nation*, lured by reverberations from the terrific impact of the Hepburn personality on an idolatrous public'.

The same issue of the magazine contained a detailed critique of the picture – and its star: 'Of course, the greatest success of the year was *Little Women*. I agree with the unanimous praise given to the production. From a standpoint of lighting, scenery, photography and casting, it was a splendid picture. However, I have yet to be convinced that Katharine Hepburn is a great actress. She has an insolent manner that fitted her characterisation in *Little Women*, but that same manner indicates a limitation to me. She is regarded as a precocious youngster and one feels that she is constantly sticking out her chest and saying, "Look at me" . . . Evidently, it is charming to most critics. But she brings the same mannerisms to all her work. I feel when I see her, that she is simply being Miss Hepburn.'

The magazine was experiencing the difficulty of getting to

know the real Miss Hepburn. She went to its offices to be photographed by their star cameraman, Russian-born Lusha Nelson. She made it her business to hide her neck – which she has always considered her least attractive feature, long and scrawny – with a scarf before she posed. When she saw the result, she said that she felt as though she looked like a young Beethoven.

But she seemed to have reached the stage when no matter what she did, it was all right by the people who paid the money at the box office. David O. Selznick came back to RKO to produce the film and as far as the company was concerned, Katharine Hepburn could write her own ticket. Which was not necessarily such a good idea.

The studio had not yet either come to terms with her dress style. They told her in no uncertain terms that if she persisted in wearing dungarees, they would find a way of breaking into her wardrobe and stealing them. One day, they actually did that. It was not the sort of thing to faze Katharine Hepburn, although there were other actresses who would have burst into floods of tears at the thought.

'Unless you give me back my pants,' she declared, 'I intend to walk through the RKO lot naked.' When one thinks about the anxiety she felt about her bony neck, to say nothing of the freckles which were as pronounced in her early adulthood as they had ever been in her youth, it seems a threat hardly likely to be exercised. But Hepburn had a reputation for doing strange, strange things. The studio wondered, worried – and decided it had to call her bluff. Of course, Kate didn't walk around stark naked. But she did come out of her dressing room in her silk panties. The trousers were returned instantly.

4

A Woman Rebels

Bʏ 1933 ᴋᴀᴛᴇ had developed a very healthy (from her point of view) sense of her own value. Jed Harris, then rapidly rising as a much respected writer, asked her to star in his play *The Lake*. She agreed – and then stayed in Hollywood instead of doing the twenty-eight-day pre-rehearsal 'training' that he insisted upon. He said that she needed private coaching from him on how the morbid psychological drama had to be played. It wasn't an argument that cut particularly deeply with her – especially now that RKO offered her £50,000 for those four weeks in Hollywood. She also thought it more important to keep at work in the studios now that she was riding so high. But Jed Harris decided it was unpardonable arrogance on her part – and would go on saying it for years afterwards.

Scripts and script ideas were being pressed on Kate continually and the studio itself was printing synopses and sending them to her. For her part, Kate was determined only to select for herself parts and stories that she particularly wanted to do. Unfortunately, according to Pandro Berman, in the selection of her material, she didn't seem to be using the intelligence she was showing in every other regard.

Kate said that while waiting to start rehearsals for *The Lake*, she wanted to make a picture called *Spitfire* – about a mountain girl driven from her village when she declares herself to be a faith healer.

'Oh my!' recalls Berman. 'What a mistake that was! Here was this cultured New England lady playing a gypsy squatter. The film was a disaster – but Kate seemed to love it.'

Berman had reason enough to recall with film the less than affection. Kate was being paid the customary £1,500 a week for her work on the picture, which on the day filming started everyone expected would take four weeks to complete. Exactly four weeks and $6,000 later, Berman knew he needed one half day's extra work from his star.

'She will do it for another $10,000,' said Leland Hayward who by now was more than just Kate's agent. The odd tale of them dating each other had turned into strong rumours of a hot affair between them.

'I thought about that,' said Berman, 'and very reluctantly concluded that I had no choice but to pay her this little bonus.' There was no doubt in Berman's mind either that the decision to press for 'this little bonus' was Kate's alone. 'I don't think Hayward wanted to do that; I was in business with him on several other deals, but Katharine insisted upon it. She knew that she had us over a barrel.'

What she, in fact, told the studio was: 'You make *us* live up to the conditions you write into contracts. It's time you learned to do so, too.' Not that it was such a big deal. 'We were spending buttons on pictures in those days. We needed fifty pictures a year for our theatre chain. Laughable what we spent on them! I was making pictures for $100,000. *Spitfire* cost us less than $150,000 all in all.'

There were people who regarded her attitude as cheeky, to say the least. Kate had other ideas. She never walked around the RKO lot worrying about the effect of her behaviour or the results of her talent on the studio's bank balance. As she explained years later: 'I've always had a deep conviction of my charms and was always well satisfied with myself. The stuff I had to work with seemed very suitable and it never really bothered me that people never considered me a beauty.'

If she *had* persuaded RKO to make *Spitfire* against their better judgment, there was no question of Kate herself doing films that she did not want to make. But no one saw *Spitfire* as a tragedy – even though it was both a box office and a critical failure. When theatres had to be filled fifty-two weeks a year with something, it didn't seem to matter very much.

[38]

But secretly it did matter to Kate, who now had to start seriously rehearsing *The Lake*. It turned out to be disastrous in every respect – and brought back too many memories of most of her previous stage work. Harris directed the play and showed how furious he was at her earlier lack of co-operation. A great deal of her self-confidence, both her strength and her weakness, quickly vanished.

There was a state of total war between herself and her director. Years later, Jed Harris told about his battles with an actress whom everyone regarded as perfection on stage but whom he himself considered now to be self-centred and incompetent. Other people working on the play say that she was badly used by the director who had little admiration for what she had done in Hollywood. It is true beyond doubt that Kate had problems. She wasn't happy that the cast included a number of actors and actresses who had been Broadway successes before she had even entered Bryn Mawr. 'Get those people away from there!' she demanded when she saw a couple of these veterans standing in the wings. 'I can't work with people staring at me.'

Harris was rough with her, but it was a message that before long got through. 'If you're to become an actress, you must learn the stage tradition of courtesy,' he told her. 'Everyone standing at that line, obeying orders is a better trouper than you.'

The Lake folded after a very shaky six weeks. Brooks Atkinson, the *New York Times*'s 'butcher of Broadway' wrote about Kate at the Martin Beck Theatre: 'She is not a fully-fledged actress yet. In the current drama, she has a sensitive and remarkably intense personality and an unworldly charm. But she has not yet developed the flexibility of first-rate acting and her voice is rather a strident instrument.'

The comments stung. But none seemed to be made with more venom than that of Dorothy Parker, who in a celebrated *bon mot* that doubtless had the Algonquin set choking over their Martinis, said that Kate 'runs the gamut of emotion, all the way from A to B'.

One critic plainly thought it easier to ask questions than provide answers: 'Will Katharine Hepburn dare to return to

[39]

Hollywood without winning a success on the stage in New York? What effect will the flip flop done by her play *The Lake* in New York have upon her picture career? Has the award of a prize by the Academy of Motion Picture Arts and Sciences saved her from a big, bad slump? What is the picture *Spitfire*, the weakest she has done, going to do to her popularity? Certainly no star has been in such a hot spot.'

Kate thought she knew the reason for it all. She felt, as she said later on, that she had lost all contact with her audiences. When she heard that, despite her unhappiness with it all, Jed Harris intended taking the play on the road she was furious. Harris has always said that he expected that she would join the road company and that he had invested money that he couldn't afford to lose. Kate, on the other hand, has maintained that he used the tour prospect as a convenient means for blackmail.

The *Saturday Evening Post* reported that she phoned Harris and said: 'There's no doubt I stink in the play, but nobody was wildly enthusiastic over the production, either. You've got your investment back and more. Why not call it off? It would be like selling a bottle of patent medicine which you knew was no good.'

Harris, they reported, replied: 'My dear, the only interest I have in you is the money I can make out of you.'

It wasn't a nice thing to hear. She asked him, 'How much?'

'How much have you got?' he countered.

She went to her bag and produced a cheque book. 'I've got exactly $15,461 and 67 cents,' she replied. 'OK,' said Harris. 'I'll take that.'

She took the comparatively easy way out and sailed for Europe instead of going to Hollywood. Once again, she went steerage. But she only stayed in Paris for four days before sailing the Atlantic once more. 'I can't explain why I do it,' she told reporters in a moment when she felt it would be more painful to avoid the press than to accept their presence. They couldn't understand why she would go to the trouble of spending so little time in a foreign city between such long sea journeys. But she was soon back on her usual form. 'I just do it and that's all there is about it. I had nothing to say when I left

[40]

and I have nothing more to say now. If I have something to say when there is a reason involved, I am perfectly willing to talk.'

In actual fact there was a reason – and for going on by seaplane to Mexico immediately after docking in New York. And the explanation for that became only too apparent as soon as she landed. She wanted to regularise her relationship with Ludlow Ogden Smith, and Mexico where it appeared they handed out divorces as regularly as they did tequila was the obvious place to get it done quickly – if not, as time would tell, tidily.

And it was very, very secret. Kate registered at the Hotel Itza at Merida, Yucatan, under her legal name, Mrs Ludlow Smith and immediately reserved a seaplane seat back to Miami four days later. She finally admitted that terms were being settled at the seaport of Progresso, although early press inquiries seemed to show that her husband knew absolutely nothing about it. Nor did his mother.

Mrs Lewis Lawrence Smith said at her Philadelphia home: 'I can't believe it is my daughter.' (She avoided calling Kate her daughter-in-law.) 'The last time I heard from her, only a few days ago, she was in New York and no such thing was contemplated. I am inclined to be very sceptical of the whole thing. I don't see how she could have got to Mexico in the short time since I heard from her.'

In fact, Kate, as wily as when she got RKO to up her fee for a film, had joined a group of tourists who visited Mayan ruins at Yucatan. It was a device she could have sold to Pandro Berman for her next film project. Her own mother was contacted at Hartford and, taking a leaf from her daughter, refused to comment. 'I do not care to discuss the matter,' she said.

Kate's marriage had been really such a non-event that until recently very few people even knew that she had a husband. Those who did know were singularly unimpressed by the relationship – which wasn't the sort that was talked about in society. In fact in December 1933 it had been announced without comment that the names of both Mr and Mrs Ogden Smith were being omitted from the following year's Philadelphia Social Register. They had both been listed in the

[41]

volumes of the previous two years with their home given as 146 East Thirty Ninth Street, Philadelphia.

The event caused little more than minor tremors among the faculty at Kate's Bryn Mawr alma mater. The impression people had was that she was taking the divorce lightly. In fact, it came after a long period of soul-searching. Years later, she would explain her attitude to marriage. 'There has to be some mysterious attraction. And it can't just be sexual. It has to be a respect, an admiration, as women, as men, as something. It's enormously difficult and getting more so now that the ladies are bored with one.'

She was fond of quoting Dorothy Dix: 'If you want to sacrifice the admiration of many for the criticism of one, get married.' As Kate commented: 'It is the most terrible, terrible truth, isn't it?' She has admitted many times that she herself 'behaved very badly' over her marriage. 'I was not fit to be married because I was fit to think only of myself. An actor, whose temperament as an actor tends this way, has to be very careful about getting married, because you're very likely to make somebody else very unhappy. And I loathe making people unhappy.'

It was for that reason that she vowed never to marry again. Neither, however, has she since then believed in marriage as a concept. 'It's an artificial relationship, because you have to sign a contract. It's a guarantee that is made for the children in the hope that they will have a solid foundation. I don't think a man and woman necessarily need the arrangement. It certainly doesn't keep them together any more. You can't ask two people who are totally disinterested in each other to live together – that's cruel. I think people often dive into marriage without knowing what they're doing or to whom they're committing themselves.'

Kate herself probably pleaded guilty to all those things. She had, as she put it later, also faced 'the issue of motherhood squarely' and decided it was not for her: 'It was a matter of becoming the best actress I could be or becoming a mother. But not both. I don't think I could do justice to both. Acting was right for me. A career was important for me.'

[42]

Perversely, this only seemed to strengthen her own family ties. When her brother Dick wrote a play about the Hepburn family, she was furious. It was an invasion of privacy she declared and threatened all sorts of things to get him to change his mind. He never offered it to a management. It could have made him, of course. He has been trying to write successful plays ever since and none of them have got very far.

Kate's own divorce seemingly over, she went back to Hollywood to make a new RKO picture *The Little Minister* in which once more she played a gypsy girl – only this time a titled lady dressing up as one. And it was set not in America's mountain country but in the highlands of Scotland.

Pandro Berman has revised his opinion of this film with the benefit of history. He had doubts about it at the time because its box office take was not as great as most people had anticipated. But now he says: 'It was a pretty good picture and all things considered, it was a success both critically and with the public. She did well in it and she was cast well.'

The movie was followed by *Break of Hearts*, in which she co-starred with Charles Boyer, which didn't amount to very much, and then by *Alice Adams*, which did.

It was the story of a poor girl desperately anxious to charge up the social ladder who is thwarted all the way. The director was George Stevens, although he was appointed by Pandro Berman over the protests of Kate, who said she thought there ought to be a more experienced man in charge of the movie. If she had known that Stevens's experience had been restricted virtually to Hal Roach comedies – custard pies, slapsticks, the lot – she would have been even less enthusiastic about her producer's choice. But Pandro Berman was insistent if diplomatic.

'I can get a very experienced, very famous director,' he told her without at that stage specifying a name, 'but I think George Stevens is a man of the future. I think he will be marvellous for you.' What he really meant was that Stevens had been newly put under contract by RKO – and was cheap. The other director would cost him dear and would only be available for the one picture.

[43]

'Who's your other man?' she asked Berman.

'Willy Wyler,' he said. 'He wants to do it.'

'Oh, that's marvellous,' said Kate. 'Thank God. He'll be wonderful. That's all our problems solved.'

'No,' said the producer. 'They're not solved yet. I still want to use George Stevens.'

The dispute went on for six weeks. Ultimately, Berman said to her: 'Come up to my office and we'll settle this thing once and for all.'

She went to the office. 'What do you want to do?' she asked him.

'I know what I want to do,' he replied. 'I want to use George Stevens.'

'And I want Willy Wyler,' she said stubbornly.

'Well,' he answered. 'I can't fault you for that. He's the best. But I'd like to persuade you to use George Stevens.' At that point, Berman told me, he had an inspiration. 'Why don't we flip a coin?' he said. Much to his surprise, Kate agreed. He took out a quarter. They agreed that heads it would be Wyler, tails Stevens.

Heads it was. But Berman could see that she was hesitating while he himself was distinctly unhappy at the outcome. 'I'll tell you what,' he said, 'let's flip it again'. This time, it was tails. And Kate said she would accept Stevens. 'There was some reason why, now that we had got to this stage, she didn't want to reject Stevens,' Berman told me.

The following day, Stevens happened to pass Kate in an open car with a man, kissing, according to a story the director was to tell. 'I'm sorry,' he said, feeling more than a little embarrassed – which was exactly how Kate herself felt. Flustered, she asked her unidentified boyfriend to drive her to the studio where she was about to be late for an important meeting with Berman.

'Well,' she said, after the producer had introduced her to Stevens, 'I guess you're the one I want for *Alice Adams*.'

Nevertheless, the relationship was not entirely free of problems. Fred MacMurray, destined for a career as a cheerful, well-liked actor who really didn't care too much about the consequences of many of the things he did on screen, remembered one disagreement between Kate and Stevens. 'I think it was in a porch or somewhere like that. Stevens said he wanted it done a certain way, and Kate wouldn't agree. "No," she said. "I think it must be done this way." "No," said Stevens. "It has to be done *this* way." That was going on all morning. He must have done it dozens of different ways. Finally, we broke for lunch. After lunch, it happened again. "I don't like your way," said Katharine. "And *I* don't like *your* way," said George. Finally, George won and had it done his way.'

It wasn't their only dispute, and for weeks it seemed highly ominous that they were still calling each other 'Miss Hepburn' and 'Mr Stevens'. The problems they had experienced on the porch were, in different ways, repeated time and again. The classic example was a scene where Alice had to enter her room and burst into tears as she threw herself on to a bed. That, at least, was how the script called for it to be done – but not how Stevens wanted it performed.

The director asked her to go over to a window to cry. 'I'll cry on the bed,' insisted Kate. And for four hours each stuck to their guns. Finally, Kate decided she had had enough. 'It's ridiculous,' she screamed. 'There's a limit to stupidity. I've put up with all of it I can. You dumb son-of-a-bitch, I'm going to cry on the bed.'

Stevens wasn't backing down that easily. After all, what is four hours in the life of a picture? Chaplin took months agonising over a single gesture, refusing to accept a shot until it was right – while the rest of the company stayed on full salary. 'Either you'll cry at the window,' he shouted back, 'or I'll go back to my custard pies!'

That was all the Hepburn temperament wanted to hear. 'Quitter,' she taunted. 'If I ever had any respect for you, it's gone now. You don't get your own way, so you quit! You're yellow!' All that in front of the assembled cast, technicians, grips, everyone on the lot. Such assaults between director and star had never been heard before at RKO or anywhere else for that matter.

[45]

It was a time for compromise. A time when, no matter what else happened, the director had to lead. 'Miss Hepburn,' George said, calmly, reasonably. 'Just walk to the window – please. And stay there awhile. You needn't weep. I'll dub someone in, in a long shot, and we can fake the sound track.'

A good fighter knows when to admit defeat, gracefully find a way to recognise the bell. She said nothing. Simply walked to the window – and as the cameras turned, her face creased. And she wept. No one could be totally sure if she were doing it because that was how the director wanted it, or simply because she really needed to cry. But after that, everything changed between them.

The relationship appeared to blossom. 'They seemed awfully fond of each other,' said Berman. 'I wouldn't be very surprised if there wasn't a romance of some kind or other between them. Of course, George was that way with all the women he worked with. He got very close to them. But that's what my imagination told me.'

When tears were called for again in this archetypal 'woman's picture', there were no more problems. Another scene required her to look at the actor playing her father as he remarked that the boyfriend who had just left was 'the nicest you have ever brought home'. Stevens told her: 'It would be nice if you could manage a tear or two on cue. Try it once, will you? If you can't bring it off, we'll use glycerine' – the classic answer to crying problems on a set.

'I can do it,' said Kate. Just as the man used the word 'home', she cried perfectly.

The director was thrilled – only to be told by the cameraman that he thought the lighting was distinctly off. 'I'll fix it somehow,' said Stevens. 'I can't lose that one.'

But Kate said that it had to be just right. She did it again – crying beautifully just as the man said 'home'. Kate was to explain: 'There was nothing so marvellous about it. Pop was played by Fred Stone, who was so sweet – he looks like a helpless baby lion – I could have cried fifty times.'

Nineteen years later, Stevens was to write: 'I never knew an actress of whom I was surer as to potentiality. It all seemed there, in her. But I never knew an actress of whom one could be less sure that the promise would come through. She not only had no technique. She didn't seem to want any. I think she believed in those days that God had smitten her very young and by a miracle made a Bernhardt.'

But he thought there was a reason for that. 'The trouble lay deeper than that. She really thought it dishonest to think about technique. She just wanted to stand – or rush around before a camera and feel. She thought that the audience would feel, too. Such mechanics as timing, build-up to a climax, plain use of stage geography, she thought meant artificially acting. That's why she would be seized with a panicky knowledge that she wasn't going over and rant.'

When *Alice Adams* was released, nothing showed of their early disagreements. Pandro Berman said the picture was his favourite of all the movies he had made with Hepburn. 'It was just a lovely, lovely picture. Katharine was marvellous in it.' In a BBC radio talk, Alistair Cooke said in 1937: 'Only once in four years, in *Alice Adams*, has she been acting a sort of girl she might reasonably be. I wish she could be given a rest from Great Loves and take, instead, a walk with the young man next door. I wish she didn't have to say lines like: "It's no use my darling, wherever we go, whatever we may become, it'll never be the same again – never." And let us hear this gangling college girl say, what she must have said a score of times when at Bryn Mawr: "Sure I like you, but I still think there is time for another hot dog."'

She was much more concerned with what she regarded as the dignity of her profession. At about this time, she heard that John Barrymore seemed destined for a speedy decline in his once brilliant fortunes. 'You know what,' she said to the studio, 'I think it would be nice to play his daughter again.' It was a gesture from the heart that before long would be seen as typical – in spite of the totally opposite public persona – but it was never acted upon. And then she was once more having to watch her own career.

Few people had much that was nice to say about *Sylvia Scarlett*. Pandro Berman remembers it as the time that Kate and

George Cukor 'ganged up on me'. She played a girl who, as part of a scheme to help her criminal father escape, dresses as a boy. 'A freak picture,' recalls Berman. 'I hated it as a book. I didn't want to do it, but they were both mad about it. I said that we should get a script, which was written for us by John Collier. George and Katharine were wildly enthusiastic – I'd never seen them so keen to do anything.'

What really persuaded him to go ahead was the fact that he discovered that Paramount were ready to release Cary Grant for the movie and he had always wanted to do a film with him. As is so often the case in movies, it was what didn't happen that turned out to be at least as interesting as what did. It was a story that had one other exciting male role. With Cary Grant sewn up for the part of a cockney, there was still another young Englishman to be cast. Berman, convinced he had been railroaded into a film he didn't want to make, thought the one redeeming feature of it all would be the chance to feature a handsome young Australian he had just discovered.

'I thought he was going to be a big star. I tested him and he was good – very good. I showed the test to George – but Cukor couldn't see him for dust. Katharine didn't like him either. I had signed him for seven years, a contract that granted us options on his services providing he did this picture for us first. But Katharine and George didn't want him for this picture at all – so we let him go. His name was Errol Flynn by the way.'

Berman adds he doesn't hold this against either Kate or Cukor. But he added forcefully: 'We didn't make any money out of the picture and I was denied the chance of having this big star working for me for years and years. I don't know – in fact, I don't care if Katharine and Errol would have got on well together in the film. The picture is secondary to what Errol Flynn would have been to us at RKO.' The role in the end went to Brian Aherne, who appears to have got on very well with Kate and everyone else connected with the film.

It was a time for enjoyment as much as work for many of the members of the company. Much of the filming was done

[48]

at Malibu and Kate, no longer married to Ogden Smith – although that had never really been a consideration – seemed to be a highly desirable target for the men who frequented the resort.

Although there were so many men in her life, her attitude to the opposite sex worried people close to her. Even her father had expressed reservations about her approach to men – although he would admit it may have had something to do if not with environment, then with geography. 'All you New England girls look at a man like a bull about to charge. You're very forthright and truthful, but you do sort of put a man off.'

At no time did she seem to have that effect on a tall, lanky moustachioed young man who took advantage of the Malibu setting to sweep in for regular visits in his seaplane. His name was Howard Hughes.

Nobody had any doubt that there was a heavy affair going on between Kate and Hughes. He would before long own the very studio for which she worked, but for the moment he was as swept up by the glamour of the film-star world as he was by building aircraft and manipulating money. He was also intoxicated by Katharine Hepburn. She probably saw in him a strength of purpose that for her seemed extremely masculine; again one of the values for which her father had always seemed to stand.

The film was nothing like as successful as the relationship between Kate and Hughes. The producer, in fact, took a long time to feel even the slightest affection for the movie. On the night of the sneak preview of *Sylvia Scarlett* at Huntington Park, Cukor and Hepburn had an early dinner together before going to see the film. They were both convinced that it would be the great success they had been predicting all along to Pan Berman. 'I can,' said Cukor, 'quit the business now and rest on my laurels.'

When Kate agreed, he laughed. 'Wouldn't it be funny if we have a flop,' he said, absolutely certain that this was beyond the bounds of decent possibility. They only had to wait for the lights to be down for about five minutes for the joke to come horrifyingly to life. It was a total disaster. Half the audience walked out and those that remained stayed to shout abuse at the screen. Nobody, apparently, could understand what it was all about. Later the cast gathered for what turned out to be a wake at Cukor's house. Berman arrived late, in a distinctly I-told-you-so mood.

'We know,' said Kate. 'We know. We caused you all this worry and we were wrong. We'll do another picture for you free of charge.'

Pandro Berman told me, 'I remember saying something at that. I can't say what.' Cukor always insisted that what Berman said was : 'God almighty! I want to get out of this house. I never want to lay eyes on either of you again.'

He was allowed a break from having to do that by Kate's own determination to get away from Hollywood at every possible opportunity. In between pictures – and this became the habit of a lifetime of film making – she would go back to Connecticut to be with her family. It was firmly inscribed in her contract. She had the studio's understanding – a binding one at that – that she could leave after every picture had been completed. As she said at the time: 'I like Hollywood and picture acting. But I still believe it's healthy to run away regularly.'

At 'home', it was as always her father, Dr Hepburn, who was treated as the star of the family – and the one feared by her sisters' beaux. Harvard student Ellsworth Grant had to find a way to pluck up sufficient courage to ask the doctor for his daughter Marion's hand. He decided that the best way of doing so was simply to make an appointment as a patient. He gave his name as 'I. M. Stuck' and said that his complaint was a 'heart case'. Kate was on hand to speed things along. There's no doubt, however, that if she hadn't approved, she would have sent any prospective brother-in-law away with a giant-sized flea in his ear.

Kate was totally involved with family affairs. While she was home, she used the time to swim, to play tennis and to play golf and, sometimes, to take charge. 'I think I'm the boss here,' her father would say. 'My wife thinks that she runs things, too. But when Kate is home, we all know that she's the boss.'

It was while she was on the golfcourse that the Hepburn

[50]

house blew down in a sudden storm. She raced back, helped her mother and sisters out of the mess and then phoned her father at his office. He listened carefully, seemingly unemotionally. Finally, he said: 'You didn't, by any chance think of setting light to the house before it blew away, did you?'

'No,' Kate said hardly knowing whether to laugh or cry.

'Oh,' her father replied. 'It's a pity. We're insured for fire – not for hurricanes.'

Fortunately, the family was still very comfortably off. Her father knew enough about finance to avoid the terrors of the Wall Street crash – and he was very profitably investing his eldest daughter's Hollywood salaries, giving her a modest if comfortable allowance from the proceeds.

At the end of this particular stay, Kate returned to Hollywood to find that despite Berman's protestations, her last movie hadn't after all lost very much – simply because it hadn't cost much in the first place. Everywhere that it did play, the theatres were empty – for the first ten years of its life. Eventually, however, it became something of a cult movie and in time, has come to be considered as a classic, a great success. But at the time it was neither of these things. It lost, RKO once worked out, $168,624.04. But if it didn't do much for Katharine Hepburn, it established Cary Grant as a comedy actor of immensely attractive potential.

As for Kate herself, she seemed to be frightening people. Her old admirer Adela Rogers St John wrote in *Liberty* magazine about her again: 'As vital as Mussolini. [Mussolini was a man to be looked up to in those days], as natural as a small boy sitting on a fence, as honest as her own freckles, Katharine Hepburn is not only a great actress and potentially the greatest we have ever had in this country, she is the finest type of girlhood and womanhood that America possesses.' Pandro S. Berman needed to be convinced. But the animosity, real or imagined, between him and his director and star was not strong enough seriously to prevent their working together again. They did so the following year in *Mary of Scotland* which, for all the producer's protestations, Berman bought with Kate in mind. He had seen Maxwell Anderson's play about the Mary Queen of Scots story on Broadway and decided that she would be just right for the title role. He had Fredric March lined up as the Earl of Bothwell, Kate's ancestor. He did not know that the Queen had a baby daughter named Bridie Hepburn. Even if he had, the knowledge would not have been enough to save the film.

Berman doesn't remember it any more affectionately than the earlier picture. And for good reasons. It cost – and lost – a great deal of money. There were, however, lighter moments on the sound stages of RKO that, in historical terms, could be said to compensate for the now forgotten box-office take.

It was one of the first times that Kate demonstrated while working on a film, her yearning to be under the power of a strong man – a not always appreciated characteristic of her makeup. She told Berman that she wanted *Mary of Scotland* to be directed by John Ford. In every way, it was a very strange choice. The sophisticated New Englander plainly had nothing in common with the hard-drinking, uncouth Irishman (another not-too-obvious connection with a film about Scotland). Even more strange, Ford, rapidly becoming established as the master of the outdoors epic, had very little experience working in other cultures – and practically none at all working with women.

Nevertheless, there was a chemistry between the two of them (later there were to be claims that there was even an affair, although no confirmation has ever come to this from Hepburn). Kate, however, her powers of observation as acute now as when she marched with her mother in the suffragette parades, was disturbed by one profound difference in their lifestyles.

'She came up to me on the set one day,' Berman recalled. '"Do you think," she asked "John ever takes a bath?"' It was a question that she thought entirely relevant. Not so much – or at least she never spelled it out that way – because the heat from the lamps magnified certain aromas coming from his direction.

Pandro Berman told her, 'Well, I imagine he does – once in a while, although I suppose he does look a bit scruffy.' 'Yes,' Kate replied. 'I'm going to tell you something. I'm convinced he's been wearing the same shirt since the picture started four weeks ago – and has never changed it!'

'I couldn't tell you,' said Berman, trying to sound diplomatic. And then spoiling it slightly added: 'You would know better than I do. You're down on the set all the time.'

'Well,' she said. 'I'm going to find out.'

About a week later, Kate brought up the subject with her producer again. 'I'm right,' she said. 'He's still wearing it.'

'How do you know?' he asked her. 'Easy,' she said. 'I got a blue pencil and when he wasn't looking and had his arm leaning over a chair, I put a blue cross on the sleeve. He's worn it every day since – and the blue cross is still there.' Since Katharine Hepburn has never been one to call an Irishman's shovel by any other name – or to be tinged by the blarney – when the film was over she put the unwashed shirt to its owner. He confessed there and then. He wore it on every picture he made. He thought it brought him luck.

Not enough luck to make *Mary of Scotland* a box office hit. The picture cost about $800,000 – more than was ever to be spent by RKO on even an Astaire–Rogers picture. It didn't recoup more than a fraction of that. If Kate wasn't so conscious of everything around her, one might have been forgiven for thinking that she was too far removed from the habits of normal Hollywood mortals to bother with such things as the money her movies did or did not make. As it was, it is fairly certain that she could tell her agent to the penny what she thought her talent was worth in terms of returns in the theatres.

But that was not the image she created for herself. Close friends were puzzled by her behaviour, even those for whom it seemed her eccentricities were charming diversions. Why else would an established star walk through the RKO lot with a monkey on her shoulder? (It was later discovered that the little primate, which she wore attached to the shoulder strap of her dungarees, was rented at a daily rate.) Why did she insist on taking perhaps seven showers a day?

And why was she rapidly gaining the reputation as Hollywood's number-one housebreaker? She wasn't anxious to

[53]

pursue any crime; simply that her always overwhelming curiosity got the better of her every time she saw a window open in an otherwise deserted house. If there was no one at home, she simply climbed through the gaping aperture and began an investigation of all that lay before her. But there wasn't much risk of anyone doing that to *her*. By another strange paradox her own privacy was what she valued above all else.

The Hepburn house, high on the Hollywood hills, seemed to deter invaders like any medieval castle placed in a similar position. Besides, she had probably let the local crime syndicate know that she would repel boarders with boiling oil. They would have had reason enough to believe her. She didn't like visitors to her film sets and the publicity outfit at the studio would try to find ways of ensuring a tactful response to requests that she meet people – men or women whom she regarded as simply interrupting the work that was in hand.

One director said he had the answer: 'Yell: "No" at her seven times. If you try to be tactful, she thinks she must be right.' She nearly always thought she was right in her choice of material – by now RKO wouldn't dream of making her take roles that didn't instantly appeal to her. But she was still frequently wrong – although in 1934, she and Wallace Beery had been awarded gold medals in the Venice Film Festival and declared 'the world's best movie actors'.

A Woman Rebels, however, did so badly – it was a suffragette story – that Pandro Berman says he can't remember a thing about it. In that BBC broadcast, Alistair Cooke described the Katharine Hepburn performances in *A Woman Rebels* and *Mary of Scotland* as 'sad'. 'There is one consolation, however, for Hepburn addicts. You don't have to have taken drawing lessons to see that Katharine Hepburn has a lovely skull and that's one thing that the studio can't change. It's on view all the time in *A Woman Rebels*.'

There were at the time, however, people who saw the title of that movie as saying a great deal about Kate's attitude to playing the Hollywood game. She continued to give her sniping comments to reporters. One or two of them diligently reported her answers to questions about her family: 'I've been married three times,' she was said to have told them. 'And I have ten children.' There was no suggestion in the subsequent reports that they knew she had been less than frank.

What they did believe was that when she went to Ivorytown, Connecticut, to play at the summer theatre in *Dark Victory* – before long to be a Bette Davis Warner Brothers film classic – and said she was going to 'show 'em' – 'show 'em' she would. But she called off the venture before the play went into production.

At home on one of her trips to Hartford she found she was being chased by a couple of photographers. She crouched in the back seat of her car. When the men stalked their way towards her, she lunged at them both with her tennis racket. They slunk away, examining their dented cameras and rubbing rapidly appearing bumps on their foreheads.

In years to come, her actions would be copied by other actors and actresses a hundred times, but until she did it, the Hepburn response was totally unknown. Stars either avoided cameramen or were not reluctant to admit that they enjoyed every moment of it – and would be deeply offended if it did not happen. But Kate's attitude was beginning to disturb the fan magazines, the journals that may not have had too great a literary reputation but which the studios regarded as one of the hands that fed them.

'Should this rebel have been tamed?' asked Mark Vyse in *'Picturegoer'* magazine at the time *A Woman Rebels* was released. The magazine suggested that she had lost a succession of much better roles because of her 'self-will', a crime of which no real lady should ever be guilty in the mid-1930s. Mr Vyse went on: '"I can't play it that way because I don't feel it that way. I don't want to do it the accepted way," this child of the individualistic upbringing would cry. Small wonder that harassed authorities turned to someone more amenable.'

And there was worse to come. After having sympathised with the problems the Hepburn personality may have faced with her directors – mostly in *Mary of Scotland*, in which, she said, there had been 'an unfortunate decline' – the writer said:

[55]

'This does not alter the fact that Katharine's accent jars and that, in spite of vitality and sincerity, her performance lacks dignity. Nor has she thoroughly mastered the art of wearing period clothes.' An unfortunate comment considering the piece was headed with a picture of Kate and Herbert Marshall in *A Woman Rebels* in which she looked quite beautiful.

But the writer was enjoying his sniping, and merely warming to his theme: '"Not goodbye, arrivederci, they say in Italian," she says to her lover in *A Woman Rebels* – a moment when a touch of sweetness would be permissible, even welcome. Yet in striving for sincerity, she delivers the line as though she were asking the milkman not to call till next week. Katharine is only twenty-eight. Those who believe – among whom I count myself – that there is something fine in her work which no adversity will kill, may live to see her give a performance which will establish her in this country as one of the greatest actresses of the screen. In the meantime, should she be in the position of having a daughter to bring up, I doubt if she would be as much indulged as her mother.'

He may not have realised at the time just how unlikely a situation that was. Once again, she said that she never wanted motherhood. 'I had no intention of doing that! I was a pig from the start! But at least I had brains enough to recognise that I was a pig. Often the eldest daughter has the sense to stay independent.' Having younger brothers and sisters helped her in that view, she always maintained. 'I watched five other people being brought up and felt not me, thank you. I think certain people are brilliant at motherhood. And I don't think those people should be forced to work in insurance companies. Women's position in life is so much more complicated than men's, isn't it?' Another time she said: 'I made the decision not to have children many years ago. And I don't regret it. I also chose not to make a career of medicine and I don't regret that either.'

Kate tried not to let the worries over some of the things being written about her bite too deep. Occasionally, however, she allowed her feelings to come to the surface – although her replies were sometimes difficult to understand and not

[56]

calculated to draw sympathy from families whose bread-winners were standing in line at soup kitchens. 'I am paying a terrible price for fame,' she said in May 1934. 'It's almost impossible to enjoy life after you achieve success in pictures.'

To some people, nothing fails like success, and the fact that a few papers, despite the attitude of the competition, were constantly calling Kate 'the new Garbo' was rankling. The same *Picturegoer* was agreeing that Hepburn was 'A Hollywood mystery woman'. But if that sounded flattering, then the reader had to read on:

'The chief mystery about Katie is – why is she still a screen star? Yes, I know she has something to offer that others haven't. I know she is practically (to coin a frightful word) unglamorisable. I know she is no beauty in the Hollywood sense, that is that she has not the facial bone structure and the figure that can be conventionally camouflaged into an exact replica of every other Hollywood leading lady. I know that she has audacity, enterprise, fire, verve, elan and a number of other spirited qualities. I admit all this, and I agree that things may be in her favour – provided they are not overdone. And they are and she survives them – and therein lies the mystery. Why has her fire not caused her to be fired?'

It was one of the few cases in which a film magazine was going all out to attack one of the idols of its readers. And doing so mercilessly. 'There seems to have been no definite official discountenancing of the – shall we say imprudent behaviour of Miss Hepburn,' noted *Picturegoer*, unable to decide why Mr Will Hays, who ran Hollywood's morals, had not acted on behalf of the studio community. 'Why? What is the mysterious power which this tall, angular red-headed woman wields, which forces Hollywood to put up with her gaucheries? It seems extremely unlikely that her company, RKO Radio, greatly enjoys the situation. For they have always been noted for smooth, peaceful inner workings and an almost idyllic standard of "personal publicity". Why should red-headed Katie be allowed to be the sole black sheep of the flock without being ba-arred: Why has her career not been interrupted by her enterprise?

[57]

And so the magazine went on to speculate. 'There is only one generally accepted excuse for this, and that is the excuse of the box office. An enormous repayment to the studio in dollars and cents, pounds and shillings, kopeks and piastres and yen and pice is the only answer that disarms criticism. But is it forthcoming? Here with the possible exception of *Little Women* is no irresistible succession of triumph such as gives the star the right to say "to heck with the front office." No. There must be something about this oddly attractive woman which disarms the full force of criticism and compels her sponsors to persevere in their efforts to make her a world beater.'

What was upsetting the press was that Kate had arrived in London and given not so much as a smile to waiting newsmen – who, compared with their treatment of some of their American colleagues, didn't realise how lucky they had been. The London *Daily Mail* had written: 'When you were accused of imitating Garbo, you retorted: "I don't want to be alone. I just want to be *left* alone." Well, Miss Hepburn, that is impossible for a star of your brilliance. You ought to know by now that complete privacy is impossible for someone so much in the public eye. I don't suggest that you put a notice on your door, saying "Interviews granted; twenty-four-hour service." I don't want you to address a mass meeting of your fans in Trafalgar Square. But I should very much like you to give me fifteen or twenty minutes of your time whenever you come to Britain.'

Her fans suffered equally. About this time she had the doors of her car electrically wired, so that they would be held back. Once she changed clothes with her maid so that the fans outside a theatre wouldn't recognise her. And there were certain celebrities whom she had upset as well. Soon after arriving in Hollywood, she had an invitation for dinner from a woman whose name she didn't quite get. 'Afterwards,' she explained, 'I discovered she was Mary Pickford and I had turned down an invitation to Pickfair! I apologised and Mary forgave me and invited me again. I went – and talked the whole time. I was never invited back.'

Why was she so difficult with the press? It was partly

because she saw no reason to offer her private life on a plate to people who were complete strangers. But Douglas Fairbanks took it a stage further for me.

'I think she was just born like that in Connecticut, and was pretty well much like that in the theatre. The attitude to the press was the same that a lot of people from the theatre felt – that this was just such a ridiculous circus and she wasn't going to contribute her end of it to this circus. If you don't like it go to hell – or lump it, whatever phrase she might have used. She had the courage to say and act in a way that a lot of other people felt but didn't have the courage to do. They thought that they had to conform or lose their jobs. She said: "To hell with it. If I lose my job, I'll just go back East." She worked hard and that was the best she could do.

'I know that people think she was abrasive. I've never felt that way about her. But I think people have teased her about it and she's become more conscious of it, until sometimes there was a period of time when it began to be deliberate and conscious, and then natural – but exaggerated a bit. If she'll talk to some friend or other, she'll be brusque and feel free to take liberties.'

Years later, Kate herself was to confirm that attitude. In a long article in *Esquire* she was quoted as saying: 'I know that I have a lot of qualities that just sort of put your back up. I can just open my mouth and my voice irritates some people. It has a sort of challenge. It just says, "What the hell are you gonna do about this," doesn't it? My tone of voice is rather aggressive and there's a certain violence in it. Well, I like that. And I feel good, so I'm violent. I come by that naturally . . .' All the stars for whom she herself had respect – and she mentioned such names ranging from William S. Hart and Tom Mix to Joan Crawford, Bette Davis and Greta Garbo – 'had strong, strong personalities.' One Hollywood producer put it like this: 'If she were cast as Little Red Riding Hood she'd end up eating the wolf.'

The American magazine *Pictorial Review* was on much the same tack as the other writer, but they seemed to concentrate on Kate's lifestyle. They couldn't understand why she wasn't fulfilling the dreams of her fans and living like a star. For instance, she had only just bought herself a big car 'which she had obtained at a rare bargain'. But it was her style of dress that really upset this guardian of the rights of moviegoers to see their idols as just that, people removed from the cares and responsibilities of mere mortals.

'When not in costume for her role, she wore faded blue denims [which shows how far ahead of her times she really was] . . . Her shoes are the worst things any woman has ever worn, away from a wheatfield. They range from canvas-wrapped atrocities to hobnailed boots and, as she is always sticking her feet high up on the most fragile piece of furniture in the room, no one in the movie city ever missed the footgear.'

There was also this barb from an actress who was never reluctant to criticise Kate's fashion foibles: 'Throw a hat at her and wherever it hits, it will hang,' she said. But what no one seemed to realise at the time was that her clothes were not some crazy affectation. She didn't wear trousers to shock or to prove that she was independent – she didn't care. What she wanted was simply to be more comfortable. Kate didn't believe any of that was anyone else's business. If they wanted to write about her, then let them publicise her work – although she wasn't talking about that either.

She took to the road in a stage version of *Jane Eyre*. It was produced by the Theatre Guild, with a view to a New York opening. Katharine Hepburn, film star (despite everything, nobody could take the appellation away from her), saw it as a marvellous opportunity to revenge what she still considered to be her earlier humiliation at the hands of the company.

She was offered $1,000 a week – and promptly demanded the figure to be upped to $1,500. The difference was the 'blood money' to which she thought she was now entitled. She didn't enjoy the play much and decided not to go with it to Broadway. But on the road, it was a box office hit – partly because the Howard Hughes circus was fully in operation. There was as much excitement in the autumn of 1937 seeking out Hughes and Hepburn as there was in seeing Kate's stage performances. As far as she was concerned, however, she still gave the impression that she didn't care in whose company she was seen.

The play was a sensation at Omaha, Nebraska, in the middle of a bitterly cold, dreadfully damp spell. When it was all over, she drove herself to the station to catch the 3.30 a.m. train. On the way, she passed the stage carpenter, driving a prop-laden horse-drawn waggon. 'That's Wally over there on that waggon,' she called to her companion. 'I think I'll go and ride with him.' There and then, in the driving rain, she left her comfortable sedan and climbed up on to the cart so that Wally wouldn't be alone.

Few people would say that she was herself alone during the run of the play. Five and a half thousand people filled the Masonic Temple at Des Moines, Iowa for *Jane Eyre* – on the same night that Shirley Temple was in town.

Other members of the Hepburn clan were not immune to the pleas of the press for news of the wayward Katharine. But when the reporters chased Mrs Hepburn Snr they were more concerned about her ever-more daring statements on birth control. 'I have ceased to worry about people being shocked,' she said after debating the issues with the American fascist Father Charles Coughlin of Detroit. 'They're shocked already and I want to get it over with. The terror of race suicide [one of the main arguments of the anti-contraception lobby] is nonsense, for women want children. But they want them when they can afford them physically and emotionally.'

Kate wasn't a great partygoer. When she was seen at one of those Hollywood functions which exist to flatter the egos of the hosts rather than to provide enjoyment for the guests, there was a fairly good chance that she would set a few film tongues a-wagging. That was partly because she was never afraid to speak her mind. Sometimes because the wrong things slipped out of her mind at quite the wrong moment.

Nothing caused more difficulty for her than the affair at which she met the actress Elissa Landi, who had just made the film version of *The Warrior's Husband*, playing the same part which Kate herself had done on stage. The two women appeared to get on like a studio on fire, talking shop, and the shop that interested them most was, of course, *The Warrior's Husband*.

'Which scene did you like best?' asked Miss Landi.

Kate's reply caused her companion to freeze and the other guests clustered around them to cough nervously into their champagne glasses. 'Oh,' she said, 'the one where you run across a field and vault a fence. It seemed to me to have so much more life and spirit than the other scenes.'

She didn't know it, of course, but that was the one scene that Miss Landi did not perform herself. A stunt girl had done it for her. For an all too long embarrassing moment, it seemed that the cats were about to scratch.

As did some of the critics about *Quality Street*, a chocolate box piece about the end of the Napoleonic wars. Franchot Tone co-starred. Like most boxes of chocolates there were some parts of *Quality Street* that weren't quite as tempting as others. Pandro Berman told me he doesn't remember very much about it.

Blessed with Gregory La Cava directing, there was never much risk of that being the case with her next movie *Stage Door*. Kate was known to have a strong antipathy to alcoholics. La Cava was a sodden drunk. 'A bum,' said Pandro Berman. 'But he was also one of the finest talents I have ever worked with.'

Not just the picture – the story of life in a New York girls' theatrical boarding house – benefitted from his delicate direction, but Kate undoubtedly did, too.

'What a brilliant man he was!' said Berman. He was brilliant because he flouted convention, yet achieved the results other great directors may have gained by doing things the way they had always been done. Other directors accepted a script, awarded roles to actors and actresses and then shot the scenes. That wasn't the way La Cava did it at all.

'He was a man who never saw a movie apart from the ones he made himself,' Berman recalled for me. 'He would say, "I don't know if So-and-So is suitable for the part" and I'd say "Well, of course you don't. You never see a film." Well, once having accepted that a person should have a certain part, he'd

[62]

spend days studying that actor or actress. He would then work with the writer in adapting the action and the dialogue to suit the personality of the player, instead of doing things the other way round.'

In fact, he changed the script so much that George Kaufman – who with Edna Ferber (the much-acclaimed writer of *Show Boat*) wrote the original story – said cryptically, 'Why the hell didn't he change it to *Screen Door*?' He was unconventional in another regard, too. He would spend the mornings doing nothing but rehearsing – and then at noon would work on rewriting the script. In the afternoon, he would shoot. 'But he was so great,' said Berman, 'he would get just as much film into the camera in that afternoon as another director would get in a whole day's shooting.'

La Cava of course had his problems, and they were mostly connected with his drinking. Once, he fell off the stage of the theatre where they were filming location shots – in a drunken stupor. But as a director he managed to make the cast feel as though they really were lodgers in the boarding house that formed the background to the movie. They were, in effect, a repertory company of young women who before long would become magic names in their own right.

Hepburn was the star. On hand, too, was the already established Ginger Rogers. And with them, a young redhead called Lucille Ball and a wisecracking thin girl named Eve Arden. 'I remember how we looked at Katharine Hepburn with a certain awe,' Eve Arden recalled for me. 'Not envy, but a respect, an admiration. She was always full of advice for us.' And she added: 'I have always admired her integrity, strength and courage. I am sorry not to be in the position of being closer friends. I'm sure we all looked up to Kate in the picture.'

That was apparent even to the extras. They were so moved by a Hepburn speech – cut for effect by La Cava from four pages to ten lines – that some of them were found weeping by the time she was finished. The director wanted Ginger Rogers to weep too – not for real, but for the camera. 'She is strictly the menthol type,' he said afterwards. 'The only way I'd ever been able to get her to cry before was to tell her her house was

[63]

burning down.' But he played a recording of the Hepburn speech to her as the cameras rolled – she hadn't been present when it was originally filmed – and she, too, wept real tears as if to order.

Kate herself, however, was not afraid to take a full ration of advice from her director. 'I think,' said Berman, 'that he was great for Katharine, for Ginger and everyone in the picture –but particularly for Katharine, because she was slipping at the time pretty badly. *Stage Door* was the picture that saved her goose.'

It had cost $900,000 to make – La Cava was to charge that Pandro Berman probably debited a couple of new buildings to the film's budget – but brought in the practically unheard of sum of $1,900,000 at the box office. Kate's goose was not just saved. It was given a lush new field in which it could run. 'She is the complete intellectual actress,' La Cava said after the film had been completed. 'She has to understand the why of everything before she can feel. Then, when the meaning has soaked in, emotion comes, and superb work.' Years later, that would be known as The Method.

RKO responded to this new lift to her career and to the effect it had on studio morale by giving her a new opportunity to work with Cary Grant, now rapidly established as Hollywood's favourite light-comedy leading man. The studio thought it had a property which would do for their joint talents what *Sylvia Scarlett* manifestly had not been able to do.

Bringing Up Baby, produced and directed by Howard Hawks, was a crazy story about a zoologist and should have had every theatre till from Hollywood to Hatfield ringing loudly. Instead, it took off with all the impact of a wet sponge on a forest fire. The mutterings of the theatre people suddenly became amplified speeches. The last straw was delivered by Mr Harry Brandt, President of the Independent Theatre Owners of America. He took a newspaper advertisement in which he declared that Joan Crawford, Kay Francis, Greta Garbo – and Katharine Hepburn were 'box office poison'. Somehow, it was the name Katharine Hepburn that really got people talking. The others were, in their way, cult figures. But Hepburn was still very young and very controversial.

The statement stung – although, as Pandro Berman told me, Kate kept her feelings well to herself. But it was obvious for days just how depressed she felt. The company in which she was placed may have looked impressive but the message was deadly. So deadly, in fact, that RKO responded by offering their one-time blue-eyed girl a film called *Carey's Chickens*.

5

Gone with the Wind

WHAT WAS NOW facing Katharine Hepburn was a seemingly glaring alternative – either toe the line and make a B-picture that you hope everyone will speedily forget, or break your contract and take the consequences.

It was a card game in which, in 1937, RKO Radio Pictures had all the aces. The contract system had been tested in the courts. More than that it had been seen to be inviolate even abroad. Hadn't, just the year before, Bette Davis been dismissed in the High Courts of Justice in London as a 'very naughty young lady' – and then sent packing? A contract, said the judge, was a contract and not even crossing 3,000 miles of Atlantic could alter that fact.

Kate's decision, based on the hard fact of reality, was to think that she had never been part of Hollywood, had a sound financial base at home in Connecticut and if saying no to RKO meant the end of her film career, that was just too bad. She told the studio bosses: 'Look fellows, don't let's mince matters. I'd like to get rid of you. You'd like to get rid of me. Let's call it a day.'

But she decided to do so honourably – and expensively. 'How much do you want?' she asked the company. It was an offer to buy her part of the agreement. The studio called in its accountants and did some accounting. The figure they came to was $220,000. With less difficulty than she had found in managing a tear for George Stevens, she got out her cheque book and wrote the figure and signed her name to it.

She was free – and desperately unhappy. She thought that, for all her protests that she didn't enjoy filming, she would find work easily elsewhere. It didn't come. The studios had an unhappy habit of letting their rivals know that they wouldn't take too kindly to their discarded properties being picked up. Kate, as always, thought she could beat the system.

Before very long, she could. She signed with Columbia to make *Holiday*, the same story by Philip Barry from which she had taken her screen test. In this she played the dowdy daughter of a patrician New York family who falls for her sister's boyfriend (Cary Grant). The scenes in the nursery of the huge Manhattan household when the rest of the family have left for Christmas Day services are some of the most memorable of her career.

It was a reunion with her old friend George Cukor, who was determined to make of the partnerhip everything that *Sylvia Scarlett* had not been. The decision to make the movie was, as much as anything, a chance for the iron dictator of Columbia, Harry Cohn, to cock a snook at the rest of the film community with whom he was in the midst of his periodic wars. Once having made that decision, he sold the picture with his traditional flair. It worked. The film was both a commercial and critical success. What was more, having made the movie, Kate was again an acceptable, marketable commodity.

There was time for her to contemplate her future. She also did that rare thing, made a speech. The young woman who was never frightened of pontificating in private, was as uninterested in getting across her views on life from a public platform as she was in a newspaper interview. Her views were precisely that, *her* views. But in 1938, she spoke to the Herald-Tribune Forum, sponsored by the New York newspaper and established to let personalities of the day reflect on the world around them.

She quoted Beth in *Little Women*, 'I have an infirmity. I am shy.' She spoke about the power that the moving picture offered. Children went to the movies because they liked them. 'We go to be entertained, to laugh, to weep, to think and to be inspired. There are a great number of brilliant and talented producers, writers and directors in Hollywood whose sole occupation is to provide us with an opportunity for just this, to say nothing of the bankers. They work day and night in a mad effort to give the public what it wants.

'Now in the field of the classics they have a comparatively

free hand, and they have done a fine job. For some reason or other we do not seem to be so touchy about the political, economic and moral problems of our grandfather's day, with the possible exception of the Constitution. We can face those problems simply and courageously without fear of the consequences. In other words, we can face the past with a clear conscience and we can allow our children to do the same.'

It was developing into a defence of the film industry – not at all the sort of thing her adversaries in the studios would have expected. 'But allow a movie to present situations in which we are all involved now; allow a movie to show people their plight and suggest a way out, allow a movie to present a political, moral or economic topic of the day, honestly and simply and they are told to do nothing, say nothing, and hear nothing.

'They are sent scurrying back to the shelves to redraft that poor old story of boy-meets-girl. Then the producers are blamed for not having any originality. We are all creatures of habit. If we are fed on innocuous platitudes we cannot develop either mentally or morally. Are you going to allow this medium of public enlightenment to be stifled? The producers apparently do not dare fight this battle alone, and I don't blame them, because their risk is too great – they must have the public back of them.'

It was not the sort of speech that men at RKO would have expected, although doubtless the exhibitors now thought that was just what they would expect. To them, it was not only highly uncommercial rubbish, it sounded downright communistic.

'Now,' she went on, warming to her theme brilliantly, 'if you want intelligent censorship, that is censorship which will give you movies which will not only entertain you but contain an idea or two, the women's clubs of America can certainly help. You can make this matter one for discussions at your meetings. You can all write to your state censorship boards, insisting on a more liberal attitude and you can write to the producers, encouraging them to produce better movies, better modern movies and guaranteeing your support.

'You who are responsible for the growth and development of the men and women of tomorrow must be very careful that in an effort to protect your children's morality, you are not crippling their minds.' And she ended by quoting George Bernard Shaw. 'A nation's morals are like its teeth, the more decayed they are, the more it hurts to touch them.

'Prevent dentists and dramatists from giving pain and not only will our morals become as carious as our teeth, but toothaches and plagues which follow neglected morality will presently cause more pain than all the dentists and dramatists have at their worst since the world began.'

What she really wanted to do was to pick up on another one of those might-have-beens that came along during her RKO stint. It had happened – or not happened – just before she made *Bringing Up Baby*.

Lillie Messenger, the talent scout who all said and done had really been responsible for Hepburn's arrival in Hollywood, had read a book which she thought was not just up Kate's street but should be sitting in her front parlour. In fact, she read it in galley form and fell hopelessly in love with both the novel and its heroine, a girl with the kind of spirit Kate was demonstrating every day she appeared before a camera.

Copies were immediately arranged to be sent to Kate herself to read, to Pandro Berman and to Leo Spitz, who was now head of the studio. Kate wasn't sure at first. So she read it again – and started what could only be described as a love affair with the story. Berman wasn't nearly as impressed. It would cost much too much to make – even though Spitz himself said he would buy it if Kate wanted to do the movie (he had never blamed her for the string of film failures while at RKO).

'How much will it cost?' she asked the mogul.

'Fifty-two thousand dollars,' he replied.

'Too much,' she said, 'for a film for me.' Why she said that, no one ever knew. It was probably another example of her frankness, this time working to her own disadvantage.

But Lillie Messenger was instructed to, just the same, make a bid for the film rights when the book came up for auction. Berman also agreed. But then when the sale was held, the producer changed his mind – and that of his boss, Mr Spitz, at the same time.

Warner Brothers withdrew, too. 'No book is worth $50,000,' said Jack Warner head of the studio and regarded as what today would be called the movie town's principal guru in such matters. And so both Warners and RKO were out of the bidding for *Gone with the Wind* – and, it seemed, Katharine Hepburn had for ever lost the chance of being Scarlett O'Hara.

The sale, as everyone now knows, went to David O. Selznick, then both an independent producer and Louis B. Mayer's son-in-law. Since, as a hundred people have since said, the son-in-law also rises, a comfortable deal was arranged between the two men – that while Selznick would make the film, MGM would distribute it.

The producer knew who he wanted for the roles of Scarlett and Rhett Butler – Bette Davis and Errol Flynn. But since Davis wouldn't work with Flynn – they had had a less than happy relationship in the films they had already made together – he settled on Clark Gable for the Butler role. What happened after that, is also film history.

He announced he was looking for a Scarlett and was ready to begin a nationwide hunt for one. Kate hadn't the slightest doubt that she was perfect for the role. If Selznick had been considering another Yankee like Bette Davis, he couldn't claim the Hepburn accident of birth as a valid reason for excluding *her*. He did, however, have other reasons, which became apparent when they met to discuss the possibility. He asked her to test for the part. Kate believed that was far too demeaning for someone of her calibre, and refused.

'You know what I look like David,' she said.

'Yes,' he replied, 'and I can't imagine Clark Gable chasing you for ten years.'

The cruelty of the remark made Kate's red hair bristle, her freckles stand out like angry goosebumps.

'I may not appeal to you David,' she thundered. 'But there *are* men with different tastes.'

Selznick was obviously very pleased with the phrasing. He was alternately suggesting that she was not at all suitable and trying to see whether they could come to financial terms. Nor was he accepting her refusal to make a test as a final decision.

In a memo to Daniel T. O'Shea, his chief aide, in October 1938, he said that the reason for his reluctance was the fact that Hepburn, like another hopeful, Paulette Goddard (who had agreed to test) had 'an audience's dislike to beat down'. And yet, only a month later, he was listing her together with Jean Arthur (whom he had previously rejected as having 'identification with other roles to overcome'), Doris Jordan, Loretta Young and the same Paulette Goddard as one of the 'best possibilities'.

He said in another memo to O'Shea: 'Presumably by the time you receive this, you will have determined whether or not it is possible to conclude an agreement with Hepburn. If an agreement *has* been concluded, Hepburn should be sent for immediately and her test should be carefully selected to include the scenes that require the most sex, because I think Hepburn has two strikes against her – first the unquestionable and very widespread intense public dislike of her at the moment, and second, the fact that she is yet to demonstrate that she possesses the sex qualities which are probably the most important of all the many requisites of Scarlett . . .'

A week later, he was saying that Kate ought to be told that she was in the final list of candidates for the role. But of course he hadn't yet heard of Vivien Leigh. The public had not heard of her either, and although no one outside of Selznick's private office knew any of the detail, word was already being leaked of the search for a Scarlett that was soon to burst as the most powerful publicity stunt of all time.

Already *The New York Times* was asking the book's author Margaret Mitchell who her favourites were. The story was that she had already stated a preference for Kate. 'Not true,' she said. 'I don't know any one in the movies who looks like Scarlett.' She said she was going to remain strictly netural – even though Mrs Ogden Reid, Vice Chairman of the *New York Herald Tribune* said she had visited her friend Miss Mitchell at her Atlanta home and had come out enthusiastically for a Hepburn O'Hara.

Now all she was saying was, 'I told her I thought Miss Hepburn looked pretty in the hoop skirts worn in *Little Women* and I liked that picture very much. I have never expressed a preference and I never will. If Mrs Reid understood me to say I felt a strong preference for Miss Hepburn in the role, I owe her and Miss Hepburn an apology.'

It was the end of the Tara road for Kate.

6

The Philadelphia Story

SHE WASN'T SURE what she wanted to do next. Secretly, she still hoped that the part of Scarlett O'Hara would be hers, that it was just a question of waiting. So she did it by trying to play hard to get. If she went back East and played, she reasoned, it would be merely a matter of time before offers of the parts that she considered suitable for her would come thundering in.

It didn't happen quite like that, and the reason still had a lot to do with her breach with the Hollywood system. She was now an independent in the age of the studio contract. The moguls didn't like that sort of player at all. With a star under contract, they could dictate terms that, while apparently mutually convenient, still suited them best. A freelance player could be a trouble-maker – and everyone knew what Katharine Hepburn's reputation had been.

Story ideas did come, however – with good money. MGM offered her a contract at $5,000 a week. One other studio was suggesting the previously unheard of sum of $125,000 for a single picture – but one she wasn't going to sell herself to make. There was even an offer for a several-pictures deal at $400,000 which she rejected in a telephone call. No. If it couldn't be Scarlett O'Hara, the alternative had to be superb. (Bette Davis had said much the same thing to Warner Brothers – and since she was under contract, she was much more limited.)

Instead of accepting any of these offers, she went home and played tennis, swam – and when she went to New York spent as much time as possible cycling in Central Park. It seems that the local journalists were more interested in her wardrobe than her career prospects. She had, one reported, a mink coat, a 'Russian scarf' and three pairs of slacks.

In the evenings she discussed her financial situation with Dr Hepburn who was no more worried about her economic stability than she was herself. The family investments were still paying handsome dividends and the number of noughts on a studio cheque were more important for the status they represented than for the things they could buy. She even spent time with her former husband, 'Luddy' Smith. He took her to the theatre in New York and agreed to handle some of her financial investments which needed a more professional eye than even her father could give.

Frequently he would go to the Hepburn summer home at Fenwick – even when Kate wasn't herself there. A room at the beach house was recognised as his – next to those of Kate's brothers, making the top floor of the house a men-only retreat.

Kate wasn't any more short of men friends now than she had been when she was busy fighting off the Hollywood cameramen. Howard Hughes was still on the scene. Together they were guests at a party at the home of the President of the forthcoming New York world's fair, Grover A. Whalen – one of the few occasions when the eccentric Hughes would agree to come out of seclusion for a semi-public function.

Another of the visitors to Fenwick was Philip Barry, who came as a private guest and stayed to be a business partner. The conversation got round to story ideas and he had one in which he wanted to involve Kate. There was a character called Tracy Lord whom he knew that she and nobody but she could play. It was the story of a young divorcee who discovers – to nobody's great surprise – on her wedding day that she prefers her first husband to the one she is about to marry. The play was *The Philadelphia Story*.

They discussed it word by word at Fenwick – and Kate fell in love with it. She knew it would make a good film, too, but for the moment there was more than a feeling of satisfaction at the thought of scoring the huge success that this could have on Broadway. That would be sweet indeed. They talked about it in the Fenwick house, and at a party. It wasn't what the urbane Mr Barry, one of the best-dressed men in the literary-dramatic set, wanted. He couldn't discuss his plans for what he was convinced could be a stage masterpiece surrounded by dozens of people competing with each other to press home the latest pro- or anti-Roosevelt argument.

'We got woods,' said Kate. 'Come out in the woods and talk.' They talked and Kate loved what she heard even more. From Fenwick, they moved their discussions to Barry's own home in Maine. It was such a good proposition, she thought, that she wanted it to be a business investment, too. The first person she asked about that was her father.

He looked at his daughter with the eye of an admiring but protective parent. There was no investment to the Wall Street community as precarious as the stage, he told her with the experience of a man who called his stockbroker as frequently as compulsive gamblers are in touch with their bookmakers or family cooks with their neighbourhood butcher shops.

But he was also able to read a script with the background of knowing every penny Kate had earned in Hollywood – and how she had earned it. He devoured *The Philadelphia Story* manuscript. 'But,' he said with due consideration. 'This one could be it. This could be it.' The recommendation was enough.

It wasn't the only one. Kate also had the backing of Howard Hughes, who was in the last phase of his relationship with her. He had taught her to fly and now put a plane at her disposal so that she could continue commuting between Fenwick and Maine with greater ease for her discussions with Barry. He also provided some of the cash for the investment – including all of that for the screen rights.

Before long, the play and the plane were hers. The Theatre Guild had agreed to present it and Kate was a fully-fledged partner in the whole operation. She put up a quarter of the money needed to get the show on to the stage, in return for 25 per cent of the stage profits. She also bought the rights for any screen production, with agreed bonuses. She secured, too, 10 per cent of the gross profits from the Broadway run of the play and 12.5 per cent of the touring profits. It was the kind of deal which show-business lawyers haggle over in the 1980s and think has never been done before.

But it didn't all go as smoothly as the conclusion of this agreement and history would appear to convey. Kate adored the first act, but didn't feel anything at all for the second and third. At one point at a Fenwick discussion, she turned to her author and business partner: 'I'm sorry, Phil. But this isn't for me.' Barry got over the huge jolt to his ego, worked on the scenes and got them the way Kate thought they ought to be.

The play was a masterpiece of casting – much of it put together by Kate herself. She had Joseph Cotten, at the beginning of his period as a member of the Orson Welles repertory company, playing her husband. Dan Tobin as her brother and Shirley Booth – who would achieve stardom late in life in the film *Come Back Little Sheba* – playing the reporter.

It was also a story made as much with Kate in mind as a pair of trousers sculpted for her in Paris. But it wasn't any easier for either Kate or Philip Barry when the play got on the road for its pre-Broadway tour. Or rather once it reached the end of that tour – for it opened to rave local reviews and marvellous audience response. Just five days out of New York and in the traditional final try-out city of Boston, Philip Barry saw a performance and decided it would be lucky to last a week.

'Your nerves have got to you,' he lectured the cast – including his star. 'You're the most congealed bunch of hams I've ever seen.'

Needless to say, Kate was not accepting that. Her language was tough and salty. 'You're conceited,' she told him in one of her more printable statements. 'You haven't the slightest understanding of sensitive people, and you should never be allowed to speak to a cast.'

But Katharine Hepburn was having problems, and not just with nerves. Her voice, already so distinctive, was now sounding much too strident. Another coach was found to knock off the less pleasant edges.

Kate arrived in New York just before opening night in a state of mild panic. Later she said she was so terrified of failure that 'it was like a kind of death'. Instead of staying in the house she now owned at Turtle Bay in the city, she moved into the Waldorf Astoria. She couldn't face the idea of worrying about running the house *and* the play.

She wouldn't allow any visitors – not even her immediate family. The curtains were drawn. Whenever a moment of utter panic overtook her, she repeated three words to herself: 'This is Indianapolis. This is Indianapolis. This is Indianapolis.' It wasn't terribly complimentary to the townspeople of Indianapolis, but they doubtless would have understood what she meant. What happened in their city really wouldn't have mattered very much to the career of Katharine Hepburn. One false move on Broadway, however, and she was washed up.

All the way in the car she hired to take her to the theatre, she kept her eyes closed. Still the same words were being whispered or said, unspoken with closed lips. 'This is Indianapolis. This is Indianapolis. This is Indianapolis.' She was saying it to herself as she walked through a flower-bedecked Shubert Alley on the way to the stage door and she was saying it, too, as the curtain went up on her adjusting some flowers in the living room set. (She insisted on changing the try-out pattern of her coming into the room in 'an entrance' – because she said she couldn't stand the effect that the audience's applause would have on her. She needed to say the lines at the very start and get them over with.)

Perhaps that was what did the trick. The play was a huge success at the Shubert Theatre. This time, Brooks Atkinson had no doubts about her. He recalled his previous reservations, however. 'A strange, tense little lady with austere beauty and metallic voice, she has consistently found it difficult to project a part in the theatre. But now she has surrendered to the central role in Mr Barry's play and she acts it like a woman who has at last found the joy she has always been seeking in the theatre.'

It was an intuitive statement. Joy was precisely the emotion she now felt.

By the 415th performance of the play in the autumn of 1939, a total of $961,310 had been earned at the box office – a phenomenal sum in those pre-World War Two days on Broadway. There were to be another 254 performances on tour. All of it meaning a magnificent return for Kate's own initial investment. More important, it did wonders for the Hepburn career. The jinx looked as if it were finally laid to rest.

In 1940, she was given the New York critics' award for the best actress of the previous season. She accepted in a two-way radio link from Dallas, Texas, where she was completing the road tour. 'I'm hysterically happy,' she told her listeners, in one of the very few public statements she had ever made. (It confirmed her own contention, of course, that when she had something to say, she would.) And then she acted out a scene from the play on the air. It was said that her honour was 'almost undisputed'. The awards came flooding in. Astonishingly, to all those women of style and film executives who had been cattily talking for so long about her tastes in fashion, the New York writers also elected her as one of the thirteen best-dressed women of the year. Significantly, she was not among the twelve who gathered at the Waldorf Astoria to show their taste to the assembled photographers.

But she did pose for a portrait – one that was said to symbolise 'The Spirit of Tolerance', commissioned by the Council Against Intolerance in America. It was used as a poster installed on the corner of 7th Avenue and 42nd Street in New York and in the Council's nationwide Independence Day ceremonies which were said to be a 'declaration of tolerance and equality'. Back home in Hartford and Fenwick, Dr and Mrs Hepburn couldn't have been more happy.

All this fitted in perfectly with Kate's other political activity – her support for her union. She came to the help of the Association of Actors and Artistes of America in their fight against the stagehands' union who wanted to organise the performers, too. Kate decided it was time to make a political stand. 'For nineteen years,' she said, 'the AAAA (it was known as the Four As) has performed ably and honestly, representing the performers in the theatrical profession.'

As much as anything it was Katharine Hepburn against the stagehands' parent body, the giant American Federation of

Labour. 'Any attempt,' she said, 'on the part of the AF of L to disregard the just claims of the AAAA will be regarded as a breach of faith not to be tolerated by the loyal members of our union.'

Kate was appointed Chairman of the Four As. As a result, she clashed head on with another daughter of Hartford, Connecticut, the vaudevillian who proudly boasted of being 'The Last of the Red Hot Mamas', Sophie Tucker, 'Soph' decided she would be very happy to join the stagehands and their union, the International Alliance of Theatrical Stage Employees. As a result, Kate's group managed to close Tucker's New York show *Leave It To Me*.

Meanwhile, James Cagney and Miriam Hopkins had offered their support for the Hepburn position, which was now being seen as out-and-out war with Sophie Tucker. 'I've been up against big billing before,' said Sophie.

The AF of L were called in to arbitrate and Kate was declared the winner. And she was victor, or victrix perhaps, in another fight closer to home. Rather, *at* home. Kate was having a nap at the East 49th street brownstone house when a burglar broke in, and found his way into her bedroom. He got as far as handling a pearl necklace worth $5,000.

Kate, for whom the nightly catnap was a necessary prelude to going on stage for *The Philadelphia Story*, saw the intruder through the corner of an eye. As he darted to the door, Kate pulled a dressing gown around her and rushed after him. She chased down the staircase. He rushed past Kate's butler and cook – who then joined their employer chasing him out on to the pavement. He managed to get away – after jumping into a waiting car, an accomplice at the wheel.

The necklace meanwhile remained safe on top of Kate's dressing table. Afterwards she was no more forthcoming about the affair to reporters than they might have expected her to be. 'I won't talk about it,' she said, telling them their job in a way that never ceased to offend her when they told her hers. 'It is not news.'

The Philadelphia Story, however, was news. And long after the original reviews, the papers were still writing about it. *The New*

York Times didn't know whether to be pleased or distressed at this development. In a long feature article, Jack Gould wrote: 'The legend of Hepburn ranks close to that of the bigness of Garbo's feet. For a decade the fable has flowered and bloomed to proportions that would made didactic Aesop turn over in his grave. Friends and foes complained that she carried her Yankee nose a notch too high . . . . hacks for the fan magazines had her squatting in the middle of Hollywood Boulevard. The headline writers had a good time.

'Alas, there has been a "great change". On every hand assurances are volunteered that to the legend of Hepburn must be added a new chapter. Sweetness and light have come to the little spitfire. Time and a hit show have wrought nothing but good, it is alleged on high authority by persons close to persons in usually well-informed circles. All may be forgiven and forgotten.'

In fact, Mr Gould was really saying a great deal; a lot of it true. The success of *The Philadelphia Story* had made Kate feel a great deal more secure. 'The truest explanation [the writer opined], is that she bets on long shots. Last season, she jolted Hollywood circles by buying up for a tidy sum her contract with a motion picture firm to stake her reputation and future on the stage . . . As is the gambler's way, Miss Hepburn has enjoyed winning. For all the fame she may have garnered in the celluloids, her real ambition has been to achieve success behind the footlights, if for no other reason than when in her teens she told her schoolmates she was going to be an actress, the schoolmates laughed. Miss Hepburn now has the last laugh at $3.30 a head at the Shubert.'

After the huge success of the stage play's New York and touring runs, she sold the screen rights to MGM. All the studios had been after it. Seemingly none of them had any reservations about the script or the star. The moguls were like circus clowns doing verbal somersaults to invite her into their centre ring.

The men who from behind desks made intentionally large – to inhibit actors and other employees who would have to walk a 'dolly-shot' length of carpet – could previously be heard muttering to aides, 'Keep that crazy broad away from me,' were now saying very different things. They were on the phone themselves – a rarity indeed – imploring 'Katharine darling' to have lunch with them in their private dining rooms – almost never available to mere actors and actresses who might pick up a morsel of gossip they weren't supposed to hear – and sign on the dotted line.

Kate signed with MGM because she believed that the sophistication that studio was beginning to show was just right for 'her' story. It also made the best financial offer – which might just possibly have been due to the kind of shoes she was wearing. Garson Kanin, who wrote a justly famed memoir that was to cost him Kate's friendship, suggested that the shoes, ugly in design but with massively high heels, made her feel that she towered over Louis B. Mayer to the point that he was inhibited by her. It is more than possible. It wasn't easy to argue with Miss Hepburn when she had a queen bee buzzing in whatever served as her bonnet. When the bee was her demand for what she considered to be only her just reward, the impression of height provided by those hideous shoes made men like Louis B. Mayer positively quake.

For other people, 'L.B.' allowed the tears to cascade down his cheek so that they *knew* the great act of charity he was performing in allowing them the privilege of being on MGM territory; let alone working at his Culver City studios.

Kate gave an instant impression of terror to a studio boss. Put her in the cage where Leo, the MGM lion, lived and it would be the beast banging on the bars asking to be let out.

Nurturing a film deal can sometimes seem more like giving birth to a baby. In the case of Hepburn and *Philadelphia Story*, the comparison was perfectly just. It took no less than nine months to get it all organised. Kate had placed certain conditions on the deal. Not only did she insist on playing the lead role of Tracy Lord herself – she wouldn't allow any other thought to come to mind – she also knew that there was only one man who was going to direct the film, George Cukor.

It was in a way a conspiracy between them. They had talked about it incessantly since she had sewn up the screen rights for herself. Cukor had been in the audience at a whole series of live performances of the play, so that he was in a position not just to know the story, but to see where his star was best, and work out the way he was going to change a scene here, adapt one there and perhaps to provide whole new episodes of the story to ease the continuity along.

Donald Ogden Stewart was retained to write the screenplay, because Cukor wasn't sure that Barry could do what he felt was needed for a filmed version of the play. Louis B. Mayer agreed with all that. But he still demanded a number of clauses inserted into his idea of an insurance policy – either because he felt he had more to lose than his opposition or because he was still secretly worried whether there could be any true antidote to a dose of box office poison.

He therefore refused to accept the idea of Joseph Cotten playing opposite Kate – a fact that, years later, Cotten himself was to tell me was one of the big disappointments of his career as a journeyman actor who became a star but never a superstar. He wanted big, big stars to play with Kate. Like Robert Taylor. 'No thanks, LB,' said the handsome actor who was not known for ever mouthing anything that had not been scripted for him.

Clark Gable made noises amounting to: it wouldn't be fair to the studio to compromise all the good he had done for MGM with *Gone with the Wind* with a tough cookie like Katharine Hepburn who might want to do unpleasant things to him. He had already once been 'sold out' to Columbia – then regarded as the positive dregs of the Hollywood studios – for disobeying a Mayer order and the result was the stupendous *It Happened One Night*. So the mogul was not inclined to argue too forcibly. He settled for two men who were under contract and whom he thought were just becoming big enough to get people to line up outside neighbourhood theatres – even if the notion of Katharine Hepburn starring in her own picture didn't persuade them to leave their firesides.

Her own first day at Metro hadn't been the most welcoming one. She was left sitting in an outer office for an hour until George Cukor arrived to identify her. The big question was, of course, whether she really could beat the 'box office poison' jinx.

[81]

All she would say about it herself was, 'I made more money doing *The Philadelphia Story* as a play than in my whole time in Hollywood.' To do the film, Kate had to accept a long-term contract with Mayer. At first, he tried to strike a hard bargain. Kate was not short of the necessary weapons for answering back. 'Look Mr Mayer,' she said. 'I know you're deliberately trying to charm me and yet I am charmed.' So charmed that they came, she said, to a 'fair' agreement. She got her own way.

The contract, unlike virtually any other in the history of that most rulebound of studios, was purely verbal. For all his lachrymose histrionics, Mayer accepted that there was something exceptional about this woman that was worth accepting on her own terms. And, she would always say, he lived up to every clause in that contract himself.

For her own part, Kate said years later in an interview with Louella Parsons: 'I get so mad at some of the things they say about Mayer.' She usually called him Mr Mayer and that was a temporary slip. 'Mr Mayer . . . understood the agonising vagaries an artist has to go through. He didn't get angry at his stars when they got drunk or did things they shouldn't.'

He put Cary Grant in the role of her former husband – he and Kate always got on well together so there could be no risk of chemistry souring the well-explored formula – and had James Stewart backing up the rear as the journalist sent to report on the family junketings.

It was a happy picture. They did silly things a lot of the time and that makes for a good atmosphere – even though, on one occasion, it was a somewhat heady one. Kate presented a gift-wrapped package to one of the company. He opened it excitedly and found inside, a satin-lined box and a very dead skunk. Not at all the sort of thing you would expect from a lady of Miss Hepburn's breeding. But it was a Kate-type thing to do. It seems that she had found the animal on the way to the studio and thought the other members of the company would enjoy a decent funeral. With due solemnity, Kate then went out on to the lot and dug a hole for the burial ceremony.

There may have been some significance in the fact that once having got the box made to her specifications, she presented it

[82]

to Jack Greenwood, the script clerk – who had the difficult task of correcting Kate when she made a mistake. Perhaps she was trying to tell him something. But it did seem like a very good joke.

Was this a new Kate? The impression she was giving was that it most certainly was. She even agreed to talk to the press and to pose for publicity stills.

The story was so right for Katharine Hepburn. The line 'Who the hell do they think they are, barging in on peaceful people, watching every little mannerism, jotting down notes on how we sit and stand and talk and eat and move', came straight out of the Kate Catechism.

But nothing was going to make her fall in line with what Hollywood decreed to be best for their performers. In fact, not long before, she had admitted that she was one of the actors and actresses who had been threatened with dismissal for upsetting her studio for a set of reasons totally different from the usual bouts with the Establishment.

This time the explanation was political. She said she would not vote for the Republican Californian Governor Sinclair. The Democrats had alleged that their opponents were demanding a day's pay from all the top stars towards campaign funds and all the big studios were co-operating in getting the players to respond. That was not the Hepburn way at all. In time, naturally enough, the furore died down.

It was intensely hard work for Kate, practically producing the film as well as starring in it. She lost eight pounds in the process – although still found time for tennis when not required either on the set or to read an edited script. Kate's own part of the deal was worth a quarter of a million dollars, a virtually unheard of sum for the time.

What was also unusual for the film was the fact that an assistant director was given a degree of authority that a senior man like Cukor would regard as an infringement of his own role, and a star, like Hepburn in particular, might consider an impertinence. Eddie Woehler, Cukor's assistant, became both a sounding board for his principal's own thoughts and a useful producer of ideas himself. As did Woehler's wife.

[83]

It was Woehler who said he thought Kate 'fluttered' too much in the play. 'My wife saw that in the play,' he reported, 'and she doesn't like that. Don't let Miss Hepburn flutter in the picture, George. All that fancy running around drives my wife mad.'

There were other people around at this time who were rather attracted to Kate's running around. Among them, President Franklin D. Roosevelt, who was one of the first American leaders to see the value of having top show business personalities around him. In 1940 a whole gaggle of stars were invited to the Roosevelt New York State home at Hyde Park to discuss their possible public-relations contributions to his coming third election campaign. Kate was among them. But instead of travelling in one of the specially hired trains that was to take the other Hollywood people, she chartered her own seaplane, flown by another pilot.

He landed in the midst of a Hyde Park river and Kate waded ashore with her slacks rolled up. But some of the mud stuck. And a man like Roosevelt wasn't beyond seeing the funny side of a situation that in voting terms could be very valuable indeed. When the President passed her in his car, he called out: 'I'm very flattered Katharine that you would go to all this trouble to see me.' It was a line that deserved to be flashed round the world. A President hob-knobbing with movie stars? The man must be human after all!

It seemed that a great many people were anxious to return that kind of compliment to Kate herself – such as Laurence Olivier and Vivien Leigh, the beautiful English girl whom Kate was not yet sure she had forgiven for being discovered by David O. Selznick and then beating her to the role of Scarlett O'Hara. The pair were in Hollywood to film *That Hamilton Woman*, in which Vivien played Lady Hamilton to Olivier's Nelson. They were also in the midst of their own very personal love affair. But it was a frustrated one. Olivier was still married to Jill Esmond, and was anxiously awaiting the date when his divorce would be finalised and so be free to marry again.

When the day arrived, Ronald Colman offered his Santa Barbara home for the ceremony. It was all arranged extraordinarily hastily and quietly in order to beat the newsmen. One of the few to be told was writer Garson Kanin, who had a mysterious phone call in which it was suggested he act as the best-man and witness, and at the same time he was asked to find another witness. How about Kate as maid of honour? he asked.

The couple had no objections. Nor did Kate, who jumped at the idea. Not only was she quite friendly with the pair who would soon be known as 'the Oliviers', she loved the notion of a conspiracy to beat reporters and photographers – at anything. It was part of her war with the press and she smelled a battle that looked all set for victory.

The Oliviers would soon be regarded as the number-one couple in the theatre, unsurping the thrones of the Lunts and the Barrymores. But the family that still counted most in America were the Roosevelts. When Eleanor Roosevelt, the President's wife and herself regarded as one of the primary political influences in the country, asked Kate for help, it was not a request to be treated lightly, even by a lady who seemed at times to have so little respect for authority.

America was still officially at peace, but Mrs Roosevelt was as determined as her husband that the country should join the fight against Nazism. When the government propaganda machine decided to make a film aimed at getting more women to think of helping their country – this was almost a year before Pearl Harbor – the First Lady offered all the assistance she could give – which meant, in turn, the help of people whom she knew. One of them was Katharine Hepburn.

'I'd like you to narrate the picture,' said Mrs Roosevelt. Kate said yes immediately.

It was certainly very different from her role in *The Philadelphia Story*, which was proving even more of a triumph than the brilliantly successful stage version. There was no false modesty from Kate about this. 'I saw it like a vision,' she herself said at the time. It turned out to be like one of those popular songs that is there for ever, the kind Tin Pan Alley calls standards. In Hollywood, they are less inhibited. They call them classics.

But it didn't win Kate the Oscar for which she had been nominated and would love to have won – for that would have proved she was firmly back in the Hollywood saddle. Instead, Ginger Rogers walked away with the statuette for her title role in *Kitty Foyle* – a part which Kate herself had been offered. There were the compensations of the box office, however.

The Philadelphia Story was to break all records at Radio City Music Hall, the place where *Little Women* had been an earlier Hepburn triumph. But Kate was not going over the top with her celebrations. No champagne parties. No new cars. Simply a few gifts – like eight swimsuits, most of which went to her sister Peggy. One of them she kept for herself. (The film was remade fifteen years later – as a musical with Grace Kelly in the Hepburn part, Bing Crosby as the former husband and Frank Sinatra as the reporter. That, too, has earned a following of its own – although largely through the Cole Porter music. In its new incarnation, it was called *High Society*.)

It was a story that would stay with Kate for a long time, one that she wasn't willing to let go. Filming done, she took the original play on to the road – almost as if that was the version which she considered to be the more pure and the one whose taste she wanted to remain on her tongue. The last performance was, inevitably, held in Philadelphia itself. When it came to the end of the very last scene, she went to the footlights and told the audience that it would never be played again. But, she wouldn't let the stage hands bring down the curtain. 'Let the people just walk away,' she commanded. 'The curtain could never come down on *The Philadelphia Story*.'

It was her classic, too. And with or without those shoes, she was walking very tall indeed.

7

Song of Love

SPENCER TRACY WAS bluff, Irish, with red hair and a temperament that fitted the image perfectly. He was also a great actor, married to a woman named Louise, had a son called Johnny and a daughter named Susie.

Johnny was born deaf – which meant that until Louise, who became a universally recognised expert in the art of dealing with deaf children, taught him he was unable to speak. Because of Louise, Johnny even went to college.

Spencer was a devoted family man with a few problems. Which is probably the way he would have liked to have been accepted. His main problem was that it all got too much for him. He didn't enjoy living at home. He also drank.

Kate and Tracy had known each other casually for some time, in the way that Hollywood people do tend to develop acquaintanceships with those in their trade who match their degree of success. They may not become intimates, but inevitably, they talk of each other much as people living on a middle-class housing estate casually know their neighbours and get to call them by first names, nicknames and diminutives – Freddie, Greg, Harry, Kate – even if they never visit each other's homes.

What brought the two together was a story idea that Garson Kanin had planned about a woman political writer who marries a sports reporter – the only thing they have in common being the love they have for each other. He immediately saw it as a partnership for his own two close friends who had never worked together but whom he thought were 'naturals'.

Kanin was called up for military service soon after convincing

Kate that she ought to play the political writer. He then handed the idea over to his brother Mike and to Ring Lardner Jnr. Before long, it would become *Woman of the Year*. How it all got to MGM has the makings of an early-1940s black-and-white Tracy–Hepburn story in itself – one of those pictures that has to feature bull-nosed Packard cars and houses with the kind of maids who answer back.

It was Garson Kanin who sent her the finished story. When it arrived, she confessed soon afterwards, she was afraid to open the envelope. But open it she did – and read it. 'It's magnificent,' she called to her friend and sent it off to Joseph L. Mankiewicz who she knew was buying stories for Metro. But before despatching the opus, she removed the front page, the one with the authors' names below the title. What was more, the men had typed it all out themselves. Kate wasn't willing to risk anything leaking by sending it to the usual agency to be completed.

There were two reasons for this. For one thing, she was convinced that the studio would either reject a story by men who were virtually unknown in Hollywood at the time – or if they did buy it, would do so at a price that didn't justify its merit. For another, if the story were rejected, tales of that rejection would fly round the other studios like news of an illicit romance. However, if the other studios didn't know the title of the piece in question or the authors . . . It was like not knowing the names of the couple involved in the juicy scandal.

Now Kate, for all the hardness that other people see in her, has a reputation for doing good turns for men and women she hardly knows – the kind of good turns that get instant attention even if she cannot always guarantee the results. In this case, she wanted the scenario to be accepted just as much as the writers did.

Mankiewicz – who, the story goes, had once dubbed her Katharine of Arrogance – was highly suspicious. He accused her of being neurotic. Her answer was simple: read it, don't quibble.

It all seemed to happen at a fairly fortuitous time. Just a day or so earlier, Mayer himself had told her: 'I'm disappointed

[88]

we've found nothing for you. I'm even more disappointed that you've found nothing for yourself.' Well now she had. Kate was going to New York. Mankiewicz promised to call her there. By the time she arrived at East 49th Street, there was already a message that he had, in fact, called.

The first question was the inevitable one: who wrote it? He had a feeling that he knew the answer. She had told him already that it was a partnership presentation. He had an inkling it must have been Ben Hecht and Charles MacArthur, who had produced the classic American newspaper story, *The Front Page*.

He also had a feeling they would come expensive. He wanted to know how much. Kate was still not saying. She had some sums of her own to do and there were going to be complicated features to those accountings. Naturally enough, the matter was not allowed to rest, even for a day. Another MGM executive, Sam Katz, rang her with the same questions. She still was not giving the answers.

That was when the name Spencer Tracy was mentioned again. Mankiewicz came back on the phone to say that he had shown the story to Tracy who liked it so much he was hoping to postpone his role of an impoverished farmer in *The Yearling* to do it.

It had got to the point when it was up to Mayer himself to conclude the negotiations. It was the typical 'L.B.' scene, the message of confidence, his appreciation of her great talent, her beauty even, his statement that it was in her interest to show complete confidence . . . The lump in his throat was growing like a snowball being rolled downhill; the tears welling in his eyes; the spectacles taken off so that he could clean the lenses as he pleaded on the long-distance phone line from Culver City to Manhattan.

She agreed to fly back to the West Coast to talk to him direct. This time, she didn't prevaricate. She said she knew all the things Mayer had told her on the phone. She also knew that she had a humdinger of a property which she was willing to sell him. She still wasn't willing to reveal the names of the authors. But the price, if he really wanted to know . . .

[89]

The rest can be imagined. 'Katharine darling . . .'

'Katharine darling' said the price was $211,000. She didn't add, 'take it or leave it'. But that was very much what it amounted to. It was a strange figure to ask. But then, she *had* been doing those calculations. She wanted $100,000 for the two authors for their story. She insisted on $111,000 for herself – for her part in bringing it all to fruition.

Mayer, without quibbling, offered $175,000. Without quibbling herself, she said no. Well, he pressed, where on earth did she get the figure of the odd $111,000? $5,000 for each of her two agents, she explained – she never could see any reason for them to take their cut from *her* money – and another $1,000 to cover 'telephone calls and things'.

It was settled. Mayer said he would pay the asking price – no doubt shedding a few *genuine* tears in the course of working out how the film's budget was going to be affected – and now he wanted to know the names of the authors. She told him, and Mayer shrugged the hunched shoulders inside his Eddie Schmidt (the number-one 'By appointment' tailor in Hollywood) pinstripe jacket.

Outside his office, Mankiewicz, who had overheard everything, hugged the star of his next production and said 'I've just kissed the blarney stone.' But it was a stone that still needed polishing. With Kate controlling it all as if she were an orchestra conductor in rehearsal, the writers and George Stevens – who everyone concerned had now decided should direct the movie – went through the script line by line until two o'clock the next morning.

It was the first time any of them could remember Kate being up after ten o'clock. Every detail was gone over like the hair of a prize dog at a competition show. Neither of them wrote 'yes' for Kate. She always said 'yah' in her normal conversation. Why let her sound anything but normal? 'Rahly' was the way she said 'really' so that was the way it appeared in the script.

George Stevens had no doubt, from the beginning, that the sports writer should be played by Spencer Tracy. The Kanin brothers and Ring Lardner were of the same opinion. MGM, who had now come to Kate with a long-term contract that

At the time of Kate's Hollywood début. (National Film Archive)

Her first film. With John Barrymore in *A Bill of Divorcement*. (RKO)

Kate's first Oscar came with *Morning Glory*. In this scene, she is between Adolphe Menjou and Douglas Fairbanks Jnr—who admitted to the author that he fell madly in love with her at the time. (RKO)

Looking more beautiful than the real *Mary of Scotland* could possibly have looked. (RKO)

In *Quality Street* with Franchot Tone. (RKO)

In life one is called upon to play many parts. In *Dragon Seed*, Kate was supposed to look Chinese. So were Walter Huston and Turhan Bey. (MGM)

Bringing Up Baby also helped bring Cary Grant to stardom. (RKO)

The Philadelphia Story suited Kate as did the hat and dress she wore in the movie—here with James Stewart and Cary Grant. (MGM)

The great love in her life—Spencer Tracy. (MGM)

Spencer and Kate in their first film together—*Woman of the Year.* (MGM)

And in their last—*Guess Who's Coming to Dinner?* The years didn't diminish their love. (Columbia)

Kate—never happier than on a bike. On her right, Robert Morley. (National Film Archive)

With Spencer in *Adam's Rib*. (MGM)

appeared to meet all her demands, wanted no one else. The only one who had any qualms was Kate herself. She was full of them when they first met.

'I'm afraid Mr Tracy,' she said politely but with the tone of voice that meant she wasn't in the least bit afraid of anything and had made up her mind to say no, no matter what, 'I'm afraid that I may be too tall for you.'

'Don't worry,' said Spencer. 'I'll soon cut you down to size.'

They laughed. They were at the beginning of the kind of partnership nobody at the time could have foreseen. It was the start of one of Hollywood's greatest love stories, and one like no other in the history of the gossip centres of the world where it seemed as though everyone knew everyone's story. There were no secrets about Gable and Lombard. The scandals of Errol Flynn's various relationships were so well documented that Jack Warner of Warner Brothers – whose own dallyings with ladies who took their clothes off for him at the drop of a contract were legion – insisted that he either stopped or married one of the women concerned. Bogart's various affairs made the scandal sheets and the showbiz papers.

Yet for reasons that have never been properly explained, people knew about the relationship that was soon to be called Tracy and Hepburn and said nothing. Of course, the details would have given ample excuses for the newsmen and women who had awarded Kate their 'Sour Apple' for lack of co-operation to have their revenge. But they never did. It may be that they knew of Spencer's home problems. Perhaps they had an infinite respect for Louise's work and didn't want to upset her. Perhaps they had simply stumbled on a love story that nobody wanted to spoil. It seems highly unlikely. The real answer is that the press didn't know. The gossip was stilled because the film town had decided to rally around two of their own. But that was still in the future when the details of *Woman of the Year* were finalised.

Already a number of people were very happy. Not least of them Mike Kanin and Ring Lardner Jnr. A new car drove up at Kate's Hollywood home the day after it had all been settled. It was left in the driveway. Attached to the ignition key was a note: 'To the Agent of the Year from the writers of *Woman of the Year*'. It perhaps made easier her favourite hobby – house-breaking.

There was no roof that was too steep for her. With the help of whichever petrified friend she was with – it took a lot more bravery to complain about Kate's actions than to aid and abet her – she would climb on to the gutter and get in through the nearest window. As she proudly told disbelieving Hollywood guests: 'Nothing keeps me out.' She simply nosed around the house, looking in one room, walking through another door, and going out through the closest window when she had seen enough.

But she always added, the presence of a friend was essential because she was – and you had to believe it – 'naturally timid'. As she explained: 'I'd go through the skylight, throw a rope to (my friend) and lug her up. I don't have too much nerve on my own. People think I do, but I don't. But I have a great ability when I get prodded.' That went for her acting as much as her burglary.

'I sometimes think that our business is personally humiliating because you are, after all, in the position of the common prostitute. You're selling yourself and everyone begins to say, "Oh boy. We've had enough of that", if you've been around too long.'

She was by now thrilled that Spencer Tracy would be co-starring with her. She had been watching some of his work and she agreed with the writers that he was the only one for the part. The conspiracy to get him had been helped by the fact that he had already started work on *The Yearling* – and was hating every moment of it. It was being shot on location, which meant swamps and flies and he detested that sort of working environment. When the cameraman finally decided he didn't like it either because he couldn't keep the flies off the camera lens, it was a gift from heaven for everyone concerned. Spencer could bow out of the picture with a clear conscience, because it wasn't working out anyway and Kate could get the co-star she wanted. (*The Yearling* would be made four years later with Gregory Peck in the lead as the farmer with the little boy who falls in love with a fawn. Greg told me that his abiding memory of the picture was the boy – Claude Jarman Jnr – who knew how to cry to order but then never stopped. Spencer wouldn't have liked that either.)

But that first meeting between Kate and Spencer hadn't been easy – even before his threats of cutting her down to size. He surveyed the way she was dressed. 'Not me boy,' he said to Joseph Mankiewicz. 'I don't want to get mixed up in anything like this.'

What he didn't want to get mixed up with was Kate's trousers. 'You see,' Mankiewicz explained haltingly, 'Spencer doesn't approve of women wearing trousers.'

Soon afterwards, explaining how she got out of that predicament, Kate said: 'I couldn't care less. Well, I've always worn trousers. Never not worn them. I know my legs are good, but I marvel that women should be sainted for keeping stockings up. That's one of the most boring tasks that anybody could ever be faced with. I don't wear makeup, not even lipstick.'

What she did wear on her face right from one of the first scenes in the film was her obvious admiration for Tracy which before the final shot was in the can had become true, unadulterated love. There was also the undeniable admiration she felt for his acting ability. In an early scene at a bar, she accidentally spilled a glass of water while the camera was whirring. Any other time, she would have stopped, the director would have called 'cut', but Stevens knew that Spencer would keep on as though nothing had happened – and he did. He got out a handkerchief, mopped it up, as if going through some bit of business required by the script.

It took time for the couple to get to know each other professionally, really know each other. Early on, she asked him what he thought of her 'play acting'. He was not impressed. 'That's the strangest remark I've ever heard,' he said. 'What's play acting? Do you mean the tricks some people pull on the stage? If that's supposed to be acting, I don't like it.' She didn't ask him that sort of question again.

Woman of the Year set a pattern that would continue through

nine films. They never rehearsed, simply went into the scene
and did it the way it had to be done. 'We didn't rehearse,' Kate
was to say, 'because we didn't need to. Our films assumed that
if the relationship between us was valid enough, the spontaneity would be there. Besides, Spencer was very quick at
getting his effects so I had to become quick, too. But we worked
long and hard on our scripts. I was the one for the finicky
details. Spencer had a mind for the total effect.'

She knew that the effect he wanted in their first film was that
it would be *his* picture. That was all right by her too, although
whether it would have been had she not fallen in love with him
is a debatable point.

Kate has always said that she takes credit for playing the film
at all times 'from his viewpoint, not through the woman's – for
she was a high-brow bossy Dorothy Parker type' [still plainly
no love lost between the two women] 'who'd get the
audience's backs up. I know I've got aspects of me like that.' It
was a daunting confession. To fit in with his requirements, too,
she once more saw some of his old MGM films. She studied
what women in Spencer Tracy films were expected to wear –
and didn't put on trousers all the time.

When filming of *Woman of the Year* began, the gossip around
the studios was that Kate and George Stevens were romantic-
ally aligned. They were affectionate to each other, although
George wasn't frightened of telling her when she was off form
and they fairly frequently dated outside the studio. By the time
the film was completed, there was plainly something very
strong developing not between Kate and her director, but
between her and her co-star.

It was the kind of love that showed itself by the tough things
they said to each other – in public. An insult can be much more
endearing than a compliment in such circumstances. Soon after
it was all wrapped up, the couple rented a house on George
Cukor's West Hollywood estate. It would remain their home
for the next quarter century – with Spencer going to visit 'the
folks on the hill', his family, at weekends, and Kate taking off
for Connecticut when the urge took her.

She could be seen sitting at his feet, asking his advice on

anything from the political situation to the art of acting. Did he have any theories on acting? she asked him once. 'Know your lines,' he replied. 'And don't bump into the furniture.' And that seemed to sum up their relationship. She was the woman smitten personified. Whatever he said, however simply it was said, was marvellous to her.

Other people called him Spence. She never used anything but his full name when referring to him to friends or fellow actors. He had a whole range of names for her which Garson Kanin recalled. They ranged from Kathy and Kath to 'Flora Finch, Olive Oyle, Laura La Plante, Madame Curie, Molly Malone, Coo-Coo, the Bird Girl, Madame Defarge, Carrie Nation, Dr Kronkheit, Miss America or Mrs Thomas Whiffen.' Sometimes he called her 'Zasu Pitts' or 'the Madam'.

Before anyone took the relationship seriously, a newspaper-man had asked her: 'Are you in love with Mr Tracy?'

For once she gave a printable answer. 'Certainly I am,' she said. 'Isn't everybody?'

Another man who may not have been aware of all that he had written between the lines said: 'When you see those two together, it makes you feel envious. They're such a couple of innocents, you couldn't do anything to hurt them.' It was the beginning of a perfect marriage without the document that said it was.

When Spencer died twenty-five years after *Woman of the Year*, Louise told Kate that she would have given him up had she known how serious it was. It seems fairly certain that she did know – and refused. Tracy, a devoted Catholic who had once considered becoming the priest he played in *Boys Town* and so many other movies, would always feel that his faith prevented his having a divorce. The matter had come up years before when he and Loretta Young were in love but, as Miss Young was to tell me herself, she was even more devoted a Catholic than Spencer.

As for Kate, she was always to feel that she had the best of both worlds. A husband she could care about to the point of adoration, but without being tied by law to a relationship she always believed was strictly of the heart. Nevertheless, no matter how strong she was and how powerful a figure she cut in her dungarees and slacks, it was Spencer who wore the trousers in their house. She loved looking after him, trying to curb his drinking, telling him to sit down and take things easy when he appeared to be feeling ill – the premature signs of the alcohol-induced illness that was to kill him.

She kept her public declarations about him restricted to their partnership on the screen: 'We balanced each other's natures. We were perfect representations of the American male and female. The woman is always pretty sharp, and she's needling the man, sort of slightly like a mosquito. The man is always slowly coming along and she needles and then he slowly puts out his big paw and slaps the lady down, and that's attractive to the American public. He's the ultimate boss of the situation and he's very challenged by her. It isn't an easy kingdom for him to maintain. That – in simple terms – is what we did.'

It was more simple than that. They were in love. Friends would come away from their house reporting how happy she was scrubbing the floors – on one occasion she could be seen on all fours washing the tiles of the dressing room in the theatre where he was about to play. At other times, she was just delighted literally to sit at his feet and hand him his slippers. Demeaning to the liberated woman she seemed to symbolise? She saw it as the fulfilment of all her dreams. It was really the perfect answer to the woman's movement.

Kate was nominated for an Academy Award for *Woman of the Year* – although the Oscar went to Greer Garson for *Mrs Miniver*. The writers, however, did get an award for Best Screenplay, and Kate was to earn a different prize: in 1941, *McCalls* magazine named her *their* own Woman of the Year. 'We honour Katharine Hepburn,' said its citation, 'as a woman, not actress though surely she is much of both. Beauty, grace, talent, devotion – Miss Hepburn has the traditional feminine virtues in untraditional ways. She is a raving individual. We should have more like her.'

George Stevens described her as like 'a pitcher who has a fast ball. He knows it's fast as any in the league. He keeps pouring it in while he begins to figure curves and drops, he learns how to cut the corner of the plate. Still got the speed. That's where Kate is now.'

Her relationship with Stevens remained perfect, despite the ending of any romance between them. And it showed itself in a peculiarly Hepburn way. When she shouts at people, they know she likes them – and can shout back. One scene in *Woman of the Year* required her to mess around in the kitchen, without appearing to do anything very sensible.

'Are you going to ask me to do that?' she shouted derisively.

'Yes I am,' said Stevens.

'Why?' she asked, plainly indicating that it was stupid.

'Because you're an actress – and an actress should be able to do anything to put over a show.'

'All right,' she replied, 'I'll do it.'

Not everybody, however, knew her quite as well as they thought. 'She is one of the hardest working actresses in the business,' reported *Colliers* magazine in 1943, 'and will wear everybody in the studio to a nubbin before giving up on a scene. She is entirely without a sense of humour but she is also a very smart girl. She watches very carefully in conversation and when the speaker shows by a glint of the eye that the wow is about to come, she breaks into merry laughter. Even if sometimes misplaced, it is better than no laugh at all.'

Those who saw Tracy and Hepburn – it was Spencer who insisted on getting the number-one billing in their films; she always said it didn't matter – at home saw that they both laughed a great deal.

What they didn't attempt to do was to flaunt the sexual part of their relationship to a world that would have been happy to gape, given half the chance. When they went away together, they always booked either into separate hotels or at least separate rooms. Tracy would have the big suite – although he would say that he didn't like the responsibilities of owning property or buying expensive things. She would take the smallest room in the hotel, and then go from her room – which was almost never used apart from hanging clothes in the closet when the bellboy and maid arrived to deliver her bags and unpack for her – to his by a back staircase; never a public elevator. Even when they shared the West Hollywood house, he kept a suite going at the Beverly Hills Hotel.

Her worry was always his drinking and the friends in similar condition with whom she would sometimes find him. Her admiration was both for his manliness and his talent. She would always say that he was the finest actor she knew. 'There are very few great actors,' she said once. 'Spencer was one. I'm not in his class. Inside him was a light that did a disservice to some poor movies he made – it made them that much shoddier.'

Kate was, however, still anxious to show that her own acting talent was more than intact in the sort of place where it mattered most, the live theatre. In April 1942 she was back on the boards in a new Philip Barry play *Without Love*, about a platonic marriage between a widow and an Irish politician. Her husband was played by Elliott Nugent, and their marriage as a stage partnership was about as successful as the play itself. It didn't work at all.

Spencer went along for part of the tour to keep an eye on Kate. But he stayed at a different hotel from her in every town they went. About the only thing that kept Kate happy while playing in *Without Love* was the fact that the title represented the total opposite of her actual situation.

One of the first places the show played was the Bushnell Memorial Stadium at Hartford – the first time in all her years of stardom that she had performed in her old home town. Her parents, her brothers and sisters came to see the show. And she forced herself to make another speech, this time from the stage. Actually, it wasn't the first time she had played before an audience at Hartford, she said. The first time was at school. 'I once recited *The Wreck of the Hesperus* in public.' The Governor of Connecticut was in the audience for *Without Love*. So was the Mayor of Hartford.

At Pittsburgh, things weren't quite so happy. She had a somewhat intense confrontation with a cameraman who attempted to take her photograph as she walked through the stagedoor just before a matinee of the play. He seemed to be most interested in Miss Hepburn's trousers. As she arrived, the photographer rushed in front of her and snapped – which is precisely what happened to Kate's temper. She took the camera and threw it to the ground, smashing it totally.

Meanwhile her relationship with Spencer may have had an effect on Kate's former husband. Giving his name as Ogden Ludlow – the one that Kate had made him take – he reopened the question of their divorce. He told the court at Hartford that he was worried about the validity of the 1934 Mexico divorce and was therefore given a new decree on the grounds of Kate's 'desertion'. He didn't tell the judge there was any significance in the case and it wasn't until the hearing was nearly over that it was realised that the defendant was, in fact, Katharine Hepburn.

Kate didn't appear herself. But her father, ever the concerned parent, did – just to establish Connecticut as being her official legal residence. Ludlow told the court that Kate had decided that she couldn't 'continue her career and be married, too'. He was perhaps upset that the title of her latest play had put into words what all along had been the condition of their marriage.

The Theatre Guild put the play on at the St James's Theatre in New York. Brooks Atkinson took up the reservations everyone else seems to have felt long before it reached Broadway. He wrote in *The New York Times:* 'Even at her best, Miss Hepburn is not a virtuoso actress. But it is hard for her to sustain a scene in a trifling play that is generally uneventful.'

She was good political capital for anyone who wanted her, but Kate was being very selective about the causes she espoused. One of them was public health. In December 1942 a very slim Kate was photographed in *The New York Times*, buying seals for the city's Tuberculosis and Health Association.

Back in Hollywood, she and Spencer had made *Keeper of the Flame*, a story with more than a few similarities to *Woman of the Year*. He played a reporter, she the widow of a politician – with a secret she would rather have hidden. The screenplay was by Donald Ogden Stewart from a novel by I. A. R. Whylie, and George Cukor directed. The story had strong allusions to fascism which Louis B. Mayer now had to accept was good patriotism – filming began in the immediate aftermath of Pearl Harbor.

She was among nearly fifty artists – from Yehudi Menuhin and Helen Hayes to Gracie Fields and Ethel Merman – who demonstrated they were doing their bit for America's war effort by playing waiters and waitresses, barmen and cigarette girls for American servicemen in *Stage Door Canteen* in 1943, a propaganda movie which was merely an excuse to show as many well-known faces as possible and a genre that was repeated time and again.

In 1944, Kate could be seen with taped eyes playing a Chinese woman in *Dragon Seed*, about peasants and their war against the Japanese. It was strong wartime propaganda but ridiculous casting in a fairly poor picture. The interesting part is that the film, which co-starred Walter Huston, saw the reunion at MGM of Kate and her old RKO producer Pandro S. Berman.

There were two directors for *Dragon Seed*. Jack Conway became ill halfway through, and had to be replaced by Harold Bucquet. It was one of those demonstrations of Hollywood's heart being worn on its pure-silk sleeves. Berman knew that Conway was so ill with TB that he might not make it to the end of the film, but he wanted to give him the dignity of trying. So Bucquet was on hand to 'mark' him. When Conway was too ill to continue, Bucquet was in full charge without a day's break.

'Not a bad movie,' Pandro Berman told me. It was shot on location in the San Fernando Valley, and the settings looked impressive on screen – much better than the conventional Metro backdrops that always looked picturesque and usually glamorous but never totally real. This did look like most people's idea of wartime China. Certainly that's what Berman hoped.

'The thing that I remember most was that we got caught up in the Chinese civil war. Both the Nationalists and the Communists wanted us to show their uniforms when it came to fighting the Japanese. I couldn't stand either of them. So you didn't see any badges or any other signs of who was on whose side in China.'

Since, to Hollywood, the racial characteristics of both the

Chinese and the Japanese always seemed interchangeable there were enough problems trying to work out who was on whose side anyway without getting involved in domestic politics. The upshot of it all was that neither General Chiang Kai-shek nor Mau Tse Tung would have liked it very much, even if they had seen it – which was highly unlikely.

That was followed by the filmed version of *Without Love* which, since it was the third Tracy–Hepburn picture was more than ever an inappropriate description of the true state of things. Once more, Kate played a widow, but this time Spencer was cast as a scientist, instead of the politician.

In a supporting role was a young actor named Keenan Wynn, a New Yorker who told me he had 'specialised in flops'. 'Kate and Spence used to come to New York all the time. I was in fifteen flops in eight years but they were good management flops, so they would come and see them. They would go backstage to see others in the cast, never me. But after a time they recognised me. '"Oh yes," they'd say. "We remember you. Young character actor. Do you want to come to California?"'

That, as Wynn told me, 'is all any young actor, I was twenty-seven at the time I think, wants to hear.' About two years after that, Spencer arranged for Keenan to make tests in New York and brought him out. *Without Love* was his first break – and a flop in the Wynn tradition up to date.

Kate was concerned that Keenan would go out to the *Without Love* location on his motor cycle. 'Don't,' said the thirty-eight-year-old actress to the man nine years her junior, sounding like an anxious mother, 'it's dangerous. Don't do it. Please.'

He'd been riding for fifteen years and was not about to give it up then. But it produced some dividends. A few years later, Kate was in a film that had a scene with a particularly nasty motorcycle cop. 'Let's get Keenan,' she said. According to the actor, 'we had a ball. The scene looked so good that they took it out of the film – because it would have distracted from the rest of the picture. That was about par for Hollywood at the time. But it shows how nice Kate was to think of me like that.'

After *Without Love*, Kate was working for Pandro Berman

again in *Undercurrent* – a suspense story about a professor's daughter who marries an industrialist. Her co-star this time was Robert Taylor. But there was also a somewhat callow youth in the film called Robert Mitchum. The film was directed by Vincente Minnelli, at the time the husband of Judy Garland and the two women became friends – with Kate, by all accounts, doing whatever she could to make the still very young star come to terms with her various problems, all of which stemmed from an MGM discipline she herself had been spared.

The amazing thing is how she managed to keep away from the normal newspaper trash to which stars were subjected – 'Sour Apple' or not. Sidney Skolsky, one of the best known columnists of the period, wrote in 1945: 'Her boldness is actually a defence front. As a matter of fact, she is a very shy person.' But people still talked about her, about her clothes and, in September 1945 about her accent. She was one of a group of women selected by *The New York Times* 'whose speaking might raise our speech standards'.

She was, said the article, a 'model for women speaking Eastern dialect and whose natural proclivity is toward drawling. Miss Hepburn's enunciation is crisp and clear cut at all times. Even when she speeds up her pace by 200 or more words a minute. Woman who mumble and treat articulation shoddily may well lend her an ear. Because of her wide and distinctive nasal inflections, adolescent girls find Miss Hepburn's speech among the easiest to "take off".'

Sea of Grass was the fourth Tracy–Hepburn film – about the conflict between a cattle baron's work and his family. There was a row, too, between Pandro Berman and Elia Kazan, the director. He had wanted to shoot on location and the studio had said no.

But it wasn't anything like as easy saying no to either Katharine Hepburn or Spencer Tracy.

8

A Delicate Balance

*T*HE BIG SECRET of the Tracy–Hepburn romance could have been blown any time someone from the studio called to see either one of them at home. If Kate was receiving the visitor, Spencer was usually there to offer a drink. If it was Tracy acting as host, they would always have a cup of coffee served by Kate. Almost none of those visitors was at first able to conceal his surprise at meeting the two in each other's company. Yet still the 'secret' was never revealed.

Among those visitors was director-producer Richard Quine, who had an idea for a Tracy picture. He rang the front bell, and Kate opened the door to him. 'We then talked about the script – and she was all the time offering advice on what he should do and which lines were not right for him. Delightful!'

Cyd Charisse had an almost identical experience. She went to the house in West Hollywood to read for the part of Spencer's daughter in a script he was at the time considering. It was before the magnificently–shaped actress had established herself as a superb dancer in *Singin' in the Rain* and with Fred Astaire in *Silk Stockings*. 'Kate brought in the tea,' she told me. 'All the time, I noticed her hovering in the background so that she could hear how I did every line – although she was supposed to have left the room by then.'

Paul Henreid, the perpetual German gentleman of 1940s Hollywood films told me how he worked with Kate in *Song of Love*, a film both of them ought to be happy to forget – allegedly the story of Robert Schumann and his wife Clara.

'She did one cute thing,' Henreid told me. 'She would disappear for a few minutes during rehearsals and then come back smelling like a rose. "Don't you think it's considerate of me?" she asked. "I put a little perfume on – just a little on my nose." Spence came round to the set practically every morning to wish us luck.'

'You know your lines?' Tracy would say to her. 'Well then, say 'em loud and clear.' Nobody, not even Cukor or Stevens, had dared talk to her like that before. 'And then,' Henreid said, 'he'd turn to me and say, "Watch her. She'll always start to smile at the wrong time." She was very definitely under his influence and control – and I've never quite understood how Hollywood respected them the way it did.'

The film has an interesting contribution to make to the Hepburn story – because she spent four months learning to play the piano properly for the picture. It wouldn't be good enough simply to fake it. She wanted her fingers to be just right. As Keenan Wynn said: 'I was around at that time and I remember she insisted on having to "feel" it. She's a complete actress. She knows it.'

But Wynn pointed out that there was one other factor at play, too. 'I know that if you couldn't deliver, couldn't act – which is fairly common; it's a word used too freely these days because there are many performers, not many actors – she wouldn't go along with them. She'd just shut off. She wouldn't try. She'd just go ahead and nothing happened. She knew it wouldn't happen. She'd go off without talking to them.

'People say now, "Why don't they make films like they used to do?" I say, "Thank God, that they don't." There were so many films that were made that were terrible – even though people like Kate and Spence were the exceptions in this case. Robert Taylor, a lovely man, he wasn't an actor. But Spence was, Kate was. And you never thought of them necessarily as big stars. Stars are the five-year people, the current people. But stardom is bullshit.'

Paul Henreid and Tracy became firm friends, playing chess together – a game that was usually interrupted by Spencer's raucous yell, 'Katie where *are* you?'

'And she'd always come running, just as soon as he called,'

said Henreid. '"Get us some Scotch," he'd say and she'd come along with two glasses, although I could see that she disapproved. She would pour it out very meagrely – two very small glasses!' Given half the chance, she would have preferred to pack him off to Alcoholics Anonymous, but Spencer wouldn't have gone.

She was on safer ground with the problems of birth control, for which she was working as keenly as her mother – helping the Planned Parenthood group fight a proposed federal Human Life Amendment. She was also walking smack into what before very long would be called simply 'McCarthyism'. In 1947, she was one of the foremost backers of the independent left-wing candidate for the Presidency, Henry Wallace – formerly Roosevelt's Vice President.

At a rally for the Wallace campaign, she broke once more her self-imposed ban on making speeches. It was a time when the Motion Picture Alliance for the Preservation of American Ideals was getting prominence in the film community. 'For myself,' she declared, 'I want none of those ideals.'

Spencer had signed to make a film with Frank Capra, called *State of the Union*, an independent production to be shot at MGM. Louis B. Mayer agreed to the deal on condition that there was a firm guarantee in the contract that it would be distributed by the Loews' theatre circuit. In the film, Tracy was to play a business tycoon who decides to run for the presidency of the United States, not for reasons of personal ambition, but simply because he thinks it his patriotic duty. It has been said that the character was based on Wendell Willkie, who ran against Roosevelt for the Republicans in 1940, but Capra told me that had never been the intention. It was a strong part for which he and Louis B. Mayer knew that Tracy would be ideal. There was also a part for his supportive, loving wife. For reasons never properly explained, Kate wasn't even considered for the role. Capra wanted Claudette Colbert and Mayer agreed.

None of that was difficult to agree to. It took weeks, however, to finalise the necessary negotiations, to have the sets prepared, the scripts printed and digested, the early conferences between director and stars, and supporting players. The wardrobe also had to be settled. Not much of a problem for Spencer. A few suits had to be made, a couple of new hats, a few pairs of shoes. But Claudette Colbert was a lady of style. Her outfits had to be designed by the finest couturières that Culver City could provide – and then made of the best materials by the finest cutters and seamstresses. MGM demanded nothing less. Miss Colbert's clothes had cost $15,000 by the time they were all made ready for her inspection at the Metro studios that day in 1948 – all to her own size and specifications – and because the designs were all of contemporary fashion, by common consent would go home with her once the film was completed.

It was at this stage of the proceedings that something very crucial happened. Capra and Colbert came to verbal blows – and an ultimatum was issued. 'We were about to start shooting on the Monday morning,' Capra told me. 'Late on the Friday before, Claudette walked into my office. She looked beautiful and I told her so. Then she told me that she had to have a quitting time at 5 o'clock each evening, because the doctor had given instructions to that effect. Well, I said, "That's impossible." And she said, "That's what I've got to do."'

It was the stuff that producers' and directors' nightmares are made of. As Capra explained: 'She was going to be in the first scene on the Monday morning. She put it up to me that I should take it or leave it.' No director wants to hear that sort of thing from one of his players. The alternatives may be unpalatable, but he likes to show he is the boss. On this occasion, faced with the choice of pandering to his star's difficult demands or having to find a new leading lady, Capra decided that his pride – and what he considered the ultimate good of the movie – had to come first.

'Just turn in your wardrobe on the way out,' he said.

'All my wardrobe?' she asked incredulously, never believing for one moment that Frank Capra, who was so popular among the people surrounding him and who had a reputation for being soft-centred, would take that step.

'All your wardrobe,' he replied.

'I really don't know what happened,' Capra told me thirty-five years later. 'She's really a very wonderful person. Not normally that kind at all – and certainly proved it afterwards. I had to do one thing or another. I made up my mind.'

There was a moment of pride – and then of panic. How was he going to get a new leading actress by Monday – and one for whom all those clothes would fit? He had to call a Metro executive, who normally would not have been involved in an independent production of this kind. But it was being shot on their lot and now there was a question of possibly having to use an MGM actress to replace Miss Colbert – short of cancelling the whole thing.

Louis B. Mayer himself was furious and called Capra into his pure-white office for an explanation. The director was in no mood for niceties. 'It's none of your business,' he told the mogul. 'We're just renting your studio. It's our picture.'

Tempers cooled. 'No,' said Mayer, remarkably calm and with no trace of a tear in either of his eyes. 'I was just going to say, don't let Tracy hear about this from anyone else. He can be kind of funny in that way.'

Capra called Tracy. 'How many girlfriends have you got?' he asked him on the phone.

Spencer laughed. 'Why you damn little Dago,' he said, 'I'm going to report you to the Guild . . . You can't do that to an actor.'

Capra explained the reons for this apparent suggestion of impropriety and Spencer seemed strangely relieved when he heard.

'You know,' he said, 'the Madam has been rehearsing with me – going over my part and giving me my cues. She knows all Claudette's lines – and she's terrific.'

Capra was delighted. 'Do you think she'd do it? Shall I call her?'

Tracy had no doubts about that and he said so. 'It's just the kind of a scene that she'd like,' he said. 'She's just that kind of girl, boy. Madam'll help us all right.'

Call her, Frank Capra did. 'I'll be right down,' she said – and late on the Friday evening, she drove through the MGM gates, hair blowing, no make-up, untidy trousers – and mercifully flat shoes.

'We didn't even mention how much she would get paid for the job, or discuss her billing – that was very, very unusual. All she wanted to do was to talk about the film.'

The next day, they discussed the matter again – at the Tracy–Hepburn house. Kate and Frank's wife talked about the clothes she would have to wear. Kate called her own designer and put him to work immediately. 'We can use the same dress for the first two days,' said the director. 'Please try and have one ready.'

On the Monday morning, Kate was at Metro at six o'clock – and so was her dress.

'We went right through – with no problems at all. As though she had been working on it for herself all the way. I'm sure she was much more suited for that character than Colbert would have been. But what struck me was that here were we, in trouble – and she came running. We needed her help, and that was all there was to it. No difficulties because she knew we were over a barrel. I had enormous respect for her.'

Tracy wasn't surprised. 'Of course not,' he told Capra. 'If she sees someone in trouble, she'll run.'

All the way through the film, Spencer referred to Kate as 'the Madam' – and, Capra now recalls, 'she didn't like it one bit. But it was plain to see that these two wonderful people were very much in love with each other. As far as knowing their craft, I never found anyone who could surpass them. I just sat in my chair and listened – there wasn't much else I had to do. Her interpretation of the role was precisely the way I had seen it – a woman who was trying to protect her husband and understood the way people were after him and that sooner or later he would wake up to the fact that they were using him.

'I never had to give any direction. They knew what the story was all about and they had seen the stage play. But she was playing the part in such a marvellous way that I wrote new scenes for her. I could see how it was all developing – how this girl was working so hard to save that silly wonderful husband of hers.'

To all intents and purposes, he *was* her 'silly wonderful

husband' in real life – and you could see it on the set, too. 'Oh yes,' Frank Capra recalls. 'You could see it. She would laugh at everything he said. And that's the greatest compliment a woman could give a man. They held hands. You could see how much they enjoyed each other's company.' The man known in Hollywood as the head of the Irish Mafia melted in her presence.

'Both were tops in their business and there are very few people today who are as good as either one of them. They plainly just loved their work. It was a marvellous thing to see these two people do a scene. They knew who they were. They, in fact, weren't acting at all. They were living it.' But privately. You never saw them at a Hollywood party. That was likely to be too public for them.

The remarkable thing was how Kate's sudden arrival at the MGM *State of the Union* set was accepted by the local community. Said Capra: 'It struck me as very odd but very Hollywoodish that when we started work on that Monday morning nobody made it seem that they thought it strange that Katharine Hepburn was on the set instead of Claudette Colbert. Nobody made out that he or she was surprised. I expected a thousand questions. I must say I felt very small. Nobody asked me anything. It seemed that they didn't give a damn. It was also an example of how at that time MGM seemed to represent Hollywood. They were the Olympians – and they didn't worry about anyone else.'

What they might have worried about, Capra recalled, was the effect on the UnAmerican Activities Committee. The Tracy presidential character seemed exceptionally left-wing. It was a wonder that the film on its own was not seen as a piece of seditious propaganda. 'I must say I was worried about that,' said Capra. 'And then we heard that President Truman was running it all the time on the presidential yacht. I guess that gave it the seal of approval.'

Not everyone on the set was so willing to do that, however. While the stars of the picture were undeniably 'progressive', a leading supporting role was occupied by the immaculate and dapper Adolphe Menjou, regarded as the most extreme

[109]

right-winger in the film capital, a man who went running to Senator McCarthy and his predecessors, naming names of people he branded as Communists because he said it was his patriotic duty.

'He and Kate hated each other,' said Capra. 'Hated each other. At the end of the day, he would go off in one direction, she in another. They never spoke.' Menjou may have been pleased that the film was no great box office hit. Perhaps a little too sophisticated for middle America. Conceivably a bit more problematical politically than the director wished to admit, it didn't do nearly as well as most people at MGM had forecast. But it was Tracy and Hepburn at their very best.

They knew everything there was to know about each other. As Spencer told Garson Kanin: 'The trouble with Kath is . . . she understands me.' Spencer would make comments on Kate's acting and she would worry about his driving. 'Totally hopeless,' she said. 'No sense of direction whatever.'

The sense of direction *was* there in his performances, however. 'He always said that the first two takes were the best and I think they were with him. But I think *I* can still go pretty well on that 23rd take . . . And . . . when Spencer and I worked together, we never rehearsed together before shooting. Never. Not ever.' Years later, she said: 'If people ask why our partnership was so successful . . . it was based on a natural and truthful completion of needs.'

Sometimes things looked so marvellous between them that it seemed as though nothing at all would ever be wrong. But it wasn't as simple as that. He was suffering from the effects of his drinking – and she was suffering along with him. It was severe enough for him to be classed as a total alcoholic and Kate more than once experienced the traumas of it all – the delirium, the pain of the drying out process which she surveyed with the care of a loving daughter who was also a trained nurse. The fact that she was neither of these things made the care that much more agonising, but also deep and thorough.

9

Adam's Rib

*T*HEY WERE TOGETHER all the time now. In London, Spencer played in *Edward My Son* and Kate went along too. In Hollywood, they decided they had to make another movie together – a decision that was really made for them by Louis B. Mayer, who thought the pair the greatest set of twin moneyspinners since Judy Garland and Mickey Rooney last made an Andy Hardy movie.

There had been disappointments, however. Kate wanted to play in *Dr Jekyll and Mr Hyde* as both the good and the bad girl, but the studio wouldn't agree. It was Garson Kanin who came up with the right formula for their next film – a courtroom drama of a kind no one had yet even conceived. There was a judge, a jury, a prosecuting attorney and a lawyer for the defence. Of course, all that had been done before. What was new was the battle of wits and witticisms between the woman defence attorney and the tough DA, who was also her husband.

Kate was not just perfect casting as the defence lawyer; she was crying out, it seemed, for all the injustices of a world she herself had never known. People at Fenwick didn't go around killing husbands who had two-timed them – if they had, it wasn't something that would ever have been hidden from Dr Hepburn's fireside conversations. Of course, Tracy and Hepburn were professional enough to see through the problems the story-line presented. They could appreciate how conflicts of professional interest could arise in an otherwise idyllic relationship – and it showed.

The fact that the director was George Cukor, who had spent days in real courtrooms studying not just the interiors of the buildings but the way the judges and other lawyers carried out their work, made it smoother still. And the screenplay was magnificent. But what people who were working on the picture remember best is the relationship between Kate and the actress playing the girl she was supposed to be defending – a young blonde with a high voice, full of ambition, and with a little too much body fat – who she knew was equally blessed with talent. Her name was Judy Holliday.

Kate did on the set of *Adam's Rib* what she has done a score of times since – advised a younger player, helped her along, tried to suggest ideas that even the director hadn't thought of. But there was a special reason for her concern. She had been told that Judy was in line for what promised to be one of the most exciting films planned for 1950, Columbia's *Born Yesterday*, with Broderick Crawford and William Holden.

The screenplay was by Garson Kanin, who also wrote *Adam's Rib*. He wanted Judy Holliday for the *Born Yesterday* not-so-dumb blonde role, but Harry Cohn was less than convinced. So a conspiracy was activated. Kate agreed that the camera should be focussed on Judy throughout a single-take seven-minute courtroom scene. If she made an impression in that scene – without even Kate herself being seen asking her questions – then perhaps Cohn could be persuaded to give her the role in his film. The generosity and concern paid off. Judy Holliday got the role – and collected an Oscar for her trouble.

Ask Kate herself, however, what she liked best about *Adam's Rib* – apart from playing with Spencer – and she would probably have said the fact that it was made in New York, not in the stultifying atmosphere of the Culver City studio, and that she had convinced her close friend Cole Porter to write a song for the picture which he called 'Farewell Amanda'.

It was also farewell to MGM for Kate. The studio system was fracturing like an abyss in a mountain range, one by one the stars were being advised that they would probably be better off on their own. Kate took the hint and decided to go back to the stage.

But now she wanted something different. Ever since the taste of *Romeo and Juliet* first touched her lips with Douglas

Fairbanks in *Morning Glory*, there had been the ambition to play Shakespeare, to take a part and make it remembered by future generations as the definitive portrayal of one of the classic roles. Few Americans had ever done that. John Barrymore's Hamlet was one of them. But Shakespeare's women's roles rarely met the parts he wrote for men on equal ground and the American women who had succeeded in playing them were all too few.

Kate thought she could lay that ghost as Hamlet had his. She decided to do it with *As You Like It*. She was Rosalind. But she was also the unofficial producer, the behind-the-scenes director, the unsung casting consultant. And she put into it the love and devotion that had gone into the films with Spencer –who discreetly travelled where she did but was never seen in any hotel or auditorium through the run of the play at the Court Theatre on Broadway or at any of the 'tanktowns' on the road before the opening.

The papers had a great deal of fun with massive picture spreads to launch the play – most of them glorying in the amount of leg displayed by an actress who was rarely seen out of trousers. The legs were the things that the critics noted, too. As *Life* magazine reported in February 1950: 'After seven years away from Broadway, Katharine Hepburn returned last month to recite poetry in *As You Like It* and disclosed to everyone's surprise that her gams are as good as her iambics.' John Chapman wrote: 'Those legs are eloquent.'

Aside from the sex appeal, hers was a role that demanded total commitment, but Kate did it with a serenity that had seemed to enter her life only when Spencer had, too. But once the writers had decided to ignore Kate's legs, the critical acclaim wasn't as satisfying as all that work and enthusiasm appeared to indicate. Brooks Atkinson said in *The New York Times* that Kate was simply wrong for Rosalind. 'Katharine Hepburn's electric and refined personality is miscast in a rustic role,' he said. Yet since the play had never lasted in America for longer than two and a half weeks, everyone was anxious to see whether it would take off now. George Jean Nathan was not so sure: 'How Orlando could recognise Miss Hepburn's Rosalind as Rosalind, even in skirts, I'll never be able to figure out.'

[113]

As the play meandered its way around the States, it was seen as something of a Hepburn folly. Why do it at all? William F. McDermott of the *Cleveland Plain Dealer* wanted to know. 'I was frightened of it,' Kate admitted. 'But good new plays are hard to find.'

The interviewer described finding her in the Governor's suite of the Carter Hotel, 'ensconced on a davenport and addressing herself with apparent heartiness to a formidable steak, cooked medium rare, her hair in curl papers and her body swathed in a bathrobe of turkish towelling. She looked very unlike the lithe and svelte Rosalind who had been enchanting local audiences. But the informal attire did not obscure the vitality, the quick, graceful movement, the sense of abundant aliveness which animate her performance. Her feet, loosely encased in yarn slippers, were on the davenport and, in talking, she emphasised the points with hands, arms and toes.'

Nevertheless, despite the doubts and the criticisms, the play, as one local reporter noted, packed a whole series of theatres right up to the rafters. All previous *As You Like It* records were smashed on the way.

She was happy to talk about the theatre and her work in it – and she noted for Louella Parsons that she was thrilled how many teenagers were discovering the magic of a stage play 'and are as quiet as mice'. As for herself, she loved the theatre, she said 'but not one bit better than motion pictures', which sounds a lot more like Louella Parsons than Katharine Hepburn. 'One thing I do not like about the studios is the long wait between pictures, which shouldn't be that way.' But then she added in a statement that had nothing if not truth about it: 'I refuse to do anything I don't believe in thoroughly. I have to be enthusiastic.'

The tour was not without incident. At Blackwell, Ohio, she was arrested for speeding. Driving at 80 mph by a policeman on the way to Witchita, Kansas. Her answer to the traffic cop was full of the feminine logic that had so enraged a gaggle of Hollywood directors. 'We would have been glad to slow down if you had just warned us,' she told him, affronted that he could have had the audacity to charge her with the offence. But

[114]

she was carted back to the police station just the same. There, she was still more direct: 'You don't have sense enough to be an officer.' At that point, she stepped back three paces – and collided with a hot stove. Her mink coat was seared in the process.

It was merely another problem to add to the others. She not only lost weight again after the play, but claimed that she had gained an inch in height – she also said that she had added an inch and a half after *The Philadelphia Story*. It was a phenomenon not common in medical science. 'My doctors say I'm hyperthyroid,' she explained.

That could have been an explanation for the way things used to upset her – things that seemingly should not have given any emotional concern. At about this time, she was having lunch in New York with the celebrated American film actress Nina Foch who had also had her baptism in Shakespeare fairly recently. At the lunch, too, was Kate's mother. Nina told them about her present role in *John Loves Mary* which was being produced by Rodgers and Hammerstein, taking one of their periodic vacations from writing hit musicals of their own. Although she was one of the stars of the show, she was not getting lead billing – a fact that incensed Kate when she heard about it, although Nina herself was relatively unbothered.

'I was quite happy about it,' she told me. 'But Kate got very, very angry. She said she thought it was perfectly terrible and said so. Then she kept banging on the table.' Ultimately, Kate said: 'You know what, I'm going to see Dick Rodgers about this.'

All the time Mrs Hepburn Snr had been a somewhat amused but disinterested bystander. Now, however, she stepped in. 'Katharine,' she said like the mother of some recalcitrant schoolgirl. 'Don't get so upset. Maybe Nina doesn't want billing.'

All through the years her mother had been a continuing strong influence on the daughter who became an international star. If her father had been a source of strength, Katharine Houghton Hepburn Snr was the woman she needed when only another woman's advice would do. In March 1951 that

[115]

influence was gone for ever. The family had gathered for tea at the house at Hartford. They always did when the 'children' were around. That day, as usual, the teapot was brewing and the table laid. For the first time that either her father or she could remember, however, Mrs Hepburn was not there to conduct 'the ceremony'.

'We just looked at each other,' Kate recalled years later, 'and without a word ran upstairs. We knew what we would find. My mother was dead.' Kate was left totally distraught by the death. But she tried not to show it. Unless one knew, she was as phlegmatic about the event as any of the middle-class New England ladies she had played on the screen. Spencer was on hand to provide the comfort she needed and there was her father, her brothers and sisters to rally round as only an immediate family could at a time like that. Before long Dr Hepburn married again – the woman who had been his nurse, which didn't make Kate very happy.

But now she was to become preoccupied with a new role in a movie that was to prove very important in the Katharine Hepburn story. It was called *The African Queen*.

10

The African Queen

*T*HE IDEA HAD been put to her by John Huston. It was based on a story by C. S. Forester, best known for his Captain Horatio Hornblower books, about a woman missionary in Africa forced by circumstances to sail through rivers and swamps in a decrepit tub of a steamboat with an uncouth sailor, a kind of man she would in other circumstances have hardly known to have existed.

It would be ideal for Kate – the part was of a no-nonsense woman made old beyond her years by the work with her simple brother (to be played by Robert Morley) in an East African mission, a woman of infinite strength. The sailor, a belching unshaven man who, nevertheless, had a dignity of his own – and an infinite respect for women – was the kind of man she was rapidly proving she enjoyed playing opposite. Huston told her who he wanted for the part and she was overjoyed: Humphrey Bogart.

The initial thoughts were exchanged in New York when both stars agreed they wanted to make the picture. The only problem was where. Huston left them both with the passing thought: 'Find me a jet-black river.' They decided they would find it in Tanganyika, the site of the original Forester story, which was basically about the good British lady and her new-found cockney friend – conveniently changed to a Canadian for the film – fleeing from the nasty Germans in their East African colony (which would one day form part of the republic of Tanzania). The river they chose was the Rukki, made black by the decaying trees and plants that had fallen to its bed in the past few thousand years. So black, in fact, that it could have been specially manufactured by the Parker company.

London acted as the unit headquarters for the enterprise. From there the crew and all their equipment came. Kate sailed in to Britain, possibly limbering up for the perils of the deep on *The African Queen*, on the very unimposing freighter, *The Media*.

Kate broke her rule and spoke to the press – only declaring 'sealed lips', as she put it, when it came to questions about her private life. Significantly, not one person asked anything about Spencer Tracy, apart from the requisite question about when they would next make a film together. But then nobody would have expected any other sort of question.

'I know I'm plain and scrawny,' she told Donald Zec of the *Daily Mirror*. 'I'm tall, skinny – but very determined.'

'Take no notice,' broke in Bogart. 'In our film she bathes in the nude, wonderful stuff. I hope it'll get past the censor.' (Audiences were not to be privileged to see anything to which a censor could take the slightest exception.)

As for Kate, she was very taken with the love interest in the film. 'Only the really plain people know about love,' she said. 'The very fascinating ones try so hard to create an impression, they soon exhaust their talents.'

Kate didn't look for creating impressions – but she created an image for herself. She decided from the time she first saw a script that this missionary lady she was playing would have her hair piled high on the top of her head. That was how she would play her – and how she would wear her hair for ever after.

The early discussions for the movie were held in the salubrious surroundings of Claridges. There, she had to slip into the hotel through a side door because the establishment didn't welcome the sight of ladies in trousers. At the hotel, columnist Ward Morehouse reported meeting a Katharine Hepburn who 'sat on the floor in front of a roaring fire in beige sweater and slacks, saying, "It's quite an adventure, this African jaunt, and thank God Lauren Bacall is coming along. We'll be shooting on a thirty-foot boat for weeks, moving miles and miles down a river. I don't play the African Queen. I play a missionary and I'm very uptight. If anybody's looking for me, the name is Kate Hepburn. Belgian Congo."'

Bogart and Lauren Bacall flew into London from Paris for the talks and, a few weeks later, all continued the journey together to Africa. Kate and Bogie got on beautifully, although that wasn't the initial impression they gave, and he had to get to understand what he called the 'zany' side of her – such as the five baths a day she told him she took, something likely to be impossible in Africa, where the sweat pouring down her face and staining her dowdy calico dress had to look real. No, she told him, she took the baths because they made it easier for her to think.

He was amazed how she sweetened her tea with strawberry jam, and rubbed alcohol into her face and, apart from a little lipstick, never wore makeup, or used jewellery or perfume. John Huston found her equally zany. But that was precisely what he was looking for. And when he explained it to Kate on the phone she agreed that she had been looking for something like it herself.

Why no one had approached her about the role before is another one of those Hollywood mystery stories – because Warner Brothers had owned the rights to the Forester novel since the 1930s when there were plans to star Bette Davis in it. 'How we ever let it out of our hands is something I'll never understand,' Bill Orr, former production chief at Warners told me. 'We had it growing dust on our shelves. Why didn't someone approach Katharine Hepburn?' It was a case of everyone, in hindsight, knowing what they should have done and didn't do. For along the way, Twentieth Century-Fox had owned it, too – and then handed over to Sam Spiegel who, in turn, passed it on to Huston.

For once Spencer was not around, either in London or when production moved to Africa. He had to remain in California, making *Father's Little Dividend*, the sequel to *Father of the Bride*, the first picture that made any impact starring an adult Elizabeth Taylor. Had he come, he doubtless would have had a similar effect on the misery of Bogart as that of a magnum of vintage malt whisky.

The actor hated the humid agony of the Congo weather and the unpleasant things flying and crawling around him, and would very much have preferred filming *The African Queen* the

[119]

way every other movie was made in Hollywood at the turn of the half-century – in an honest-to-goodness studio with a tank doubling for the river and a craftily made toy standing in for the dirty, leaky boat they were using. One that would conveniently break in two and tip over when it was required to do so, just as studio boats had been doing for well nigh fifty years. (In fact, there would be one at Shepperton studios near London, which was used for the final destruction scene.)

He got himself blind drunk every night – if that wasn't consciously an attempt to forget being where he was, it certainly had that effect. John Huston wasn't beyond sharing a bottle or two with him. But his co-star, who had had enough of the problems of alcoholism with Spencer, was kept far away from this side of working with him.

'You boys believe you're being awfully wicked, don't you?' she said one evening when she came across their transplanted bar. 'Well, you don't know what the word wicked means.'

'What the hell is she driving at with that crack?' asked Bogie.

'I don't know,' said Huston. 'But I think she's one of us.'

She and Huston didn't hit it off all that well when they first got down to work in the jungle. 'Look Katie,' he said to her after three anxious days, 'you're playing this missionary lady as though she was somebody perverted. You'll kill the film if you go on that way. She's not perverted. She's a maiden lady whose slow awakening to love we have to see through.'

As Bogart wrote when the episode was comfortably behind him: 'While I was griping, Kate was in her glory. She couldn't pass a fern or berry without wanting to know its pedigree and insisted on getting the Latin name for everything she saw walking, swimming, flying or crawling. I wanted to cut our 10-week schedule, but the way she was wallowing in the stinking hole, we'd be there for years.' Of Kate he said: 'Here is a 24-carat nut or a great actress working mighty hard at being one.'

It was hardly surprising that Kate loved it. 'Divine,' she kept saying. 'Divine.' Once the studio craftsman had constructed her own lavatory – oil drums and palm leaves – and built a shower and given her a full-length mirror, she was as happy as . . . well, a river girl. But after a couple of days, it all collapsed and Kate had to dress and look after her toilet in the bushes, the same as everyone else. She didn't appear to mind and with Lauren Bacall spent much of the time making sure everyone else washed as properly as they could, and took their regular does of quinine.

The boat itself was pulled along the river by another ship and all the equipment followed behind – including a raft for the cameras. If the film team didn't know it was the supreme compliment – and not many of them did at this stage – it would have seemed that the two stars were hating each other almost as much as Bogie detested the location. He kept telling her that she was ridiculous, liking everything the way that she said she did.

'You ought to come down to earth,' he told her. To which she replied, 'you mean down to where you're crawling?' She then called him 'an ugly bag of bones' – which was as close to a mating call with Katharine Hepburn as you could get.

Said Bogie at the time: 'She won't let anybody get a word in edgewise and she keeps repeating what a superior person she is. Later, you get a load of the babe stalking through the African jungle as though she had beaten Livingstone to it. Her shirt tail is carefully torn for casual effect and is flapping out of her jeans. She pounces on the flora and the fauna with a home-movie camera like a kid going to his first Christmas tree and she blunders within ten feet of a wild boar's tusks for a closeup of the beast.

'About every other minute she wrings her hands in ecstasy and says, "What divine natives! What divine morning glories." Brother, your brow goes up – is this something from *The Philadelphia Story*?'

That sort of thing either brought a raucous laugh from Kate or made the teller of such stories an outcast. Kate laughed at all the right moments. She and Bogie were getting on very well indeed. John Huston admitted afterwards that he was surprised that they were. He didn't understand at the time the unexpected affinity between a 'refined lady' and a tough-talking, hard-drinking man like Bogie.

[121]

'One brought out a vein of humour in the other,' he said afterwards. 'And this comic sense, which had been missing from the book and the screenplay, grew out of our day-to-day shooting. Of course, humour underlies the story and was behind the action, but it was the offbeat combination of Bogart and Hepburn which enabled this element to emerge.'

Once Kate asked Bogart to help her to find a bamboo forest. 'What the hell for?' he asked.

'To sit in and contemplate, Humphrey,' she answered, as if there could be any other possible reason for asking such a natural question.

That was the time that Kate was wading her way through the jungle armed with a cine camera, a recording machine – not at all an easy thing to lug around in those days before miniature tape players – fly swatters and butterfly nets. Bogie saw her and decided it was worth taking advantage of the situation. 'Can you help me?' he asked her.

'To do what?' she queried.

'Carry my makeup kit,' he replied.

At one stage, the whole crew had to contemplate moving camp because they were surrounded by giant poisonous ants. Leeches were a different matter. Huston insisted that both Kate and Bogie be attacked by the real thing, which he produced from jars. That was the only way he could be sure they would shudder properly as Bogie killed them off with a lighted cigarette end. But there was worse to come. Nine members of the crew came down with dysentery and had to be sent back to London.

Kate developed a severe bout of the illness, too – which she confessed was due in no small way to her not sharing the pleasures of the bottle with 'the boys'. She tried to 'shame' them at meal times on the boat – which had by now become their floating headquarters and hotel; no ants on board as far as anyone could see – by drinking water instead of liquor. The liquor was perfectly safe. The water was as polluted as a stagnant pond. At one time shooting stopped for nearly two weeks.

There were other things that Kate disapproved of. When she

[122]

heard that Huston had actually tried to shoot an elephant, she said that she would go on strike the moment he did so. 'You murderer,' she called.

He gave her a lightweight rifle one day and insisted that she join him on an elephant hunt. She took it for protection – but her real aim was to reform him. Unexpectedly, they found themselves in the midst of an elephant charge – led by a hulking male beast. Huston jumped up into a tree. Kate stayed where she was, the gun trained on the elephant, although it would have done little more than stung him.

'Katie didn't lecture me any more after that,' he recalled later. 'She liked my hunting and I liked her acting. She turned out to be a simple, gay and rather shy woman who loves to be liked.' Not the tough emancipated woman he had expected to work with.

Sometimes torrential rain stopped production for days on end – for which Bogie was grateful until he realised it might add precious time on to the shooting schedules in this godforsaken place.

Kate would say about Bogart afterwards that he was a 'very interesting actor. He was one of the few men I've ever known who was proud of being an actor. He thought acting was a fine profession. His work was based a little on his personality. I don't mean in a cute or affected way. It was an actor functioning. He was also a very interesting man. He watched out for me like a father . . . A total gentleman.'

In the end the African shooting went on for three days beyond the scheduled time scale – and the company then moved back to London, for the final scenes to be shot at Shepperton Studios – which at least pleased Bogie. The water there suited Katie better too.

The African Queen, from practically everybody's point of view, was worth every minute of discomfort, every itch, every sneeze and all the unmentionable things that sent members of the well-paid company home. Bogart won an Oscar. Kate only picked up a nomination but audiences all over the world sat and enjoyed a marvellous yarn – and one that they keep on watching all over again every time it turns up on their television screens.

[123]

'For once, [said *The Times* in an anonymous review] the cinema has made a good job of telling a story. It has gone even further – it has produced a reasonable and reasonably accurate translation of a work of a born story teller . . . The acting of Miss Katharine Hepburn in the part of the missionary's sister is a tour de force.'

It was her finest hour.

11

As You Like It

*T*HE AFRICAN QUEEN was not just a critical and professional triumph, it was a watershed. In 1952, at the age of forty-two – playing a woman supposed to be at least ten years older – Katharine Hepburn had at last come of age.

It marked the end of the time when it was fashionable to mock. The sour apples were put away and prepared for someone else. Those who had for the best part of twenty years complained about her behaviour had a rethink. She wasn't really any different, although people thought she was. If she had begun to change, it was to accept that she was her own person and that her standards didn't have to be those of everybody else, too. But she wasn't going to be any the less – to use Humphrey Bogart's term – zany or charmingly eccentric because of it. Nor was she going to accept the Hollywood dictum that without an audience she would be nowhere.

When another actress suggested that it was the public who put her where she was, she was able to reply in suitably cryptic form: 'The hell they did.' It was her reaction when fans approached her for autographs. She almost never gave them – and when she did, it was almost in spite of herself. More than once, she slapped a Hepburn enthusiast when she thought he was being too pushy. Her tennis racket was a useful weapon for warding off fans she thought were taking their interest in her a little too far. On a number of occasions, she was known to scribble her name right in the centre of the face on a photograph handed to her for signature – thus rendering it practically useless. Sometimes, she would scribble her name in ink in a book, and then close it tight, smudging it – and everything else on the page – to oblivion.

It wasn't just a twisted kind of response to small, defenceless people in the hope that they won't waste her time. More, she would insist, that her privacy needed protecting – and the fans had to be protected from themselves, from an unhealthy personality cult.

Elizabeth Taylor has a renowned autograph collection. She asked Kate to contribute to it. She categorically refused. 'I don't give autographs,' she said bluntly and that had to be that.

Scenes were never less pleasant than when Kate came to London with Spencer in the wake of the *African Queen* triumph to play on the West End stage for the first time. Tracy practically came to blows with a London fan who couldn't understand why the idol he had worshipped from afar wouldn't merely write her signature when they were close. And yet she was giving of her talent in the way she thought she knew best and there was no more important thing for her to do – except go on loving her Spencer. Once more, at Claridges, the routine was the same – he had the big suite, she the small one.

The talent she showed to the British audiences was in a revival of a previously neglected Bernard Shaw play *The Millionairess*. She had thought of doing it years before as a film, but had got sidetracked on to other things. Now, after the experience of *As You Like It*, she wanted to do it on stage. And she thought that Britain was the place for it.

She went into it with all the enthusiasm and singlemindedness of a greyhound chasing a hare – from her detailed research into what Shaw himself was doing at the time of his writing the play to the fitting of costumes. Katharine Hepburn may have been happiest of all in a pair of sloppy trousers, but the millionairess on stage had to dress like one. So she went to Paris for her stage clothes, to the House of Balmain. Ginette Spanier, directrix of the couture house was a close friend of 'Binky' Beaumont who was to produce the play. She soon became equally close to Kate and Spencer.

'If she were the richest woman in the world, then she had to wear the most beautiful clothes in the world,' said Mme. Spanier, who was used to dealing with such a simple equation. 'But I must say there was a certain amazement that we were going to make Katharine Hepburn of all people the best dressed woman in the world.' It must have been quite a job. 'No job at all,' Ginette told me.

She came to Paris to discuss the clothes she would need, and there was the usual procedure of first meeting M. Balmain himself. At that meeting, he did the first sketches and asked the first questions. 'How many scenes are we talking about? What do you have to do in each scene? Do you go up a lot of stairs? Are the staircases wide or narrow?'

'I remember her first scene,' said Ginette. 'We made her a black velvet coat, very wide, lined with pleated taffeta. She had to have an evening dress which we made for her in straw coloured organza, mid calf and embroidered all over. She looked wonderful in it. It was simply divine and she adored it.'

There was only one difficulty. In the play, she was called upon to lift up a heavy electric fire. Michael Benthall, her director, said he would have a specially lightweight one made for her. But she wouldn't accept that at all. 'No,' she answered. 'If I'm going to have to apppear to pick up something heavy, I have to make it look as if it's heavy, too.'

The problem that brought was that the arms of this exquisitely made, extraordinarily expensive dress, costing even then thousands of pounds, would have to be specially reinforced – couture dresses are rarely worn more than a handful of times. It would have to last for the run of the play – which hopefully would be for months – and who knew, years?

'I said, "Kate. An organza dress! It won't last with all that effort!" and Kate replied: "Well, you'll just have to do something." She is not an easy lady. But compared with some of the other people we have had to dress, she was marvellous.'

Ginette Spanier went over to London to see the first rehearsals. She noticed that the buttoned cuffs of her dress kept coming undone. 'I told her: "That's just not possible! You can't have that. What I'll do is fix two tiny zips in the sleeve which you just won't notice."'

Kate was not impressed. 'She screamed!' Ginette remembered. '"Me? Having something tin there? Something on my wrist? Tragedy!" That was the only time she got nearly hysterical.'

Kate made one trip to Paris for a fitting – insisting before she arrived that they guaranteed there would be no publicity. Robert Helpmann her co-star and Michael Benthall flew over with her on a Sunday, expecting Paris to be deserted. Instead, the street outside the Balmain building on La Rue François I was jam-packed with people, most of them appearing to carry cameras.

'The word had got out that she was here and the fact was that Katharine Hepburn had never been photographed wearing haute-couture clothes in her life. There was drama, discussions – with Bobbie Helpmann and Michael Benthall telling her that it would only be polite for her to agree to having, say, two shots taken. That's all.'

She agreed. But only on one condition – that she be allowed to wear her own clothes. Nobody objected, although the Balmain staff could be seen to look none too approvingly as she walked out, wearing her much too wide brown trousers and a T-shirt fastened at the back with a safety pin, so that it wouldn't look too loose around her neck. 'I remember Noel Coward being with her at my house in Paris once and saying, "Kate. Your trousers are too wide!"'

When, after several months' use, the dress began to tear, Ginette Spanier and her head fitter flew over to London to work on instant repairs. Their solution was in principle not strange for Kate. Between them, they darned the dress – but the darning itself was a work of art, two days' worth of darning which Kate appreciated. There are not many Balmain dresses that have been darned. 'Kate wrote the most charming note to the fitter, saying how kind she thought she was. There were very few people who ever did that.'

Ginette and the fitter made several visits to London for running repairs. Sometimes the couturière and Kate met in Paris, but just socially. 'She and Spencer would come to our house. But because no one knew of their relationship in those days, they always came separately.'

Kate didn't start the play in London. Before it reached the capital, it shunted its way through the provinces. The *Manchester Guardian* was moderately pleased with the result.

'Katharine Hepburn must have convinced most of her Manchester audience last night that she had produced the definitive version of Shaw's volcanic heroine in *The Millionairess*. She was the natural boss in this play about bosses and her eruptions were always a great pleasure to watch. A question mark, it must be confessed, hung uneasily above the lively expectations one took to the Opera House. It was not the fear that the wine would prove too strong for the bottle. *The Millionairess* may be no great shakes, but it is tough enough to contain even this rather alarmingly vital actress.

'The question was rather one of Miss Hepburn's voice. Her most devoted admirers would not claim among her virtues any marked musical quality of speech; it is a voice that would hardly charm, though on occasion, it might startle a bird from a tree. There was so much for her to say; would it not be sounding, long before the end, like the wind lost in some enormous primeval forest of dry branches?

'As things turned out, the Hepburn voice was well attuned to the demands of this divertingly hag-ridden play, in which she throws one character several times round the room and then downstairs with the words, "Take that for calling my father a bore", tells another that he is a fish with the soul of a black beetle and complains bitterly that she has a mere seven hundred thousand a year after death duties. Talk like this calls for no great richness of vocal orchestration. It was a performance of great charm, sharpened like a sword-point and yet sheathed time and again in those sudden softnesses at which Miss Hepburn is so adept. It all,' said the critic 'N.S.', was 'an engaging mixture of personal modesty and artistic arrogance that must be dear to his heroine's heart'.

Michael Benthall received ample praise from the London critics when it opened in June 1952 at the New Theatre. It was the first time it had ever been performed in central London. (The play first opened in Vienna in 1936. Dame Edith Evans toured Britain before her scheduled opening at the Queen's Theatre, but this was cancelled in the wake of the Blitz.) Shaw was said to have been inspired by the teachings of Lenin to write what he saw as an attack on the undeserving rich. The

London critics were not using that adjective to describe Kate's thundering performance. *The Times* said:

'The millionairess, having compelled the unwilling Egyptian doctor to marry her, reconciles him to defeat by revealing him "the rhythmic beauty of her sledgehammer pulse". Miss Katharine Hepburn does much the same thing. She fills the awful Epifania with such a furious, raw-boned strident vitality that it sweeps away likes and dislikes and presents the creature as a force of nature. It is a force which threatens the peace of every one about her . . . She is indeed so vivid in her vicious arrogance that she brings us quite as close as we would want to come to feeling the same horrid fascination that Shaw felt in the middle thirties for unprincipled men and women who are born to boss the world by sheer force of personality.'

The *Daily Telegraph's* W. A. Darlington said that Kate was like a tornado. The vitality, he said, 'comes bursting out of her, driving her hither and thither across the stage and forcing her into strange, tense attitudes. It may be that some actresses would make sly fun of Epifania's complete humourlessness, but Miss Hepburn is satisfied to bring out the formidable qualities of a woman booted and spurred by nature to ride roughshod over her fellows. We cannot reasonably ask for more. The part is not a particularly rewarding one. Miss Hepburn fills it with life and thus fitted the part reconciles us to the deficiencies of the play as a whole.'

And in the *Sunday Times* Harold Hobson wrote: 'To inhabitants of the tropics, to people, that is, who are used to having their homes swallowed by earthquakes and ripped up by hurricanes, Miss Hepburn must seem a very naturalistic actress. For creating her staggering effect, Miss Hepburn is gifted with outstanding advantages. She is lovely in the sense that there is no excellent beauty without some strangeness in the proportions – indeed remarkably lovely, for the strangeness in her proportions is very great. Her voice is musical within the meaning of Dr Johnson's definition of music as a disagreeable noise made on purpose . . . I hope I have said enough to show that her performance, like the Grand Canyon, the Taj Mahal and the two-headed pig is quite something . . .

In fact, Miss Hepburn gives a performance that will never be rivalled in this country unless Miss Hermione Gingold unexpectedly devotes her great genius to becoming a serious actress.'

Kate did her job so thoroughly that Cyril Ritchard, the actor who played her husband, complained that even during rehearsals he was battered and bruised – because Kate was called upon to throw him about the place. And yet she was going out of her way – fans and autograph hunters to the contrary – to show that she was really a very nice lady. 'I'm a romantic, really,' she told the London *News Chronicle* 'I'm supposed to to be the cold-hearted girl, skinny, plain. What am I really? Well, everyone thinks they are sweet at heart.'

She told *Time* magazine that she thought the play went well in London because 'American vitality has a great appeal for the British. You can see that in the popularity in England of Judy Garland, Danny Kaye and others. But back home, vitality is not so bloody unique.' They were words that were to be proved awesomely correct. But she wasn't going to worry about it. Life, she said, she saw as a 'comedy. If people talked about you the way they talked about me, you'd think so, too.' As she spoke, she chain-smoked. 'Yes,' she admitted. 'I'm a heavy smoker. Sometimes I stop.'

It seemed that she really made an impact with London. Yet just a few months later, her latest film with Spencer, *Pat and Mike* (1952) was being withdrawn from the Empire Theatre in Leicester Square after only eleven days. It wasn't that the box-office poison bug had set in again. Simply that the story of a sports promoter who takes a woman athlete and shapes her into the sensation of the age at every sport she takes up wasn't the way Britain saw either sportsmen or women who were moulded by them.

But as a piece of Tracy–Hepburnia it looked good and did very much better at home. Bosley Crowther told his *New York Times* readers: 'Katharine Hepburn and Spencer Tracy, who lost their amateur standing years ago as far as their popular rating as theatrical entertainers goes, are proving themselves equally able as a couple of professional sports in *Pat and Mike*.'

[131]

George Cukor had rarely felt happier with a picture and the whole touch of Garson Kanin's script was as light as Kate's with a tennis racket. She was in a mood to do *The Millionairess* on Broadway. And like all Hepburn moods and inspirations it had to be assuaged. But it didn't work out well, either critically or commercially when it played at the Shubert Theatre. Everything about it seemed less sure than it had at the New in London. In *The New York Herald Tribune*, critic Walter Kerr wrote: 'Katharine Hepburn is beautiful, radiant, vital and not very good. At times, she sounds like an alarm clock that no one can shut off . . . She doesn't walk, she marches. She doesn't speak to other characters, she clutches them in a vice-like grip . . . When she gets off a sofa, she simply throws her two feet into the air and lands on them.'

And William Hawkins in the *New York World Telegram* said that far from being the blockbuster they had all expected, the play 'fizzled and grumbled but never detonated'. As for its being a tour-de-force, the *Journal American's* John McClaim said: 'I get the force, but I don't dig the tour.'

But it was part of the deal of being a new-look Katharine Hepburn that it didn't seem to matter. She liked the play and her peformance. In fact, she said, she was so happy with it that the logical thing to do now was to film it. Again she went to London and in 1954 she was convinced that she was heiress to everything she saw around her. She loved London. London did its best to love her and she set about a massive series of story conferences. Preston Sturges agreed to direct and a perfect shooting script was devised. But there were financial problems. No studio would take it on although there was a producer on hand, ready to turn the wheels just as soon as the financial switch was thrown. Lester Cowan would be producing, Kate announced.

'The first thing I knew that I was producing it was when Kate phoned to tell me,' he said at the time. 'So here I am in England to produce it.' It was easier said than done. 'I may be called the producer but it's Miss Hepburn who's really doing most of the producing. It happens in all her films.'

There was a great more razzamataz about the preliminary

meetings for this film than for virtually any other Hepburn picture – which meant that anyone who knew Kate should have been ready to smell a particularly noxious rat. It was a means, they all thought, of attracting the capital. When money was offered, it was on condition that the work of Kate and Preston Sturges be totally emasculated, so that it fitted into what the film industry would consider a fairly low-risk commercial proposition. After months and months of shillyshallying, everyone concerned decided that it had been a good idea once. Now it was not worth the agony of pursuing the matter any further. There would be a lot more satisfaction and happiness making a picture that other people liked, too, and without sacrificing any principles.

Kate's principle on privacy was the last that she was going to sacrifice – to the point of being told ever so politely that really her refusal to give interviews other than when she needed to sell something for a film or stage company was really rather rude. 'To be frank Miss Hepburn [wrote Moore Raymond in the London *Sunday Dispatch* in one of those occasional articles in which a journalist hopes his readers sympathise with his plight] you are a damned exasperating woman. You've been variously described as temperamental, thorny, tempestuous, and unpredictable. People have since called you shy, retiring, timid and really friendly at heart. The fact is that nobody really knows you except your close friends and maybe some of the people who have associated with you and your work. But I should like to know you better. And I am quite sure a great many of my readers would.'

If Miss Hepburn read the *Sunday Dispatch* that day – and she has always protested that she never reads anything about herself – it had little effect on her attitude to reporters or the success of *The Millionairess* film project. It was up to Sophia Loren and Peter Sellers to make the film six years later – and nobody liked that either.

But the bug of the classics – British style – had bitten well and truly by then. In January 1955, Kate was a fully fledged member of one of the most prestigious theatrical companies in the world, the London Old Vic, not to play at its century-old

[133]

theatre in the Waterloo Road but on tour with the company in Australia. She would play Portia in *The Merchant of Venice*, Katharina in *The Taming of the Shrew* and Isabella in *Measure for Measure*.

Her *Millionairess* co-star, the Australian-born actor-ballet dancer Robert Helpmann was leading the company, which again was being directed by Michael Benthall. The *Sydney Morning Herald* was delighted to have her among them 'down under'. They praised her 'fitness and security' in the part of the shrew – no one made any comments about the appropriate name of the character she was playing – and said: 'If there was a curious falsity or feeling in the vocal tremors that Miss Hepburn brought to her angrier and more sentimental lines, there was no mistaking the sincerity and value of the explosive comic spirit she brought to hundreds of moments in this classic slanging match.'

It was a success wherever they went – not just in Sydney, but in Adelaide, Brisbane and Perth. The only dark cloud on the horizon was at Melbourne where a local journalist managed to find reasons for upsetting practically everyone – Robert Helpmann for pointing out that his dancing days were over, and Kate for making it clear, so they believed, that she had 'sunk' to a touring theatre company simply because her days as a film star were over.

That, needless to say, was not the way Kate saw it at all. She simply believed that her job as an actress was to take part in every activity involved in that craft. The disappointment during the six-month season was that Spencer was not able to join her on the tour. He was busy filming in California and still had to make the requisite visits to his family.

After the Shakespearean jaunt, and in New York again, she compared notes once more with Nina Foch. Nina had been doing *The Taming of the Shrew* and *Measure for Measure* at Stratford, Conn. 'She said, "I just loved *Shrew*, hated *Measure*". I said I felt precisely the same way. Then Kate said that she was going to ask me to work for the company she was going to set up, Katharine Hepburn Productions. One of the first rules of the company would be that neither of us would be allowed to do *Measure for Measure*. We had a great laugh.' Katharine Hepburn Productions would have been a very interesting feature indeed on the theatrical scene. But it never happened.

The trip to Australia wasn't Kate's only overseas visit at the time. She was also working in Italy, filming a picture called *Summertime*, about a lonely American spinster who tries to pretend she is totally self-contained and immune to the pressures of nature and Signor Rossano Brazzi. He played the Venice antique dealer who falls both in love with Kate and for her hard-to-get ruses. It was directed by David Lean.

Said *The New York Times Magazine:* 'A wondrous creature from a planet called Hollywood has descended on old Venice.' That said a great deal about a woman who, according to the magazine, believed 'When in Venice, do as Hepburn does.'

The film was based on Arthur Laurents's play *The Time of the Cuckoo*. Its screenplay was a collaboration between David Lean himself and H. E. Bates. London, on the whole, liked it better than New York. Dilys Powell in the *Sunday Times* said it had 'two assets. It has Katharine Hepburn and it has Venice.' It had been directed and photographed 'with love and passion'. 'Yet,' she wrote, 'without Katharine Hepburn we should, I fancy, have been left watching a novelette within a documentary. Miss Hepburn adds human distinction to the scene; and she adds it not only by the nervous vitality of her playing but by her own physical beauty. Throughout the film she insists that she is old and faded and all the time we look at a woman with an austerity of profile, an elongated wiry elegance of beauty which will make her worth looking at if she lives to be a hundred.'

The Times put it succinctly: 'For much of the time . . . the film resolves itself into a kind of championship fight with Venice in one corner and Miss Katharine Hepburn in the other – and it says much for Mr Jack Hildyard's photography that Venice is able for so long to survive. For Venice is up against a true champion, and a champion persuaded by Mr Lean to fight at the top of her form. Miss Hepburn, holding her own against the enchantments of the colour and the natural beauty of Venice, by herself being passive, keeping herself in the attitudes of loneliness and inarticulate longings, in the end persuades, which is surely the aim of the script, Venice herself to play a vital part in the telling of the story.'

There were plenty of opportunities for her to wear her trousers on screen – as well as for lunch, for sightseeing, and for dinner. She also wore what was described by one writer as 'the floppiest hat Venice ever saw'. Naturally enough, she took charge of everything around her. Taking a trip on a gondola, she was convinced she knew more about navigating the craft than the gondolier – and told him so.

In the film she doesn't want anyone at a canalside café to think she is alone, so she turns a chair sideways to make it seem she is waiting for a visitor. When she sees the man she yearned to have as her lover approach, she tries to find a way to rectify the situation. But Brazzi, at first thrilled to see her, notices the chair and walks away miserably. Neither is happy. It had been done a hundred times before and another hundred since. So had the discovery that he really had a wife and three children.

In England, the film was called *Summer Madness*. Campbell Dixon in the London *Daily Telegraph* couldn't understand why Mr Lean hadn't entered it in the Venice Film Festival. 'With all faults,' said Mr Dixon, the picture 'will be remembered as one of the films of 1955'. Which could, of course, be read any number of ways.

What was remarkable for 1955 was that when Kate fell into a Venice canal – she was, well, falling into a Venice canal. It was the scene where, standing on the water's edge, she steps backwards to take a photograph, tourist style, and falls off. Jack Hildyard, the brilliant cameraman whose work perfectly captures the beauty of the Venice millions know, told me how every step was carefully measured. 'Before we were ready to shoot, she had to measure the number of paces backwards it would require before she actually fell. She did it time and again until she was mathematically perfect – otherwise she could have had a nasty accident. But she wasn't in the least bit worried about the fall. No suggestion of using a double or anything. She's a marvellous swimmer – although those canals are not exactly perfect swimming water.'

[136]

She had taken the most remarkable precautions before doing the jump, special shoes to make sure she wouldn't be waterlogged, tight clothing, antiseptic rubbed into her hair. But she had neglected to do anything to help her eyes. As a result, the filthy murky mess of it all gave her an eye infection that has never cleared up. She thinks about it stoically now. 'Just Venice canal,' she says, when people ask why her eyes give her so much trouble.

The city wasn't the easiest place to work, Hildyard recalled. 'It was in the height of summer and the Venetians and the tourists were milling around us all the time. But Katharine showed no signs of any concern about having them there.' In fact, Kate had got the location bug and was proving that it was better to do things properly than the way everyone else thought they should be done.

Despite having to make the canal plunge, Kate did enjoy Venice, even to the extent of flashing her teeth sweetly at Art Buchwald who remarked they represented 'the greatest calcium deposit since the white cliffs of Dover'.

Kate's search for privacy seemed all-pervasive. But it was misinterpreted. While she didn't want to talk about the film to strangers, or went off the set to plan her next scene in a kind of self-imposed purdah, she would have been very happy to socialise with those with whom she felt she had things in common. But that wasn't understood. She would have liked to have been asked occasionally to have dinner with David Lean or Sig. Brazzi.

'I felt rather angry about that,' she said afterwards. 'I wandered off by myself through Venice, feeling very lonely and neglected and sat down by a canal and looked in the water – and while I was sitting like that a man came over to me and said, "May I come and talk to you?"' The talkative one turned out to be a French plumber and both apparently had a pleasant evening. 'I was glad to talk to anyone who looked reasonably all right, so we went out together for a walk through Venice.' She wondered for years why she was left to her own resources like that. 'I suppose they all thought I would have madly exciting things to do and left me to it. It happens everywhere to me.'

[137]

But she really was asking for it. One British film offer led to another and she was enjoying the atmosphere of London's studios, which seemed to be more relaxed and less 'showbizy' than Hollywood. But some of the things she did didn't fit in with that approach at all.

'Keep out,' declared the sign on her door at Pinewood where she was making *The Iron Petticoat* – yet another reworking of the *Ninotchka* theme. She was a Soviet aviatrix who flies West and realises that there are sweeter things in life than the next five-year-plan. Kate's message did not automatically give that impression, however – although the declaration in huge red letters *was* slightly softened by the additional message 'To save embarrassment to yourself, keep out unless on official business.'

She didn't eat with the rest of the cast or the technicians. She had a bottle of mineral water served with some light snack which she had, accompanied by the inevitable cigarette, in her dressing room. That wasn't snobbery or unsociability on her part – when in a film studio every actor is a model of sociability to the next. She simply couldn't eat in restaurants of any description at any time – she had perhaps been in only five or six in her life. 'It gives me indigestion,' she explained. 'It's a very unnatural way to eat . . . with people staring at you.' When visitors did manage to break through the security barrier, she greeted them with her legs perched on the dressing table.

'Yes,' she told writer Thomas Wiseman, 'it's my own fault.' It had to be her own actions that gave people the impression that she was such a difficult person to get along with. 'I have brought it upon myself. I am a rather sharp person. I have a sharp face and a sharp voice. When I speak on the telephone I snap into it. It puts people off I suppose. I am lucky that I have a few good friends, but I don't care much for acquaintances.' And then, in a very revealing moment, she admitted: 'I'm mean . . . I'm real mean to reporters. They ask me things they have no business knowing – why I wear pants.'

That was one of the questions a whole lot of people on the set of *The Iron Petticoat* – it set out being called *Not For Money* –

wanted answered. But they weren't satisfied. Again she probably said that she was more concerned about the movie – and didn't add that what worried her more than anything was the condition of Spencer Tracy, still back in Hollywood fighting off depression, alcoholism and physical illnesses caused by a whole variety of reasons; among them the fact that in a ski scene in a picture he was making he was left aloft in a broken-down cable car. It unnerved him, and agonised Kate when she heard about it.

She did, however, have what she believed was a marvellous film to take her mind off domestic matters. Ben Hecht had come to her with a script that she thought was going to be superb. She would be the woman flyer. She had William Holden to play a reporter and the story would work out beautifully.

Kate decided on impulse who she wanted for her director. She had just seen the Dirk Bogarde–Kenneth More film *Doctor in the House* and had thought it was the funniest thing she had ever seen. As the daughter of a doctor brought up on stories of medical student pranks, she could relate to all of it. Ralph Thomas directed that picture and she thought he would be just right for hers, too. At the time, he was making a sequel *Doctor at Sea* with Brigitte Bardot and was on a ship sailing between Alexandria and Piraeus when the telephone call from Kate came.

'I thought someone was pulling my leg,' he told me. 'Her voice was quite easy to impersonate and frankly I didn't believe it for one minute.'

'I'd like you to direct my next picture,' she told him. 'Can I send you the script?'

Well, as he told me, he would have dropped anything to do just that – had he only believed her. 'I'd have said yes to doing the London telephone directory.'

Nevertheless, the mysterious voice asked where she could send the script and he told her that he would next be landing in Piraeus.

'Right,' said the voice, 'I'll send it there.'

He thought it was a good joke, but there was work to get on

with and didn't give it a moment's further consideration. But when the ship did dock at the Greek port, a script *was* waiting for him. 'And it was *the* most delightful story by Ben Hecht I had ever read. I wanted to do it badly.' And after their next conversation, it was clear that Kate wanted him to do it – equally badly.

The initial discussions were held in America and were continued a few weeks later in the Connaught Hotel, Kate, Thomas, Hecht all closeted together. It was agreed it would be shot at Pinewood Studios in rural Buckinghamshire and that, for Britain at the time, it would be a huge budget operation. But the picture didn't turn out the way any of them wanted it to. In fact, Thomas says, he himself became more a referee than a director.

Harry Saltzman had taken over as producer of the film and from the moment he entered the scene, the script, the concept and the cast of the film changed. Holden was out. Instead, Bob Hope was brought in to play an American Air Force officer – who would end up loving the East almost as much as the Russian had become an admirer of the West.

Now, it was a novel idea having Kate playing opposite America's top comedian, and at first she thought it could present an opportunity for a brilliant tour de force on her part. Bob Hope had the idea, said Ralph Thomas, that it would be like playing opposite Garbo – a mysterious, soothing force, two things that the direct, powerful Katharine Hepburn would never aspire to be. As soon as details were finalised and contracts signed, Hope sent Kate dozens of red roses.

But mixing the acerbic actress with the best-loved comedy actor in the history of the cinema was like blending oil with water. Saltzman and Hope insisted on the story being changed out of all recognition – to fit Hope's personality and his thirst for jokes which were being manufactured for him at the speed of a Detroit automobile plant's assembly line.

At first, all Thomas could hope for was that they would agree to respect each other's work. 'Before they started filming, however, I realised that they were both working in totally different movies.' Kate was trying to work on the script she had agreed to make in the first place. Bob Hope, meanwhile, cosseted by his own team of writers, was adding cryptic one-liners all along the way, dropping them around the dialogue like the organiser of a paper chase.

'I was on Kate's side all the way,' Thomas told me. 'But it was very obvious that they weren't talking the same language.'

Kate got so annoyed at Bob's changing lines as he went along that she got a young man she knew to come on the set and pretend to be one of her own team of writers – just to unnerve the Hope outfit. It ended up by Bob's organisation deciding to be even stronger and putting in even more words. 'After only two days, I realised there was no point of contact between the two of them. It was a great baptism of fire for me, I can tell you. There was Bob inserting his one-liners – and she telling him very forcibly, very chillingly what she thought of his lack of professionalism.'

Once Kate protested about a perfectly good scene being ruined by Hope's inserting jokes about Yogi Bear. So the director sat in his caravan until three or four o'clock in the morning rewriting again.

Not that Bob Hope himself didn't make his contribution to the film. He arranged with friends at the United States Third Air Force base at Northolt, just outside London, which was doubling in the movie for Moscow Airport, to paint no fewer than five military planes with red hammers and sickles – no easy thing to do at any time, but in 1955 when every loyal American was being taught by rote to say 'Better dead than red', quite an achievement.

Kate managed to remain immune to a number of the problems involved in the film. She got on exceptionally well with Ralph Thomas – whom she declared was 'like a hamster' – and with James Robertson Justice, a supporting actor in this film but who had, of course, been one of the great successes of *Doctor in the House*. 'You can't but fall in love with her,' Thomas told me.

But you did have to get to know her ways. One weekend, she was a guest for lunch at the home of Thomas and his wife, Betty Box, who was the producer of the film. They had young children. 'Half way through the meal,' he recalled for me, 'she stopped eating and ordered the entire family to go out for a long run. She said it wasn't good to have a heavy meal without a break.'

What impressed him most about her, said Thomas, was the fact that, despite her forceful ways and her objection to bowing to the needs of a publicity machine, 'there was nothing of the big star about her'.

Once some equipment needed to be picked up from a warehouse quite a distance away. 'You're all too busy to go,' she said, laying down an order Hepburn style. 'But I've nothing to do for the moment. Have you got a car?' Thomas said there was one just outside. 'Right, well tell me what to do and I'll got down to pick it up myself.' And she did.

She found that no more difficult than trying on the decadent clothes and underwear that had to be flown in for her from the Maison Balmain in Paris – to complete the image of the communist who had sold out to capitalism. Huntsman of Savile Row made her uniform, although no Red Air Force officer had ever been known to wear anything of that quality before. But underneath the khaki . . . a black wasp-waist corset, complete with frills. That was designed and made for her by Balmain.

Ginette Spanier came once more from Paris to fit her and M. Balmain himself couldn't resist again the temptation of meeting the great Kate. But she was much happier wearing her trousers, which she covered with a long mackintosh to walk in and out of the Connaught. Sometimes, she used the staff service lift to make the trip to and from her room.

There was an innate kindness about her on this film which, as on so many others, showed itself with the way she talked to lesser players and technicians. It was near the end of filming when she heard the story of a sound engineer who was building his own house, only to realise that he had run out of money before he could put in a bathroom. In 1955 it was not totally unknown for houses to be built without bathrooms, so he resigned himself to having to make do for the moment with a tin bath in his kitchen.

'Kate got to hear about this,' said Ralph Thomas, 'not

through the man but because we were all talking about it. So she decided to do something.' The next time the engineer visited the site of his house, he was in time to see an entire bathroom suite being delivered. Pinned to the packing cases was a card that said simply: 'An end-of-film present. Love Kate.'

The British character actor David Kossoff, who played a KGB man in the film, had a similar experience himself. 'It was a very ambitious time for me, making that film,' he told me, 'and she got to know that there was a certain professional problem that I very much wanted to get settled. "Don't worry about it," she said. "I know someone who'll phone someone else in America. We'll probably have the answer by, say, Wednesday."' On the Wednesday, an answer there was – and precisely the one that Kossoff wanted to hear.

The impression that he had of the relationship between Hepburn and Hope was slightly different from that of the director. 'The word right at the beginning for us at our echelon was that here were these two very big stars and that they weren't going to get along. James Robertson Justice – who was big and bluff and not quite as secure as he would have us believe in those days – and all the other people working on the film were called together on what I think was the first day of shooting. It was a very big set, a comedy KGB office.

'We came on this very large set, and I sensed in Ralph Thomas a certain nervousness – which there always is on the first day but in this case was based entirely on Katharine Hepburn. And then, kind of suddenly, she was with us. She walked on wearing a safari jacket with wide, quite ungraceful safari trousers. I don't think she was wearing shoes. She hadn't yet gone into makeup or had her hair done, and I remember looking at her with astonishment – because she looked like Katharine Hepburn, but an extraordinarily untidy, unkempt version of Katharine Hepburn.

'And all I could see was somebody with an undistinguished skin, not very good eyes – they were kind of red-rimmed – and very poor hair. No figure at all to speak of and stringy, long hands. But I was immediately, kind of enchanted by her. Now,

I don't know if I was enchanted by her as a kind of latent beauty or because I was enchanted before I got there. But then what came from her was a very great naturalness. There was no affectation from her at all – sounding exactly as she does in the films, with the accent, the product of the very good school to which she went.'

Almost everything about her was unexpected – like the first thing she did, sitting on the floor. 'She dominated us by being at a lower level from us. That has never happened before. She sat on the floor, as far as I remember, because no one offered her a chair and neither was there a ring of chairs. She discussed various things with us all standing near her and circling her.

'Then she disappeared and we didn't see her again until later on when she arrived in full uniform as a Russian aviatrix. And that peculiar accent which great actresses have and has nothing to do with makeup; there is the weirdest kind of alchemy which means they can be whoever they want to be.

'As the film went on, I was full of admiration for somebody I knew was 22-carat all the way through – and you're lucky to find one carat in most film people. I remember feeling quite humble.'

He does not remember feeling conscious of a referee being needed between Kate and Hope, who he found one of the nicest men in the business. 'We were all frightened that there would be temperamental dissimilarities and we were going to be in trouble with them – because films can be very unpleasant occasions. I must say there wasn't a vestige of this. It was a lesson to everybody on studio behaviour. On the one hand we watched this master of inventive comedy working out his bits, and she, entirely enclosed, as she always was in her own part, and at the end of the day, they walked off in different directions.

'There were no needless jokes. Bob Hope had jokes for us, and not for her. He seemed to treat her with a remarkable kind of delicacy. Like other good comedians, he had the sensitivities of a cat.' In other words, he was inhibited by her. But the only time she seemed to Kossoff to be opinionated was in the kind of food that she ate. When he did notice her eating alone – and not many got an exhibition of this – it was to see her special order of wheat germ bread and other health foods.

One thing about her impressed David Kossoff and the other lesser players on the film. 'Katharine Hepburn always turned up knowing the day's work. She worked at it. She knew every word. She took direction without argument. If she had a suggestion to make, it was a suggestion made without argument and listened to with very great respect. I also knew that Ralph Thomas, a *very* successful comedy director, believed that she was the one who knew best.'

But there were the difficult moments. 'Her mind,' recalled Kossoff, 'was very clear on everything. She had no time for small talk – and I suppose in the parasitic world of films at the time, that could be offensive.'

Not only did she not eat with the rest of the company. Even worse in some eyes, she didn't drink with them either. One moment that David Kossoff remembers is when the coffee trolley trundled by. 'Cup of coffee, Miss Hepburn?' the cockney coffee boy called.

'Black tea,' she answered. 'Weak, lukewarm – with a tiny piece of lemon,' like James Bond giving his orders for a shaken-not-stirred Martini.

'Although she didn't say it, you had the feeling she was going to add – "and in a spotlessly clean glass", too.'

The main scene in which they worked together was an important one. 'The lights were up in the roof because you had to start off with very big establishing shots – so you had to make sure you didn't see the lights. It was an emotional scene which finished up with her fairly much in close up and in tears. She did the rehearsals as perfectly as she would do the take. Then they did the take, and her feet fell into the same footprints almost. They landed on the same mark, she was so perfect.

'The director said "Cut" – and from behind the tears she could be heard saying: "A light went out, honey." It had been an emotional scene in which she was supposed to be looking only at camera. But in that moment, she had noticed just one of fifty lights – lamps that were so big they were known as "brutes" – had gone out.

[145]

'"Do you think we ought to go again?" Ralph Thomas asked.

'"Only if you think so," she said. Of course, the scene was done again once the light was fixed. And again, she trod those same footprints. She was just a superb film actress, doing things as a professional. I remember Katharine Hepburn with immense admiration.'

David Kossoff has not the slightest doubt that Kate knew then – as she had known on every previous occasion and as she has subsequently – the effect she had on people around her, little people, people who would never aspire to her power. 'I remember a ballroom scene in which she had spent her KGB allowance on this marvellous ballgown. Then you had the feeling of her suddenly being with you. There she suddenly was on the set – and I remember very clearly there was a silence. Suddenly there was this stringy lady we had seen in the morning with no chest at all – in fact, I don't know where she kept her breasts – but everything about her now was glamorous. Everything about her was beautiful. She glittered. Her voice was like a bell. It's a moment I have never forgotten.'

Alas for all concerned, it wasn't to be a film that would be equally well remembered, although the critics on the whole thought Kate, in particular, did marvellously well in coping with the comparisons that were inevitably to be made with *Ninotchka* and with the competition from Mr Hope.

In London, *The Times*'s still anonymous critic wrote: 'her acting has the impact of the stamp of a jackboot, the precision of a military salute at a ceremonial parade. And when she melts at the absurd frivolousness, the elegant fripperies of the West, she melts enchantingly, and here Miss Garbo seems to merge into her while the scene which sees her condemned by a secret Soviet court martial sitting in London and standing at attention while the insignia of her rank are stripped from her is made by her into pure tragedy . . .'

That was what a lot of people found when working with her, too. David Kossoff remembers that she could be sharp without necessarily having to be offensive. 'I think it was an economy of words. She didn't see too much point in saying "please" or "thank you" more than once in one sentence. You knew precisely what she wanted – and she normally got it. If she stopped and made the tiniest suggestion, it was not based on ego. Only that the scene should work better. In fact, she knew when a light went out.'

12

Keeper of the Flame

IN 1957, KATHARINE HEPBURN was only forty-eight. But already the question was being asked: 'Are you going to retire?'

'Retire,' she replied as though being told that the mineral water she had been drinking all day was contaminated. 'Retire? Not unless they make me. My father is past seventy. He's still a practising physician. He's hale, hearty and tireless.'

There wasn't much more to say after that. You didn't argue with Katharine Hepburn then any more than you ever had before. She had spoken. She wasn't even going to contemplate retirement – and that was that. Not that anyone wanted her to. A shadow was gradually creeping over what many fans were regarding as the golden generation of film stars and honest-to-goodness individualists like Kate had to be treasured for that as for their God-given talent.

It was a year when Kate herself was made painfully aware of the frailty of human life. Humphrey Bogart, so recent a friend and now so close a one, was losing a valiant battle with cancer. Still smoking, still coughing, still drinking, still choking, still joking, still laughing. But every night, the wasted form of the dominating tough guy who had won his Oscar just five years before for at turns bullying and then being bullied by Kate on *The African Queen* was now so light he could be folded up and taken to his bedroom via a dumb waiter.

He was in remarkably good spirits. Gregory Peck recalled for me telling him a particularly long, rambling story. 'If you don't get around to it quick, Greg,' he said, 'I won't be here for the punchline.'

Kate and Spencer called on him daily. The last time they called, Bogie knew that he wouldn't be around for another visit. But neither Kate nor Spencer acted any differently for fear of upsetting him. She was still there with the words of advice; he still punching his host on the shoulder as he told another gag. As they left, Bogie gripped their hands as tightly as he could – and said goodbye. He had never done that before. Kate cried as she left. She hadn't done that before either.

When Bogart died, there was an intense sadness about her – and a sense recognised by others around her that she was treasuring Spencer all the more; a feeling that she had to keep saying how grateful she was to have his now white hair and gnarled features by her side whenever possible.

Kate decided to remember Bogie in a way that was distinctly unique. She asked Lauren Bacall – Bogie's Baby as she was known – for one of his sweaters. She started wearing it in 1957 and does so to this day, darning it and cleaning it lovingly whenever the need arises. His 'zany' colleague was showing her profound love.

As for Spencer, he kept on working, although the problems of illness and premature ageing were making every day before the cameras that much harder. He sought solace in Kate always – and in the bottle all too regularly.

He was making *The Old Man and the Sea* both on location in Cuba and at the Warner Brothers studios at Burbank. Kate was around at both places, just to smile at him when that was what she felt like doing, or to offer comfort when it was required.

Milton Sperling, a senior producer at the studios and son-in-law of the company president, Harry Warner, remembered the day that she answered an SOS. 'Spencer was in the midst of one of his most serious drinking binges,' he told me. 'We knew that the only thing to do was to call Katharine Hepburn and ask for her help. Lovingly, she succeeded in drying him out for that day.'

She was as tough with the people at Warner Brothers – a studio for which she had never worked herself – as with any of the companies where she was filming. Jack Warner Jnr, son of the studio's production head, remembers her being given the star-studded welcome by his father. Jack Junior was already a senior producer at the studio himself by then.

'Could you get me some cigarettes?' Kate asked him, as though he were the office junior. 'Anything. Just so long as they're not Camels.'

The Iron Petticoat had flopped at the box office, but that didn't make her any the less enthusiastic to get down to her next piece of work. And as always the offers came rushing in, the scripts piling up daily in her mailbox, the flattering phone calls from producers asking her to give their latest find her kindest and speediest consideration.

The only one she was willing to respond to in 1957 with any kind of enthusiasm was a gentleman born in Stratford on Avon. The American Stratford, the one in Kate's own state of Connecticut, invited her to play Portia in their season of *The Merchant of Venice* and she accepted the invitation to play for the Equity minimum with a great deal more alacrity than she had agreed to an additional $10,000 all those years before at RKO.

The New York Times's critic Lewis Funke said of that role: 'She draws a buoyant, lighthearted, girlish portrait of the lady . . . a nice airy way of playing the part.' When she played Beatrice in *Much Ado About Nothing*, Brooks Atkinson wrote: 'Miss Hepburn is very much the modern actress, the hard surface of modern wit, the brittle remarks, the sophisticated eyes become her.'

In his *Tracy and Hepburn* book, Garson Kanin recalled that she was happier living in what had once been a fisherman's boat house than he had seen her for years. 'It's perfect,' he remembered her saying. 'Of course it does have its inconveniences. Sometimes when the tide comes in, if it's really high tide, it comes right up through the floor.'

Then Kate herself had to do the bailing out. On hands and knees again, which anyone not knowing her better might have decided was her favourite position. More than once a complete stranger to any of the places that she has from time to time called home has been handed a scrubbing brush or a polishing rag and ordered to get to work.

The Stratford shack was, she told Kanin, the reason she came to the place. It meant 'a hell of a lot to me'. But she did keep going back to Hollywood. And rarely more enthusiastically – although enthusiasm was an emotion she expressed over every single project in which she was engaged – than when the veteran producer Hal Wallis came to her with a property called *The Rainmaker*.

Hal Wallis is undoubtedly one of the great names of Hollywood. He was the genius behind much of the success that was Warner Brothers from the days of Al Jolson's *The Jazz Singer* right through to *Casablanca*. Afterwards, he had a similar brilliant success at Paramount. When he had a story idea and a star ready to play in it, he generally had a hit on his hands and the studios all knew it.

The Rainmaker was about a dowdy spinster called Lizzie –everyone remarked at the time how similar the role was to the one Kate played in *Summertime* – who falls for a con man. It was different in that it was set in rural America and Kate was the only woman in a family of men – her father and brothers who dearly wanted to marry her off. They saw Starbuck, the con man who told them he could bring rain in the midst of a deadly drought, as their salvation, and if only to promote Lizzie's chances, went along with all his crazy hocus-pocus posturings.

The story was based on the New York play by N. Richard Nash. 'I bought it especially for her,' Wallis told me. It was a happy memory for him. They got on well together, mainly, one imagines, out of a sense of mutual respect. He for all that the name Katharine Hepburn stood for; she for a man who had to be regarded as a seer in the world of motion pictures.

Burt Lancaster very much wanted to play the part of Starbuck. So much so that he was ready to do a deal with Wallis. The producer had been trying to inveigle him to join Kirk Douglas in *Gunfight at the OK Corral,* the story of Wyatt Earp. Lancaster, who had a justified reputation for the image cut by his superb circus-trained physique, wasn't sure it gave sufficient scope to what he believed were his undoubted dramatic talents. They were dithering on the subject, seemingly getting nowhere. But then he heard that Wallis had bought *The Rainmaker* and that Hepburn was to star in it.

[151]

'It had been one of his ambitions,' said Wallis, 'to play opposite Katharine Hepburn, so he saw this as an opportunity to fulfil it.'

'I understand you own *The Rainmaker?*' said Lancaster.

'That's right, I do,' replied Wallis.

'And you're going to star Kate Hepburn in it?'

'Correct,' said the producer. 'I am.'

'Well then,' said Lancaster, 'if you still want me to play in *OK Corral*, I will just so long as you let me play in *The Rainmaker* opposite Kate.'

(The director, Joseph Anthony maintained to Charles Higham that Lancaster was somewhat less enthusiastic, calling the story 'crap', and refusing to learn lines more than one day in advance, in contrast to Hepburn's habit of having the whole script under control before filming began.)

Lancaster, who was now at the peak of his fame and perhaps the most popular actor around in 1957, was offering a compromise that Wallis, a man better skilled in that art than almost anyone else in Hollywood at the time, had no wish to reject.

'You've got a deal,' Wallis said.

'And so the two projects were put together,' he told me. He had reason to be grateful that they were. 'Kate was a joy to work with,' he remembered. 'She was *so* professional.' Which didn't help her relationship with Lancaster.

The first day of the picture, everyone was ready for a prompt start. Kate was there at 9.30 in costume and makeup. But it was twenty or twenty-five minutes before Burt Lancaster arrived. When he did make his appearance on stage, Kate stepped into the middle of the entire company and made a speech: 'Mr Lancaster,' she declaimed, 'we have all been here, but you have not been here. If this is to be your pattern for the rest of the production, kindly let us know and we shall *all* get here at 9.55. Otherwise, we expect you to be here on time.'

'From that time on, he was on time,' Wallis recalled. 'It was in front of the whole company – something I've never known happen before. She made her position very clear – she wasn't going to stand any nonsense. She's so professional and expects

[152]

everyone else to be, too. From that moment on, she and Lancaster got on very well indeed.'

When it was all over, she gave Wallis a painting – a self portrait. It was an extension of herself; a new form of relaxation and stimulation. Someone asked her at the time what she thought she would be wearing in 1999. 'The same old costume,' she said. 'And still painting.'

She liked the film so much that when she made what most film people regard as the customary statement, once work on the project was complete, that she wanted to work with the producer again, it was taken a lot more seriously than usual.

She told him: 'You know, I'd like to work with John Wayne.' Wallis promised to give it every consideration. It took almost twenty-five years before that promise was brought to fruition. Kate did however talk over another project with Wallis. But she demanded more money. All she got from the producer was . . . silence. Like granite, as she put it in her foreword to Wallis's autobiography (written with Charles Higham) *Starmaker*. She said that she never made that sort of demand to him again.

Meanwhile Kate and Spencer were learning how to wrestle with the age of the computer in their next joint film *Desk Set* – about a television station librarian who finds to her disgust and sorrow that a machine was able to provide the answers to questions for which only she, as the resident mastermind, could previously be relied upon to find instant solutions.

For a week, she sat in a real-live office, intending to study technique. All that she really did see, however, were a gang of mooning girls studying Katharine Hepburn.

The film was a marvellous reflection on the new world of science with Kate as the librarian and Spencer as the engineer seeing her off the premises, gently sparring with each other as of old. They were, in fact, at all times playing themselves. One knew that the loving, cynical comments made on the screen were reflected in their own living room in West Hollywood.

Years later, she told Alexander Walker, film critic of the London *Evening Standard*: 'Our films assumed that if the relationship between us was valid enough, the spontaneity would be there. Besides, Spencer was very quick at getting his effects.' For that reason, they never rehearsed together. When they went through lines in each other's company, it was usually for a film or play in which only one of them was appearing.

'If people ask why our partnership was so successful,' she said, 'it was based on a natural and truthful completion of needs.'

In later years, she would admit that the idea of marriage had crossed their minds – 'during periods of soul-searching'. But, she said, 'I knew Spencer would know the answer. I never pressed him. I always knew he would do what was best for both of us.' She would look around and contemplate what life had given her. 'I've had all these years of companionship with a man among men. He is a rock and protector. I've never regretted it.'

The American Shakespeare Festival Theatre was generally excited by her, too. When they made their 1958 awards, she was one of a small batch of players – Laurence Olivier was another – who received their prize. It was in response to her Portia.

Kate was not unaware of her success and the ingredients that contributed to it. 'Stone cold sober,' she said one day reflecting on all she had achieved, 'I found myself absolutely fascinating!' Of course, there were people who – even in the 'poison' days – always had.

13

Long Day's
Journey into Night

*T*HE 1960s WERE going to be a troubled decade
for Kate. The woman who while still young had played
middle-aged characters was now middle-aged herself. Not that
she would ever admit to it, but the onset of her own fifties
brought problems that she was unable to resolve.

She still played tennis and golf, rode her bicycle, went
swimming. She was still thoroughly devoted to Spencer. But
he was now physically an old man. She wasn't old, but she was
finding that she was doing some of the things older people did
– like falling over. If anyone had told her it was a symptom of
her years, she would probably have hit them over the head
with her tennis racket, yet she was no longer finding life the
picnic she would have wished.

Nor was she selecting the right material. She went back to
Stratford, Connecticut and played Viola in *Twelfth Night* but
although her portrayal was competent, it wasn't really the part for
a woman of her age. One couldn't really say either that Cleopatra
in *Antony and Cleopatra* was written for a fifty-year-old.

And yet Garson Kanin could write in his book that with all
the other fine actresses who had played the role, only Kate
really justified the statement by Enobarbus:

> *Age cannot wither her, nor custom stale*
> *Her infinite variety; other women cloy*
> *The appetites they feed, but she makes hungry*
> *When most she satisfies; for vilest things*
> *Become themselves in her, that the holy priests*
> *Bless her when she is riggish.*

'Riggish', as Mr Kanin pointed out, meant sexy.

It was partly so because she was working in something that she desperately wanted to do. When the company looked for words to explain that they couldn't pay her anything like her accustomed fee, she said that money wasn't in it – and did the job for the Equity minimum of $300 a week.

And for the first time in her life, this professional among professionals made a mental as well as a physical slip. She was enjoying a lazy fishing expedition one afternoon when she suddenly realised she had a matinee to play. It was something she had never done before. Indeed, the very notion of missing a performance was so foreign to her nature that she would probably have rather been taken seriously ill.

Kate quite literally jumped from her fishing pose – and fell over in the mud. She tried her best to clean herself up, but that wasn't easy when sprinkled with wet, clinging mud. But she ran, nevertheless – and reached the theatre, only to find a line of people waiting to get in. She must have looked a little like a blackface minstrel when she forced her way into the playhouse. But, of course, the show went on.

In a way, that incident was indicative of the way things were moving for her professionally. *Life* magazine said of her at this time: 'She makes dialogue sound better than it is by matchless beauty and clarity of diction and by a fineness of intelligence and sensibility that illuminates every shade of meaning in every line she speaks. She invests every scene, every "bit" with the intuition of an artist born into her art. She is limited only by her ladylike voice and manner. Miss Hepburn could never play a tramp or a tenement housewife. No matter. There will always be parts for "ladies" and we need Kate Hepburn to play them.'

She was, however, playing a number of sombre, intro-spective parts, including one that she hated from the moment she signed the contract – as Mrs Venables in *Suddenly Last Summer*. She played it as seriously as any other, but she disappointed practically everyone who saw her as the cruel, dominating mother. Her co-stars were Elizabeth Taylor and Montgomery Clift. Clift had barely recovered from a serious car crash in which his face had been crushed and she spent much of her time acting as a psychiatrist-social worker helping him not just learn his lines, but deal with all the problems that he was facing in his own life.

Kate and Elizabeth Taylor were not exactly made for each other, however. There was a sense of competition among them. Both were – to use a phrase that took another fifteen years to enter the language but says a great deal – megastars and it is never easy for women in that category in particular to work together, sharing not just scenes but billing.

Kate, by all accounts, was deeply suspicious of the much younger Elizabeth, not totally respecting her acting ability, worrying that she was about to be upstaged. Taylor, on the other hand, seemed concerned that the more senior actress would try to put her in her place. There is no evidence that any of these things happened. But the fear was there and it showed itself.

Suddenly Last Summer may have been a financial success for Tennessee Williams, its author, but it is not a film that either Hepburn or Hepburn fans have much pleasure in remembering. Kate would have justified the role by saying that it was anti-heroine and helped to show just how much she was sneering at 'the whole bloody glamour racket'. But it didn't please people.

For the second time in her career, Kate worked with Jack Hildyard operating the camera. It may not have been a brilliant example of cinematic logic, but he was as enchanted with the star as he had been before. 'She was very, very kind. She never tried to do any of the things that people say she does, like working the camera herself. And she was very generous.'

Filming coincided with the christening of Hildyard's daughter Janine. When Kate got to hear about it, she sent a silver goblet as a present. It was inscribed: 'To Janine from one of your father's great admirers'. At the foot of the inscription were the titles of the two films on which they had worked together, *Summertime* and *Suddenly Last Summer*.

But, it must be confessed, not everyone she met was overwhelmed by the experience. Wilfrid Hyde White, who had made a reputation for himself by playing dignified English colonels and lovable grey-haired con men, met her at a party at George Cukor's house. 'Didn't like her at all,' he told me. 'After dinner, she stood in the centre of the room pontificating, biting her fingernails to the quick – and spitting them out on the floor.'

She may have been in training for another of her tormented women of the period, Mary Tyrone, the drug-addict matriarch of Eugene O'Neill's *Long Day's Journey into Night*, which was, in effect, a filmed play. Kate said right at the beginning that she wouldn't offer any directional advice or try to tamper with the original O'Neill script. She didn't even go to see any of the rushes.

'The play is so brilliant,' she said, 'I wanted to play it really without acting it. I did not want to be fascinating or colourful or exciting.' (Although, in truth, she would prove to be all those things.) 'I just wanted to keep out of its way and let it happen.'

So much so that again she dismissed any idea that it was a job she thought she could make money out of. She signed her contract for £25,000 – a tenth of what she got for *Suddenly Last Summer*, although the experience was at least ten times as rewarding in other ways. The film's total budget was only $400,000. She said that she had never 'given a damn about money', which was true only in so far as it wasn't both a sign of status and a convenient weapon with which to browbeat producers.

'I don't give a damn about clothes and I don't care about possessions. I've gotten tremendous fees when the material was boring and the only time I've ever really kicked myself is when I've done something I didn't want to do just because of the money involved.' In fact, she would say: 'It's far damn well the best thing I ever did. I never had such an interesting time in my life. We all liked each other enormously. With this part, it just sort of happened. I didn't have to guide it.'

She was tipped for an Oscar. It didn't happen. But the film *was* selected as the official United States entry in the 1962 Cannes Film Festival. It won a number of awards.

One of the great satisfactions for Kate was the cast with whom she was working – names like Sir Ralph Richardson (she had hoped Spencer would play Richardson's role of her husband, but he didn't fancy the idea of that at all) and Jason Robards Jnr – then something of an enigma in the American theatre because nobody could be sure whether he was really an actor of great talent or simply a commercial success because he had married Lauren Bacall who was said to have regarded him as a look-alike Humphrey Bogart. Kate was impressed by his performance as her son, James Tyrone Jnr.

But the greatest satisfaction of all was playing in a work by O'Neill for the first time, a writer she said she had admired since she was a child. She had once tried to persuade Louis B. Mayer to make *Mourning Becomes Electra*. The idea doubtless made the water in his eyes freeze because he refused to discuss the matter seriously. As much as anything Kate was moved by O'Neill's personal life; how one son had committed suicide, another became a drug addict.

Great artists, she maintained – and in that she was also seeing something of herself – 'should be sterilised. You shouldn't have children simply as an egotistical reflection of yourself. I think it's very difficult to have a career and a family. Suppose I had a child and on opening night Johnny got the mumps or something. I think I'd be tempted to strangle Johnny.'

Yet again, the critical reaction was not as exciting as she might have hoped. In the London *Daily Express*, Leonard Mosley wrote: 'If I say that Miss Hepburn, all tears, fluttering hands, anguished expressions, really does chew up the scenery here, she has good reason. The other players are so busy chewing up the rug that she needs to do it simply to keep the audience's attention. You will gather from this that *Long Day's Journey into Night* failed to impress me, except as an exercise in pyrotechnics.'

Yet *The Times* was more enthusiastic about it all. 'Miss Katharine Hepburn as the drug-addict mother . . . does not, of course, shed her familiar mannerisms, but she manages in the most extraordinary way to put them to work for her, so that they become convincingly part of the character she is playing rather than something the actress happened to bring along with her.'

She did a great deal of research into the part. She even visited sanatoria and studied the way drug addicts were being treated and how they reacted to that treatment. With the background to the story she needed less help. It was set in her own New England and every sound of the waves, every gust of wind, every particle of fog was as intimate to her as her own blood or heartbeat.

But the picture itself was helped, if help were required with something to which she was basically so committed, by the director Sidney Lumet. 'He was so enthusiastic,' Jason Robards recalled. 'He believes in everything he does. Even if it's the worst picture ever made, people think it's the greatest.'

Lumet himself said he saw the tragedy in the story by watching the way Hepburn played a broken woman, ruined. He said that technique was something she looked for only when she was in trouble. 'When it flows, technique flies out of the window. She is totally intuitive.' That was something that had come from childhood, from the time her parents let her make up her own mind and didn't shield her from theirs.

Dean Stockwell who was also in the cast remembers her help at this time with affection. As he told me: 'It was great working with her and great knowing her – I loved her very much. I rehearsed with her extensively, which was unusual for me. I usually just preferred to wait till the cameras were rolling and go, but she used to like to run the scene, and really rehearse beforehand. It may have been the only instance in my career in which I rehearsed like that.

'She was a little bit of a mother to both Jason and me. She didn't like us drinking – was always trying to make us "pay" as if we were bad boys. I remember that it was winter, and it was cold there, and she bought me a coat. I loved her sense of humour. Her and Ralph Richardson – she had a wonderful outlook on life, and a great sense of humour. With such heavy material, that was important. I do remember that she had some difficulty at the beginning of the project getting a fix on the effect of the narcotic (morphine) her character was supposed to be taking. I had had the misfortune to know some people who had used it, and was able to describe to her what some of the reactions to the drug were like. She picked it right up and worked with it.

'I've seen her a couple of times since. I really love and respect her a great deal.'

She had just finished *Long Day's Journey into Night* when childhood came flooding back, and she had cause to reflect once more on one of her speeches in the O'Neill play: 'What is it, something I'm looking for? It's something I lost . . . something I need terribly . . . I can't have lost it for ever.'

Not long before, her octogenarian father and she had toured Athens. Kate had met the doctor at the airport. 'Where's the Parthenon?' he asked. Did he not want to go to the hotel and rest first, perhaps have a wash? Absolutely not, said the old man. He had come to Greece to see the sights. He could have a wash and a rest at home. That was a particular kind of man.

But now, after a painful, slow debilitating illness, Dr Thomas Norval Hepburn, inspiration, adviser, and father of this remarkable actress, was dead. In a way that was typically Hepburn, Kate decided not to mourn publicly. Other people had talked of merciful releases when loved ones died. Kate put it more bluntly, almost brutally – if you didn't understand what she really meant. In a note to Leland Hayward she wrote: 'Daddy all worn out – so we were really glad to see him slide into "Whatever".'

'Whatever' seemed to say a great deal about Kate's own prognosis on the future. She wasn't sure if she ever wanted to work again – and when she heard that Spencer had collapsed with what was diagnosed as a respiratory infection, she decided that she was going to have a break. Spencer was released from hospital – and then went home to be looked after by Kate with, by all accounts, the approval of Mrs Tracy.

It was near the end of the long, steep slope of physical decline for the man she loved.

14

Guess Who's
Coming to Dinner

SPENCER WAS HER rock. Intimates knew that – although until an article in *Look* magazine revealed that there was perhaps more to their life than friendship, the pretence was still being accepted even into the 1960s. Writers had noted that he needed Kate's strength and they described seeing the way she would coax him into a line of dialogue or a piece of business on a film, but they said little else.

They may have shared the house on George Cukor's estate when both were in Hollywood, but when Spencer was away, Kate had a home of her own. Not always the same home. In fact, she changed it so often that real-estate agents in the town would sometimes be competing with each other in selling the Hepburn house. They were different houses, but they were both at some time during their lives Hepburn homes.

There were certain priorities that Kate insisted upon in any structure in which she lived. Garson Kanin recalled the time when he went house-hunting with her. He and the agent were talking alone in the hallway of the house when they realised that Kate hadn't been with them for some time. In fact, she didn't reappear for another fifteen minutes. When, with great relief, they did see her, both men asked where she had been.

'Taking a shower,' she said. Since that was one of the most important things she did when she lived anywhere, it was vital to see how she enjoyed doing it in a house before she contemplated buying it.

The other priority was, of course, privacy. That was why she could generally be found – or, rather, not found – with a home on top of a mountain or something serving as such. In New

York, a former boxer named Charles Newhill for years served as both chauffeur and bodyguard to keep away anyone Kate classified as undesirable. She also had a close confidante – a personal secretary who before long would double as companion, an Englishwoman named Phyllis Wilbourn, who had formerly worked with Katharine Cornell and who, when Spencer wasn't around, went where Kate went.

Now that she thought she was in retirement, she allowed herself time to contemplate just how essential that gift of privacy was for her. Quite astonishingly she accepted an invitation from the *Virginia Law Weekly* to contribute an article that would be read by the learned men and women of the legal profession. It couldn't have been on a more appropriate subject – indeed, it is probable that the editors of that much respected organ would not have wanted her to write on anything else. The subject was The Right of Privacy.

She took as her sub-heading, 'The Predicament of The Public Figure'. For a by-line, she used the name Katharine Houghton Hepburn. More commercial publications might have preferred to use the exact name that audiences all over the world would recognise. It would have sold more copies. But the legal gentlemen had no such consideration. Instead, they wanted her to reflect on how serious were the intrusions into privacy that people like her suffered.

It began (and it has to be understood that Kate never uses full stops or commas in her writings; she says she doesn't like them. Dashes are more exciting, more expressive. She used the same formula in the Law Review) by demonstrating the research she did into the subject. As if planning a new film role, she got out the relevant documents.

1890 – Boston – Samuel D. Warren and Louis D. Brandeis – The right to life – the right to enjoy life – the right to be let alone – Earliest Common Law – that the individual should have full protection in person and in property – BUT THE DEFINITION OF PROTECTION WAS ALTERABLE ACCORDING TO THE DEMANDS OF SOCIETY. It came to recognize man's spiritual nature – his feelings – his intellect as well as his person and his property. The principle which protects is the principle of an inviolate personality –

If then the decisions indicate a general right to privacy for thoughts – emotions – sensations – these should receive the same protection whether expressed in writing – conduct – conversations – attitudes or facial expression –

The right to one's personality – The right not merely to prevent inaccurate portrayal of private life – but to prevent it being depicted at all – BUT THE DEFINITION OF PROTECTION WAS ALTERABLE ACCORDING TO THE DEMANDS OF SOCIETY.

The right to privacy – Fifty years from now this word as we have understood it – will have no meaning at all – if our world continues in its present direction – and it must or it will cease to exist – So it is probably necessary that we sacrifice privacy. [Which was quite a statement considering the way she felt. But she was not leaving it there.]

In the beginning of my career – in 1932 – I had a right to consider privacy my right – and so I fought for it – a wild and vigorous battle – Quite successful – I thought – I went to a great deal of trouble – I went away – way out of my way – the few people I knew could keep their mouths shut – it was thirty-five years ago – and the opposition accepted a limit –

Today it is extremely difficult to control one's privacy – even if one is not a public figure – Who are you – How old are you – Who are your father – mother – sisters – brothers – grandparents – Of what did they die – what were they when they lived – What diseases have you had – What is your religion – have you ever been a Communist – What is your income – Whom do you support – How much did your house cost – the furnishings – Your wife's clothes – her jewels – fur coats – how much do you spend on your children's schools – Travel – Entertaining – Books – Liquor – Flowers – Teeth – Do you wear glasses – Do you still menstruate – Are your periods regular – your bowels – What operations have you had – do you sleep in the room

[164]

with your wife – and how long has that been going on –
Have you ever been involved with the law – do you drink
– Let's just have a fingerprint now – How much – These
are among the questions which must be answered – if –
you are insured by your employer – (an actor is) – drive a
car – pay an income tax – get social security – etc.

She said she particularly wanted to concentrate on the
hard-done-by actor.

We are worse off than the politician – the politician is
selling his body – and/or his own peculiar personality and
this does not command high esteem – There is always a
'Well, what can you expect' back of derogatory comment –
Both the public and Press feel that they have an absolute
right of access to the most intimate details of your life –
and by life you must read largely sex life – for this is the
department of an actor's life which is most titilating to
press and public

She did not like to appear at 'public places' because she said,
that would have to be recognised as 'the territory' of the nosy
parkers who were ready to ask the awkward questions. (The
worst offenders were, she said, not reporters, but insurance
salesmen. 'You can be protected against anything, but you
must sacrifice you privacy for it.')

My territory was my own home – a friend's house – a
private club – this is all very well – But then you have the
public place on a private matter – the hospital – the church
– the cemetery – where a public character is forced by
illness or death to use a public facility – It would seem
that, in such a case he or she should have a right to be
protected from the peering eye of the outsider – a
courtroom – But even here – or should I say especially
here – the tastes of the public have been geared to a diet of
such extravagance – that the magazines and Press – so

[165]

called respectable ones – must continue to feed it – cater to it – in the manner to which they have accustomed it.'

She had a phrase for that.

Polite pornography is no longer interesting – No more subterfuge – The naked fact – Tell it – Do it – There it is – That is the fact – The truth – The four-letter word – The naked body – Nothing withheld – You feel sad – low – take a benzedrine – you feel too lively – take an aspirin – you want to sleep – take a secanol – you feel pain – take codeine – you are confused – go to a psychoanalyst – Don't hide it – Talk – tell it – It is never your fault – We'll fix the blame – Mama – Papa – Uncle Sam – Teacher – Employer – They are responsible – I would seem to wander – but if you have a public feed on these intimate details – if you have a public geared to listen – read – speak – about the most intimate details of another's life (to say nothing of their own) and geared to 'understand' any vagary – because nothing is either right or wrong – and geared to the divine right of life – to joy – to freedom – Run – Jump – Go – Go – Go – Happy – Happy – Happy – Happy.

The article went on. What she was doing was saying a great deal not only of what Katharine Houghton Hepburn felt, but of what Katharine Houghton Hepburn was. A public figure, who knew she was a public figure, who was glad to be a public figure – yet who wished time and time again that she wasn't. Reading between the dashes, you could see a woman escaping from her confusion.

The article went round the world. Whether she objected or not to this intrusion into her privacy by having it reprinted as first-person articles written specially for those publications none of them ever subsequently said. But she did later tell the *Chicago Tribune:* 'You learn in life that the only person you can really correct is yourself, not anyone else. But you can do it with yourself, if you want to sufficiently.'

[166]

She hoped that not many people realised just how ill Spencer Tracy was. For two years, she cared for him when he was stricken with a particularly serious prostate condition, not unusual for aged men, but Tracy had it harder than most.

Kate said she had retired. 'Cooking and cleaning have got to be more interesting than acting,' she said. And she appeared to mean it. Spencer, however, was getting back to work in films like *It's a Mad, Mad, Mad, Mad World*. That was a fortuitous exercise for Spencer. He played a police chief in the midst of what was more a procession of stars – Milton Berle, Phil Silvers, Terry-Thomas, Joe E. Brown, Buster Keaton, Ethel Merman, Dorothy Provine, William Demarest, Jimmy Durante were just a few of them – than anything else.

The script was by William Rose who was before long to tell Spencer about an idea he had for a project that would make a marvellous film subject for himself and Kate. That is, if she wanted to make what would be regarded as a comeback – because it would be her first work since *Long Day's Journey*. Apart from that, it would be her first work since 1959 – which, as they say, is a long time in show business. *Guess Who's Coming to Dinner* would break the retirement.

She was aware of the difficulties. Would Spencer be able to cope with another major role, for that was undoubtedly what it was? There would be the required scene in which she tied his bow tie – few people had noticed; but she did it in every Tracy–Hepburn picture – but a lot of hard anguish, too. She knew that she would be watching him, studying every facial twitch to see how he was coping under the strain, as well as remembering her own lines and actions – and, as Spencer had said so long ago now – trying not to bump into the furniture.

And she said soon afterwards: 'It's hard to make what people call a comeback, you know. When you stop acting, you're really *out*. In this business, people just forget you.' But they wouldn't forget this film.

It was about a WASPish (in the White, Anglo Saxon Protestant meaning of the term although the frequent visits of their friend the priest seemed to indicate they were Catholic) couple with a doting pretty daughter, who doesn't realise just how liberal they are. Until, that is, she brings home her intended husband, a charming, brilliant, farseeing young man with political sympathies that practically coincide with their own. The problem – and the part of the story that makes it so interesting – is that his background isn't quite the same as theirs.

He comes from working-class parents, who live in a home so very different from the elegant surroundings of his prospective wife's house. More complicated still, he is black.

As usual, Kate was in on everything around her. She insisted on detailed conversations with the hairdresser about the art of shampooing. As she explained to her: 'I'm the best hair washer in the world.' When the director, Stanley Kramer, was asked whether Kate was right about all the things on which she so freely offered advice, he replied: 'Half the time she is.' Nobody asked too many questions about the other half.

The film was to be a spectacular success. The ninth and the most successful of the series. It was also the last of the series. Its success was due as much as anything to the wonderful blend of reality and acting the couple were able to offer. They had never played parents together in a film before – and yet here they were playing precisely the sort of parents everyone imagined they would be – pleasant, funny, caring and understanding.

Kate was to say that she based the role of the wife on her own mother – and for those who knew, it showed. There was also the genius of Stanley Kramer's directing – and choosing Sidney Poitier as the quietly angry prospective son-in-law – and the young girl Kate chose to play her daughter, an unknown actress whom she knew very well indeed, her own niece Katharine Houghton.

Kate was, as usual, totally prepared for work the day she stepped on to the set the first time. More than that, she said, 'In case my niece drops dead from the excitement, I'm here, and I know all her lines, too.'

This was Kate's thirty-second major film and Spencer's thirty-eighth. He looked at least ten years older than his sixty-seven years, his hair was white and people were no longer sure that it was kind to talk about his face being like 'a beat-up barn door'. It was made much more 'beat up' by his physical condition. He said he thought it would be his last movie.

He couldn't bear to watch the films of his contemporaries like Humphrey Bogart, Gary Cooper and Clark Gable. They were no longer there and Spencer, always something of a hypochondriac, wondered whether it was sensible to push his own boat out too far.

Kate's love and care for Spencer was matched only by the watch she kept on her niece, Kathy – daughter of her sister Marion and of the same Ellsworth Grant who had had such trouble getting Dr Hepburn to see him when he was 'stuck'. She was teaching Kathy both her lines and her approach to the part. 'And I find,' she said proudly at the time, 'that I'm not a bad teacher. I think I've helped Kathy quite a lot. Naturally, I told her things that I would never tell anyone else.'

But she also said that she was still, twenty-five years after their first film together and ten years since the one they had last done, learning from Spencer. 'He is really the great master of the film. To me he is the great master of acting. He creates something which is totally believable and gets down to the bedrock of it. It's like Greek art. It is simplified. It's as beautiful as one of the columns on the Parthenon. The proportion is perfect and it relies on total concentration and truth. It's as simple as saying, "Thank you" and it isn't Thank *you*. There's nothing phony about it.'

It was a difficult subject to film and Columbia were taking a huge risk in agreeing to make it. But they hedged their bets. Instead of paying salaries to the principals, they insisted that they take all their money as percentages of the box office take. Kate was to do very well by that agreement. Spencer wasn't.

It was June 1967. The weather was pleasantly summery. The world's attention was fixed on the recently ended Six Day War in the Middle East. But Kate was desperately worried. When one night, she heard a stirring in Spencer's room, she sat up in bed anxiously. Relieved, she realised that he was merely taking a walk to the kitchen. She heard the clink of a milk bottle, the

[169]

gentle nudge of a well-padded and lubricated refrigerator door, of milk being steadily poured into a glass, another chink, another nudge – and then a sound she never wanted to hear again.

She rushed into the kitchen – and found Spencer staring at the glass of milk in front of him. With eyes that would never see again. He had died from a massive heart attack. And with him went the most beautiful part of her own life.

15

Woman of the Year

*T*HERE HAD BEEN long separations for them before
– when she did her European films and her plays at Stratford,
in particular. But inwardly she felt they had always been
together. Even in the days before direct-dialling, they would
make long telephone calls to each other to discuss nothing
much more than the weather – and that was enough.

She knew, now that he was gone, just how much the partnership had been based on what she called, 'a natural and truthful
completion of needs.'

Kate decided immediately after his death that perhaps truth
ought to give way to convention – and to what other people
would regard as the decent way to behave. Spencer's body was
discreetly removed to what he would call 'the folks on the hill'
– the home that he had bought for his wife Louise and their two
children, which was never really his. There was a Catholic
funeral. Kate's own memorial for him was a much more
intimate and private affair and one that perfectly suited her
own definitions of privacy. She mourned – and is still mourning
today.

Intellect has nothing to do with a person's emotions, so it is
easy and trite to say that Katharine Hepburn accepted the
death of her loved one in the sensible way – by carrying on her
own life and remembering him with simple affection.

What she decided to do was to keep his memory alive in the
way that was most comfortable to her. Instead of pretending,
as she had in life, that Spencer and she were just good friends,
she would now tell everyone how they had cared about each
other. On film sets, she would say: 'Now Spencer used to do

[171]

this' or 'Spencer had his own way for saying that sort of thing.' It was a kind of verbal memorial – and much more comfortable for visiting than the granite kind in a cemetery.

She also did something that she has continued to do ever since – which others may have considered bizarre if not downright eccentric, but which she knows was the perfect way for *her* to do her remembering. She started wearing his clothes, a pair of trousers there, a comfortable sweater there. She never tried to explain it. After all, everyone knew she simply found men's clothes so much comfortable than the things women were supposed to wear. She still thought that a pair of trousers was the most sensible garment anyone could be expected to put on.

'Spencer never changed,' she likes to say. 'Whatever the role.' What she liked about him most, she has said since, was that he was a real man. 'The ideal American man. He has a bull neck, a man's neck. I like a man's neck on a man. Too many of our men today have boys' necks . . .'

She repeated how well Americans thought they went together. 'I would needle him, irritate him and try to compete with him, or even beat him. And every once in a while, he would turn and I'd tremble. Finally, he would subdue me. And isn't that what the average man–woman relationship is all about?'

Some people would say that the finest memorial to Spencer Tracy was *Guess Who's Coming to Dinner*. It won Kate an Oscar, which she heard about while working in the South of France – getting back to work *was* the best cure for her sadness. There had been speculation that Spencer would get the Award, both for his talent and for sentimental reasons. Had he done so, he would have been the first ever three-times winner and the first to win posthumously. As it turned out, she was to break records, too.

News of the Academy Award came as a surprise. When the caller on the transatlantic line told her of the Oscar, she had only one question. 'Did Mr Tracy get one, too?'

When she was told, no he didn't, she answered: 'Well I guess this one was for both of us.'

Gregory Peck told me how moved he was by that. He was President of the Academy at the time, an office he took as seriously as flying a plane in *Twelve O'Clock High* or catching a *Mocking Bird*.

A telegram from Kate in the Peck archive said a great deal:

IT WAS DELIGHTFUL A TOTAL SURPRISE I AM ENORMOUSLY
TOUCHED BECAUSE I FEEL I HAVE RECEIVED A GREAT
AFFECTIONATE HUG FROM MY FELLOW WORKERS AND FOR
A VARIETY OF REASONS NOT THE LEAST OF WHICH BEING
SPENCER STANLEY SIDNEY KATHY AND BILL ROSE STOP ROSE
WROTE ABOUT A NORMAL MIDDLE AGED UNSPECTACULAR
UNGLAMOROUS CREATURE WITH A GOOD BRAIN AND A WARM
HEART WHO'S DOING THE BEST SHE CAN TO DO THE DECENT
THING IN A DIFFICULT SITUATION STOP IN OTHER WORDS SHE
WAS A GOOD WIFE OUR MOST UNSUNG AND IMPORTANT
HEROINE I'M GLAD SHE'S COMING BACK IN STYLE I MODELLED
HER AFTER MY MOTHER THANKS AGAIN THEY DON'T USUALLY
GIVE THESE THINGS TO THE OLD GIRLS YOU KNOW

It was her first Oscar since *Morning Glory*.

She told *Look* magazine that she regarded herself as 'a battle axe with a heart of gold'. What was more, she understood the 'old eye of youth that says "She's pretty long in the tooth, isn't she?"'

Her characteristics were precisely what Peter O'Toole wanted for the role of Eleanor of Aquitaine in his forthcoming film *The Lion in Winter* in which he would play her husband, Henry II. At first glance, however, this seemed a strange marriage indeed. It was 1968 and Kate was almost sixty. Peter was still in his thirties – although his lifestyle had introduced a certain look of dissipation to his features and Kate seemed as trim as ever. It was also easier to make an actor look older than younger. And he was heavily bearded.

In many ways they were birds of the same theatrical feather.

[173]

Neither could ever have been called conventional – and the months that followed their first meeting discussing the film were to prove it. O'Toole was not completely joking when he said: 'It is terrifying working with her – sheer masochism. She's been sent by some dark fate to nag and torment me.'

Kate was taking his statements for what she hoped they were. 'No,' she said. 'We're going to get on very well. He's Irish and makes me laugh. In any case I'm on to him. And he's on to me.'

And she was certain that everything would be all right because she was 'at a time of life when people are sweet to me. and I don't mind people being sweet to me. In fact, 'I'm getting rather sweet back at them.' Those were words that were made to be eaten. And she knew it. As she also admitted: 'I'm a madly irritating person and I irritated them for years. Anything definite is irritating – and stimulating. I think they're beginning to think I'm not going to be around much longer.'

She was from the first impressed with the part she was about to play. Eleanor, she declared, 'must have been as tough as nails to have lived to be eighty-two years old and full of beans'. She and her husband were 'big-time operators who played for whole countries like big-time operators'.

It would be O'Toole's second time playing Henry. Four years earlier he had played a younger edition of the king opposite Richard Burton in *Becket*. Then, it was the torment of sending his friend the Archbishop of Canterbury to his death. Now, he was even less sympathetic. Having conveniently locked his queen away in a royal dungeon, he now agreed to have her home for a bizarre Christmas family reunion.

The king was having a heatwave-in-winter romance with a French princess whose breasts were driving him out of his mind. But international diplomacy was being geared towards a more sensible arrangement – that the princess should marry one of his two sons. The queen was there to try to help sort matters out. For the princess wasn't struck with either of the two royal offspring. One was the French king's own lover (which didn't augur particularly well for their creating an heir); the other, said the princess, 'has pimples and smells of compost'. A strange marriage indeed.

[174]

No expense is spared to allow Eleanor a truly royal passage home. The king's barge is put at her disposal and Henry is there to welcome here at the quay.

'How dear of you to let me out of jail,' says Her Majesty as the man, still her husband, bows low to kiss her hand.

'It's only for the holidays,' he replies.

Both parts were crafted by the writer James Goldman more to the personalities of the people he had in mind for them right from the beginning, than from an abstract look at Plantagenet history. The play was variously described as a 'medieval *Who's Afraid of Virginia Woolf?* and 'anti-*Camelot*'. It was also brilliant. And that was why both decided that they were as suited to the roles as though playing themselves in some strange auto-biographical amalgam.

It wasn't a smooth relationship. Both had amazingly strong personalities and gave quite as well as they took. And Kate considered it her duty to give quite a lot. She told him that he didn't eat enough and drank too much. When he argued, she decided not to call him Peter any more. From that moment on, her name for him was 'Pig'. He, on the other hand, called her 'Old Nags'.

But they hadn't been together very long before he decided that the relationship was worthwhile. Just being with Katharine Hepburn was enough to get his dramatic juices going. 'She's like a bloody poultice,' he said. 'She pulls a performance out of you.'

Those first performances were held on the stage of the Haymarket Theatre in London, which was chosen by the director because he thought it better to rehearse there without the pressures of film technicians hanging about. She was plainly in charge from the moment she set foot on the stage, after having been dropped at the theatre in her chauffeured Rolls.

'I just want to make one little suggestion,' she told the director, Tony Harvey, with the sort of smile that had the promise of disaster in it if he didn't accept that 'little suggestion'. 'It seems to me,' she said referring to a scene that had been considered diffi-cult, 'it is a helluva lot easier for Peter to play this way and much easier for me, too.'

James Goldman agreed with her. But she was not satisfied

with a mere verbal agreement. 'Would you like to write it in?' she asked them. And, of course, they did just that. She then decided she had to offer some words of apology. 'Isn't that *terrible* of me?' she asked. Knowing full well that they would have to say it was perfectly correct of her and were very grateful for her understanding of the problems that were likely to arise. She explained it was all part of her professionalism. An amateur might accept scenes that were not quite perfect. She wouldn't. 'I know the difference between an amateur and a professional,' she said.

She changed the opening scene, too. The script said that she was sitting by the fire. 'No, no,' said Kate as this was being explained to her. 'She wouldn't. She'd be chopping wood.'

In London she fled as usual from the press. One cameraman did manage to catch up with her. When an assistant director brought her a newspaper, she looked at it with disgust. 'Don't I look awful!' she exclaimed – and added, 'I thought we'd got rid of that son of a bitch. He chased us all over the West End. We could have saved on the gas.'

That was her only hesitation in travelling all around London at that time the way she wanted to do it. In Camden Town, she stopped a young boy on a bicycle. 'Where did you get that?' she asked him. 'I want one.' And get one she did – a folding machine which she kept in the Rolls boot and used for early morning jaunts around Regents Park. Peter was singularly unimpressed. 'The only exercise I ever take,' he said, 'is jumping to conclusions.'

Both had earlier taken it upon themselves to choose the supporting cast – even the most minor characters. Neither felt comfortable acting with someone who didn't justify their definitions of actor. Because it was essentially a theatrical piece, they found the supporting cast in the repertory and other small theatres in provincial Britain – calling on a leading man here to play a fairly small role in the film; spotting a small-part actress there who might do well in a comparatively large screen portrayal.

There were also bigger names – like Anthony Hopkins, whom they wanted for the part of Richard I (he delayed filming when he fell off his horse) and Nigel Stock with whom Peter had worked at the Bristol Old Vic and in his film *Night of the Generals*. The princess was played by the beautiful Jane Merrow.

No sooner had the company been gathered together than Kate and Peter developed a strange kind of relationship with them. Suddenly, they were both thrust into a parental role – the girls asking O'Toole advice about their men friends and Kate having to solve more than one marital problem for the young men in the cast. She was quick with sympathy – and with her scorn when she thought that the young person deserved all that he got.

Kate wasn't slow with advice for Peter either. She gave him much the sort of treatment she had meted out to Nina Foch. She couldn't understand how he could allow managements to put him in the films he had made. True, she approved of *Lawrence of Arabia* and, of course, *Becket*. But *How to Steal a Million?* and *Great Catherine? This* Katharine didn't approve of that at all. 'You're a bad picker, Pig,' she admonished him, leaving the usually eloquent Mr O'Toole entirely speechless.

'Only one flop since I started,' Peter attempted to correct her. But it wasn't as simple as that – as anyone else who had worked with Kate could have told him.

'Don't argue,' she said. At which he decided to give her another name. 'You're just an old female impersonator,' he said. She appeared to like that.

His work was not her only complaint. She also forcefully told him that he drank too much. 'She also told another member of the company that he was too fat,' Nigel Stock told me. Peter's answer to her complaints was to go out to her car when she was busy filming a scene without him – and fill it from top to bottom with empty beer and spirit bottles. 'It made her look like a raving alcoholic,' said Stock. 'But she knew immediately who had done it – and thought it was a great joke.'

It was not the end of the somewhat abrasive relationship between them – born, it has to be emphasised, out of the kind of mutual respect that few others express in this way, but which to any bystander looked a pretty eccentric way of expressing it.

[177]

Both thought they knew the way the other felt and most of the way were on a single course as far as the work on the film was concerned.

There were no disputes, for instance, when it came to selecting the director. They both agreed totally on Anthony Harvey – whose work in a low budget film called *Dutchman* had impressed Peter tremendously. Kate hadn't heard of him and at first needed convincing. The only place the film was showing within reach of Kate's East Coast home was in one of those rather smelly unpleasant neighbourhood cinemas which have a closer relationship to a Skid Row hostel than to a theatre. They walked across spreadeagled feet and over bony knees, kicking the odd meths bottle on the way, before they could find a reasonably satisfactory seat. They saw *Dutchman* and Kate was as convinced as Peter.

Filming began at the Bray Studios in Dublin – as much as anything because Peter was more comfortable and happy working in his native Ireland than anywhere else and Kate liked seeing new venues. There was also a good financial arrangement. The Irish government were delighted to have an international film being shot in their capital city, something that didn't happen nearly often enough as far as they were concerned.

Kate looked remarkably fit, although she still had the Venice canal eye and there were unpleasant blemishes on her face. She knew what they were. She had told her doctor and then her dermatologist what they were. Skin cancer. But it is a form of cancer that is easily treatable and she had hesitated no more about having it attended to than she would have pondered on the way she played a part. As someone once said, 'she enjoyed being a patient' without suffering from hypochondria.

They were in Ireland for Christmas 1968. Other people in the company wanted to go to parties or rest. She was up before dawn had shown any sign of disruption, let alone cracked, and drove to Arklow – so that she could climb the cliffs on Christmas morning.

Once various interiors had been shot at Bray, the entire company moved to the South of France, where there were sufficient ancient chateaux and a picturesque if also seasonably bleak seascape to fit into the wintery story. It had been a horrifying flight over the Channel. The plane chartered by the company was filled to the point of being overloaded with camera and lighting equipment.

'We only just managed to take off,' Nigel Stock recalled. 'Quite terrifying.' And so was the rest of the flight from Dublin to Marseilles. Headquarters for the company was Jules Cesar at Arles and a series of nearby chateaux and monasteries in which Kate immediately held court as though they were as natural a habitat for her as for the queen she played.

She could adopt that pose when she was in one of the draughty, dusty rooms by herself or with just another actor or actress. 'I found myself alone with her on a number of occasions,' Nigel Stock recalled. But it wasn't the attitude of queenliness that struck him. It was the pullovers she wore to keep out the cold. 'There were two of them,' he recalled. 'Both moth-eaten. One was red and one was blue – worn on alternate days. The red one, she told me belonged to Bogie. The blue to Spencer. She said they were the two men she really loved.' She also told him quite frankly of her relationship with Spencer and his family.

It was January and every member of the team benefited from the fire that was radiated from Katharine Hepburn and Peter O'Toole seemingly in mortal combat – on screen and off. O'Toole is a sociable man with people whom he likes – he can be just the reverse with people he doesn't like and his attitude to the press looks as though he took a diploma course set by Kate herself – and he is not afraid to mix with men and women other big stars might regard as beneath their station.

Kate's makeup man and Peter became firm friends. One day when she needed her face attended to, the man was not to be found. She sent out a Hepburn search party – an instrument not to be tangled with lightly. Finally word got out that O'Toole and the man were deep in conversation in Peter's dressing room.

It was not a time, Kate decided, to send one of her cryptic messages. Instead, she tore up the stairs to the room at the

[179]

monastery where they were shooting, kicked open his door and shouted in the kind of voice rarely heard since the time she herself played that other Kate in *Taming of the Shrew*. 'Why won't you let me have my makeup man?' she demanded.

Peter looked at her with one of the lovable, charming smiles that had won a few hundred thousand female hearts, and hoped that a peck on the cheek of his co-star would be enough to calm the stormy waters. It wasn't. Kate instead went for his cheek – with an almighty punch, the kind that Cyril Ritchard had experienced on stage in *The Millionairess*. O'Toole had to steady himself, but by then Kate had already gone – saying as she tore down the stairs: 'Next time I want a makeup man, send him down to me when I ask.' That was not a request likely to be ignored a second time and indeed it wasn't.

Next day they made it up. Peter paraded for her inspection before filming began – bandaged from head to toe like a fugitive from a new series of *Invisible Man* movies or an extra in *General Hospital*. This time, she saw the joke – except that when extracurricular behaviour interfered with the hard, solid work of completing the film they were all there to make, there really wasn't anything to laugh about at all.

But she did, unwittingly, inflict an injury or two on Peter. The scene in which Henry meets his Queen as she sails in for their holiday reunion looked majestic. He was in one barge, she in the other. As the two boats came close to each other, the top of Peter's right index finger got wedged between them and was practically torn off. Ironically almost an identical thing had happened to Kate in rehearsal. A thumb had got caught in an iron door on the stage and was nearly torn from its socket. She had refused to have any medical attention, let alone allow anyone to take her to hospital and she conducted the rest of the proceedings with her hand wrapped in a series of blood-soaked handkerchiefs. It was, of course, no more than anyone would have expected of a Hartford Hepburn.

Equally to be expected was the care and attention she gave other members of the company who were ill, too – Anthony Hopkins after his fall and Anthony Harvey when he was taken to hospital suffering from a high fever. She rushed around them both with the devotion of a nurse, the commitment of a mother hen. It was just a factor in what she considered to be her total involvement in the film.

She herself was not involved in everything. There was, for instance, the night that Peter gave a party for the company at his hotel which served the best Marseilles-type food and the strongest liquor to go with it. Car loads of actors, extras and technicians arrived at the hotel at which Peter was the perfect host, solicitously offering them food and drink that seemed deceptively mild. As Nigel Stock remembered, however, one by one the O'Toole guests were overcome with the combined effects of the food and the alcohol. Even O'Toole's business manager was seen to be getting down on his knees to perform a Russian dance. Peter knew the power of the liquor he was serving, but nobody else did. They should, of course, have smelled a rat. He was the only one not drinking at the party.

'Peter didn't invite Kate to that party,' Nigel Stock remarked. 'I don't think he would have dared. Or I think she would have seen through it – which none of us did.'

She did, however, think that he was drinking too much. 'You're ruining your life,' she told him. 'Why do it?' And she demonstrated how easy it was to give up things that are lifelong habits. She stopped smoking.

Peter wasn't convinced. 'Why, you New England puritan!' he exclaimed. 'I've seen you swill vodka like a Russian commissar.' If he had, it was a secret he should have kept. She didn't enjoy hearing it even though it was patently untrue.

Kate has always had a massive appetite, despite her still thin, girlish figure. O'Toole was thin, too. 'Old Bones,' she called him – and insisted that he started putting solid food where all that liquid had gone before. It didn't appear to have any great effect on him.

It wasn't just her somewhat eccentric attitude to leisure activities that made an impact on the company. Few of them had ever been with someone who knew her business quite as well as she did.

'I was terrified by her because she was such an awe-inspiring person,' Stock told me. 'As soon as she got on the set, she knew exactly what the lighting, for instance, should be. In fact, I think she knew more than the lighting-cameraman. And it was borne out every time she told him – "I want that light here, another one over there."'

There were the usual altercations with the press – and a particularly unpleasant one with one reporter who she thought was asking questions that were much too personal. But Stock didn't stay terrified of her. 'In fact,' he told me, 'I grew to love her. She was exceedingly kind to me. We sort of understood each other without having to express ourselves in any way. She went out of her way to invite me to be with her. There was no nonsense with her.'

Shortly afterwards, Kate came to London to see him playing Winston Churchill in the play *A Man and His Wife* at the Peggy Ashcroft Theatre in suburban Croydon. 'She caught me after the last matinee, trying to take make-up out of my eyes. And there was this woman standing in the doorway whom I could hardly see. "It's marvellous," she kept saying. "You really must take this into the West End."'

That was music to his ears, and precisely what he himself had long thought. 'She got hold of everybody and started to get things going. But she was defeated in a most extraordinary and sad way.' The play was directed by her old friend Michael Benthall, who also had a sixty per cent share in the production. 'He was making all the arrangements – and then died ten days after Kate first came to see me.' It was, nevertheless, a marvellous tribute from an actress to an actor, and a perfect demonstration of the way she cared – and kept her promises.

By this time, *The Lion in Winter* had reached the cinemas and received its just critical acclaim. But in the London *Sun*, Ann Pacey wrote of her doubts: 'Miss Hepburn plays Miss Hepburn magnificently and Mr O'Toole gets on with the job of pretending to be the fiftyish Henry quite effectively and the spark of great teaming positively refuses to ignite against the cold backdrop of cold medieval castles and conditions. *The Lion in Winter*, beautifully photographed by Britain's Douglas Slocombe is very clever and classy and culture conscious, but enjoyable only in certain set-piece situations in which the obvious actually happens.'

No mind. Others thought differently.

The following spring, Kate won another Oscar – for the second successive year. She shared the award for Best Actress with Barbra Streisand. It was the first time an actress had won the Award three times.

As was inevitable with a woman so much in the public eye who so much tried not to be, there was talk whenever anything remotely different happened to her. There were suggestions that she was going to be married – this time to William Rose, the writer of *Guess Who's Coming to Dinner* and *It's a Mad, Mad, Mad, Mad World* as well as such popular British productions as *Genevieve* and *The Lady Killers*.

They were frequently being seen in each other's company. Rose tried to block any ideas of romance by saying: 'We've been friends for a long time because we both knew Spencer Tracy well.' People were still refusing to admit that a spade was shaped very much like a . . . spade. 'I've got the highest admiration and regard for her and everything.' And then he added: 'I'm rich, fat, burned out and I'm looking for someone to come with me in my claret-coloured Maserati in Italy.' Kate was not willing to make that particular trip.

In fact, it was very much the year of France for her. No sooner had she finished the film with O'Toole than she took on a job that was to prove much less satisfactory, both as far as the film and the role she played in it were concerned.

The Madwoman of Chaillot was an old story full of fantasies, the best of which would have been that it never really happened. Unfortunately, happen it did and nobody concerned with the picture was in the least bit happy that it had. It was based on the play by Jean Giraudoux and was as crammed full with stars as an Academy Award presentation – which should have proved a warning. Movies ought to be released with a Government Health Warning – the quality of the picture is inversely related to the number of stars featured in it.

Here was not only Katharine Hepburn playing the eccentric

Parisienne but gathering around her in an exercise of pure tedium: Yul Brynner (with hair), Danny Kaye, Dame Edith Evans, Charles Boyer, Claude Dauphin, Jean Gavin (later to be appointed by Ronald Reagan as US Ambassador to Mexico), Paul Henreid, Nanette Newman, Oscar Homolka, Margaret Leighton, and Richard Chamberlain.

One of the earliest problems with the piece was that less than halfway through, the director was replaced – which augured not well at all for what happened afterwards.

The story was basically that of a crazy woman who is convinced that the whole of Paris is about to be converted into a giant oil field and asks her friends to do what they can to avoid it happening. The film was produced by Ely Landau, to whom Kate felt she owed a debt for the work he had put into *A Long Day's Journey into Night*. And it was to be directed by John Huston, whose ideas for the film struck her as being imaginative. But Landau didn't think so and Huston, the giant of *The African Queen*, was replaced by the English wunderkind Bryan Forbes.

'That's when it all fell apart,' Paul Henreid, who played a French Army officer – a change from the German and Central European roles to which he was condemned at Warner Brothers, told me. 'We rehearsed a number of the scenes at the Renoir Museum at Nice, which was my idea. It seemed to work out very well. She asked Huston to direct her there and stage the scene. We were all quite happy – until Landau replaced Huston with Bryan Forbes without our knowledge.'

One imagines that Kate – who has casting and director approval on all her projects – did know. 'But Bryan Forbes didn't know what was good and what was bad and ruined a brilliant script.' But that wasn't the most difficult aspect of the change. Said Henreid: 'Somehow Katie, who basically has a very good instinct for things, seemed to be very insecure and gave in to his direction at all times – which was absolutely disastrous.

'The first part with Brynner, Boyer, Homolka and myself who end up in the sewers of Paris went very well. But then, when Forbes took over, it all broke up. Kate had Danny Kaye in deep conversation, and there were a few other characters, but when I saw their scenes on the screen, it was absolutely ridiculous. Kate herself was made to become very cute. It was unspeakably bad.

'For so long as the old guard was there, it was amusing. After the change, it was dreadful. I remember once when Forbes asked me for dinner, I asked him to leave me alone, I thought what he did was so bad. As far as Kate was concerned, all he seemed to do was to make her smile and show her gums.'

Henreid said he was very aware of the impact that Tracy's death had had on her at that time. 'She talked about him all the time and the way she talked I had the feeling that she had taken the film in a kind of state of shock.' He told me that he and Kate were very friendly all the time they were on the set of the film. Once, he bought her a five-pound box of chocolates. 'She loved chocolates, I knew, so I bought her this box in a confectionery shop in Nice. She was very pleased. She proceeded to eat half the box there and then – without offering me a single one of them!'

They had lunch together once, a rarity indeed for Kate who still told people that she had only been in about half a dozen restaurants in her life. 'It was the *most* fantastic lunch you can imagine,' he told me. 'And you've never seen anyone devour what that woman could eat. The hors d'oeuvres trolley practically disappeared in one go.'

The worry that other members of the cast had over Bryan Forbes was apparently not shared by Kate herself, who became friendly enough with him to go to dinner at his house and give a few home truths to his wife, Nanette Newman, who was in the film, too.

'She is overwhelming in the best possible way,' Miss Newman recalled in a BBC radio programme. 'She has this extraordinary larger-than-life personality. She also has an incredible kindness when you get to know her and get used to that forthright thing . . .'

The first day they met on the set, Kate was typically abrupt: 'What have you done to your hair?' she asked her, which may have been considered by some to be a surprising thing for Katharine Hepburn to worry about.

'Well Miss Hepburn,' Nanette replied. 'Bryan thought I should wear it like this for a change.'

'Well,' Kate replied, looking the younger actress up and down, 'it's a change for the worse!'

But, Nanette said, 'She was genuinely interested. And she has a great ability to enjoy life, and I think that is a great gift.'

The gift that she had was undoubtedly class. Director Billy Wilder told me that he stood by every word he had once written about her. 'There are two class girls in Hollywood movies,' he said, 'and both of them are named Hepburn. There is nobody else. Just a lot of drive-in waitresses, wriggling their behinds at the Cinerama camera. But the Hepburns are like salmon swimming upstream and they do it with very small bazooms. Here is class, somebody who went to school, can spell and possibly play the piano.'

One writer who saw her at the time, Alexander Walker, said that he hadn't had the feeling of actually meeting her. 'I *felt* her,' he wrote after the experience. Why was there this extraordinary impact? Perhaps Walker again had the right idea when he quoted what she said about the deaf. 'Deaf people love me to talk to them,' she said. 'No one who's hard of hearing has any trouble making *me* out.'

She was conserving her energy by doing the things she wanted to do – and always by being in bed by 8.30 every evening. How else can you be up at five and take your first bath of the day? Kate wasn't making any concessions to anyone. She cycled everywhere. She wore torn white tennis shoes, old slacks and a man's white shirt hanging out of her trousers which had probably been Spencer's.

She had rented a villa at St Jean Cap-Ferrat that seemed to fit in with the kind of regimen she had chosen for herself. 'It's the only house I found here I like,' she explained – as if anything she did ever needed explanation. 'Real privacy. It's quite simply furnished. I like the texture of old wood. I like the feel of it and look of it. People should be like old wood. I hope I'm like old wood. Some people are like boxes made out of jewels or of beads. I prefer things made of plainer materials. It's not just the basic texture. It's the natural colour, and the ordinary plain

[186]

Guess Who's Coming to Dinner? (Columbia)

Kate the sport—in *Pat and Mike*. (MGM)

With George Cukor on the set of *Adam's Rib*. (MGM)

She loved working with Humphrey Bogart on *The African Queen*. (National Film Archive)

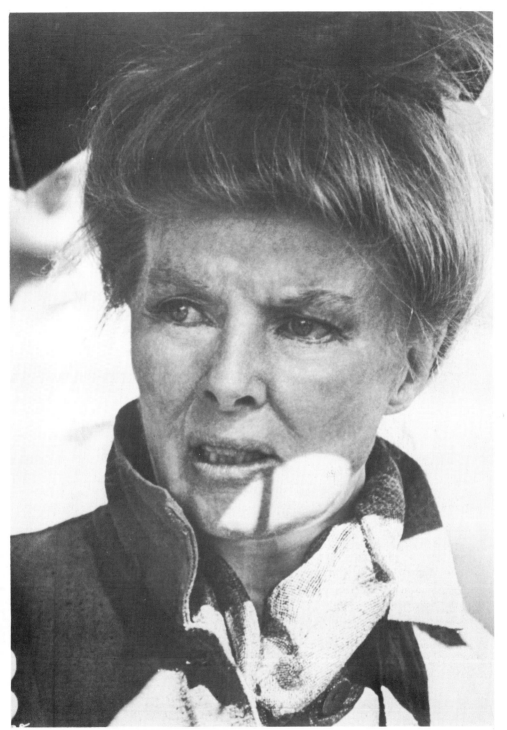

Left: As easy as falling into a canal — in *Summer Madness*. She would never recover from the eye damage she suffered in this scene. (National Film Archive)

Above: Kate as she appeared in *Rooster Cogburn*. (Universal)

She loves he-men—and none more than John Wayne, with whom she made *Rooster Cogburn*. She asked Hal Wallis to be given the chance to work with 'Duke'. (Universal)

With her niece Katherine Houghton, whom she introduced in *Guess Who's Coming to Dinner?* (Columbia)

She put Peter O'Toole in his place in *The Lion in Winter*. (Avco Embassy)

Her golden hour — with Henry Fonda in *On Golden Pond*. (ITC/IPC)

In *The Corn is Green*. A photograph taken by actress Patricia Hayes

look. I suppose it's nice to see things gussied up – (That's typical Katharine Hepburn, making up a word when she can't find one in the dictionary that says what she wants it to say) – for a change. I think the same is true of acting, don't you? You could never see them acting at it, the way you can with actors today.'

She saw the whole *Madwoman of Chaillot* story as being allegorical for the state of the universe. 'It has more relevance than twenty years ago. The world has gone cuckoo. We're still dominated by greed. Sad. That's what Giraudoux was talking about.'

She also admitted that her roles contained 'a lot of me'. And she gave Alexander Walker an example: 'There's a marvellous moment in *The Madwoman of Chaillot* when Danny Kaye, who plays the Ragpicker, says to me: "Countess, the world has changed. The world is not beautiful any more. The world is not happy." And she says: "But why wasn't I told?" She's been living in a dream . . . but is it any better to wake up? Or is it worse? Keep the dream. That's what matters. That's what keeps me going. Keep the dream. The rest is unimportant.'

Kate enjoyed working with some of the great women of the European cinema, like Irene Papas and Giulietta Masina, who played a couple of other mad ladies similarly affected. Mme Masina told her that she still had a photograph of Kate in *Little Women*.

'Mon dieu!' said Kate. 'That was a very long time ago. And now so many interesting parts have come at once. I regret that, I live to savour parts.' That was why she got on so very well with her French cook, who produced food for her the way a good director managed to get a film completed. 'That woman has reached the same values as I have,' she said.

As usual, Kate used every chance being 'in the neighbourhood' gave her to go sightseeing – including a trip to what she termed 'a pimple on the chin of the south of France, Monaco'. Other people went there, spellbound, mouths hanging open and watering, eyes glistening green as they thought of Hollywood's own princess, the former Grace Kelly living in style in the principality's palace. Not Kate. 'That poor girl,' she said. But her sympathy did not stretch to avoiding an opportunity that seemed to present itself to inspect their Serene Highnesses' home.

And as though breaking into yet another Beverly Hills mansion, Kate climbed a ladder leaning against the palace wall. She allowed herself to say, 'I hope we won't get arrested,' but kept climbing just the same. 'This must be the palace we're climbing into. I mean, it has to be here. It couldn't be on the other side of the hill. There's no sun over there.'

Having done her inspection of the palace grounds – even she didn't dare any real housebreaking – she decided to go back the way she came. Fortunately, there was another ladder leaning against the wall. She could have found a gate through which to walk, but she had lost one of her moth-eaten cardigans – a red garment with a string of holes at the bottom. There were other things that interested her in the area – wild flowers. She knew the names of them all. From primroses to hepatica. But then, she always did. Wild flowers had always been a Hepburn passion.

A mad, carefree adventure. And a lot to talk about. Except, that it wasn't the palace she and her companion had been in at all. It was just a park!

What counted in the world of the theatre, either live or on the screen, was personality, as she told Alexander Walker: 'Within limits you can diversify your roles, but your personality must stay a familiar object. Me? I'm just like the Flatiron Building. A nice old building nobody wants to see torn down.'

Few people had that sort of affection for *The Madwoman of Chaillot*. It was the disaster Paul Henreid predicted, both in the theatres and among the critics. Typical was this comment from John Simon: 'One of Giraudoux's less good and most fragile plays has been rewritten, bloated with inept contemporary references, drawn out of gigantic proportions of humourless vacuity and peopled with a barrelful of non-acting stars.' And Rex Reed, the most fashionable American critic of the day, said: 'The intentions are honourable – defeat is inevitable.'

Even the brightest ideas of Katharine Hepburn were

occasionally to fail to reach fruition. After years of directing her directors, she decided to try her hand at officially being a director herself. She decided late in 1968 to accept an offer from Irene Selznick, widow of David O. Selznick and daughter of Louis B. Mayer, to direct the film that she herself was going to produce. It would be called *Martha* and would be an adaptation of both *Martha, Eric and George* and of *Martha in Paris*, two stories by the British writer Margery Sharp. It would, in short, be very much a woman's venture, perhaps the logical culmination of everything Kate had ever felt about the feminist movement. But there were problems over the script and it all fizzled out like a firework party in the rain.

Kate was much more concerned with what she saw as her duty to put the world to rights. If she did agree to see pressmen, it was to declaim on the way she saw human values being abused. She had thoughts about youth, she told the eminent British show business writer David Lewin. 'The young are marvellous,' she said, 'because they are young. I don't envy them. That is a waste of time yearning over things that you can't recover. The point about young people is that there are more of them today and they are all jostling to be noticed. That is why they wear their mini skirts and strange dress, in an effort to be noticed. In my time . . . it was easier to be picked out. Young people still have to make the fifty-yard dash. They will have to find out how many sparks there will be in an old flint.'

As for sex, she thought that too much was written about it. 'And it is all bunk. Sex is classified and coded and fed into a computer today and that's not what it is at all. You shouldn't examine your own sex life too closely. What's the purpose? My father, who was a surgeon . . . studied sex professionally all his life and before he died at eighty-two, he told me that he hadn't come to any conclusions about it at all.

'Marriage I do not believe is a natural institution – despite the fact that my mother and father were so happy. It is difficult enough making good friends with your own sex – let alone deciding to spend your life with someone of the opposite sex. It is not easy to be interested – and marriage means to be interested – in someone else all the time.'

She also discussed discipline – 'out of style now, but is the basis for a satisfying life'; beauty – 'It is fashionable to say that I am a beauty with a well-proportioned face. But when I was beginning they thought I was a freak with all those freckles'; possessions – 'I am not jealous of possessions and I have never surrounded myself with them.' And then there was, inevitably, the Hepburn Theory on Death:

'I don't want to leave any monument for myself. I have enough vanity to be satisfied with and to enjoy what I'm doing – although acting is not all that important in the scheme of things. You cannot have everything, so I do not nag about what I've missed. When I see a new baby I look first at its feet, not its head and I say, "You have a long way to go – I hope your feet will carry you." Mine have. Life is just about the right length, although some people say it is too short. To me, it seems so long.'

And a whole new decade of Hepburn activity had not yet begun.

16

State of the Union

SHE WAS, AS she began to contemplate her
sixtieth birthday, coming to terms with that word thrust on
people who have become venerable in their professions:
legendary. Spencer would have huffed and puffed about it, but
demanded that she got the sort of care, attention and respect
that usually only went alongside legends. It wasn't par for the
course for anyone to have been in the business for as long as
she had, and at the top, without that phrase being locked into
the writers' memory banks and dragged out every time
someone pressed the appropriate computer key.

Yes, of course, she was a legend. Sometimes a bad-
tempered, irascible, difficult legend. But a legend just the
same. She saw it slightly differently – and more intelligently. It
wasn't being a legend that interested her. She was much more
concerned with a simple word – survival. 'If you survive long
enough,' she said about this time, 'you're revered, rather like
an old building. The great trick is to get over the middle period.
That's the tricky bit.'

She was thinking of the time between her first Oscar for
Morning Glory – ignoring all that had gone before it on the
stage, of course – and the latter years with Tracy. If you could
get over those, then you were on the way. She didn't mention a
little thing like talent, but even legends were entitled to be
modest now and then.

'I suppose people are more interested in you if you appear
unconventional. But I don't dress the way I do for effect. I can't
change my character now, not at my age. Though sometimes I
think I should or I may wind up in a cage. And although I'll

[191]

probably be stricken for going through this two-pound box of chocolates [not Paul Henreid's], I do like keeping fit.'

And she admitted she had been lucky with her upbringing. 'I was brought up in an age which believed in individuals; before the insurance companies took over our lives.' Kate would have had to have been offered the complete resources of the Prudential – with bonus clauses stipulating she had approval of the choice of directors – before letting any insurance company take over her. And in late 1969, she was in no mood to contemplate any such thing. There was a new challenge on the horizon. She was going into her first Broadway musical. For the first time since she had sang 'Auld Lang Syne' in one of the less memorable moments of *The Little Minister*, she was going to be singing before an audience.

She was also going to be meeting a woman with a reputation for being even more formidable than herself. The idea for the show was put to her by the man who was its creator, Alan Jay Lerner, working without his long-time collaborator Fritz Loewe – between them they had crafted a repertory of musical successes from *Paint Your Wagon* to *My Fair Lady*, making them seem the logical heirs to Rodgers and Hammerstein – but this time with music by André Previn.

Lerner's idea was for *Coco*, a show based on the career of Paris couturière Coco Chanel. He had a book, he had his music, he had his lyrics. He at one time thought he had a leading lady, too, Rosalind Russell, who had done so well about seven years earlier with the screen version of *Gypsy*. But Miss Russell was already stricken with the early effects of the cancer that would kill her before long, and couldn't contemplate it.

Then he thought of Katharine Hepburn. To Kate, the phone call suggesting the role was another one of those challenges that sound hackneyed to everybody but the person who needs it. For once, however, the cheque wasn't all made up and waiting for the amount to be filled in. Lerner wanted Kate. But only if she could sing. And not even she was certain that she could.

But she did remember *The Little Minister* and 'Auld Lang Syne'. That was the number she sang for him. Or rather he heard her give her own interpretation of singing. She did it while Lerner himself thumped the keys of the grand piano at the New York apartment of Irene Selznick. He wasn't after one of the sweet lyrical voices that stars of Broadway shows used to have. Rex Harrison in that classic of his own had proved it unnecessary every time he threw one of his carpet slippers or put on his porkpie hat. *My Fair Lady*, with its nightly demonstrations of Professor Higgins reciting on pitch had changed everything. Now a reasonably pleasant voice that got over the message that behind the words there was a tune was enough.

When he heard Kate and 'Auld Lang Syne', a kiss and a thank you were enough to guarantee that Katharine Hepburn and *Coco* were about to be a going concern. When she met the musical director Roger Edens and went through a song or two with him, he said he felt an excitement matched only by the time he worked with Ethel Merman and Judy Garland, neither of them exactly Hepburn stereotypes.

He recalled: 'When she came to my house that first Sunday morning, I got out about fifty songs, but she just moaned about her repertoire. "I might just sing 'Onward Christian Soldiers'," she said. So we started from scratch to learn a few songs. At six o'clock I knew she was the third woman in my life.'

From then on, she would practise her singing at the Selznick suite at Manhattan's plush Pierre Hotel. She found her friend Cole Porter's repertoire most suited to her needs. So day after day, she stood at the piano, thanking 'Mrs Lowsborough Goodbody for that Infinite Weekend with You' or passing on the message from the regretting Miss Otis. Sometimes, she was even more ambitious and went through the *Camelot* songbook – also by Lerner and Loewe.

Said Lerner at the time: 'She's remarkably musical and unlike most actors who forget to act when they're singing, she's always acting.' I'm not sure Miss Hepburn would have regarded that as a compliment, since she believes that acting is an extension of oneself.

When Kate was sufficiently satisfied that Lerner and the others responsible for getting the show on to the stage were really happy with her and not being deferentially polite, she said: 'They seemed to like me. They must be desperate.'

As far as Kate herself was concerned, it was a new medium with all the excitement that that meant. Again, there would be no time to mope about Spencer. What it would demand would be never getting into bed much before 11.30, but she was even willing to make that sacrifice. Her baths would have been another matter, but nobody was going to prevent those.

Lerner thought that Kate would fit well into Mme Chanel's elegant court shoes – the dresses she would have to wear in the show were mere working clothes, her trousers as always were sacrosanct – because they were built in a similar way. 'Architecturally speaking,' he explained. 'Not physically.' What he meant was that both were fiercely independent women. 'Both career women without losing one ounce of their femininity.'

As Chanel herself had told him: 'There's no future for a woman trying to be a man.' Which, despite the odd hopelessly misguided suggestions over the years that that was what Kate *was* trying to be, was exactly the Hepburn philosophy. Clothes never made this woman, but now she was going to be professional enough to play a woman who made clothes.

The original idea for the show had come from Rosalind Russell's husband, Frederick Brisson, at least twelve years earlier. It was he who brought in Alan Jay Lerner, for whom the show became every bit as much a fixation as converting a flower seller into a lady had been for the vexatious professor.

It was going to be a totally independent production. Mme Chanel would have no say in who played her – nor would she be designing the wardrobe for the show; this would be done by Cecil Beaton as he had for *My Fair Lady*, although he would be expected to be strongly influenced by the Chanel style.

Eighty-seven-year-old Chanel did however watch developments with the eye of both an artist and a mother suspiciously guarding her children. Chanel's 'children' were her style, personality. Indeed, her own life. When Kate actually met her, she felt for once what it must be like for the few privileged people who had been able to meet Katharine Hepburn. She quaked. And, for the first time in her life, worried about the coat that she confessed to have worn for forty years. But once she had made the trip to Paris, she thought, 'What the hell?', she really *was* too old to change now.

The story, to quote one wag, was that Coco surveyed the sight before her. Looked Kate up – but not down. As *Newsweek* magazine said, she really didn't care what Kate was wearing, just so long as it wasn't by Courreges.

After lunch, Kate and Lerner were shown the current collection. When that was over, she crept back into Coco's room to say goodbye. The old lady was fast asleep on a sofa. With her hat on. And her glasses. There was, however, one reservation. She thought that Kate was too *old*. 'Why,' said Chanel, 'she must be almost sixty!'

But they got on well enough when they met in Coco's suite at the Paris Ritz, just a squirt of No. 5 away from Maison Chanel in the Rue Cambon. Kate herself even bought a dress or two at the salon – more to feel part of the story than to wear in the street or at home. But the actress who still admitted to using alcohol for washing her face wouldn't go so far as to say that she wore the Chanel perfume. For the granddaughter of a man who used to use ordinary soap for cleaning his teeth, that would be going too far. 'God,' she said at the time. 'My mother used to use 4711 toilet water. It had a faint fragrance. I do like the way the boxwood used to smell at my grandfather's farm in Virginia, but I don't use anything that smells good.'

She wasn't so sure about that show, however. And the doubts tended to multiply as the months towards opening dwindled to weeks, the weeks to days. By the time it was a matter of only hours, she was wondering whether she ought not to try telling herself again that she was really in Indianapolis.

And as she said afterwards, she and Coco weren't quite the same sort of woman as she had so blithely said at the beginning: Coco was 'very grand and knew all the people; and I fancied myself as rather a country bumpkin. I liked the script, but I knew I would not be able to play her if I didn't like her, too.'

Coco was pleased enough with what she saw – and was sitting out front on the opening night on 18 December 1969 at the Mark Hellinger Theatre, cheering as enthusiastically as her age and ideas of decorum – bred from years of gold chairs in the audience at her own seasonal shows – would allow.

There were no out-of-town try-outs. Lerner and Brisson had

decided that this was a big-city show or it was nothing. Besides, it was such an expensively dressed show with so much intricate scenery to cart around, the risks entailed in opening anywhere at all before moving to Broadway were just too great to justify. Certainly, nobody would dare say it was a 'nothing'. In fact, they were saying that it was the most 'showy' show since the days when Ziegfeld was enthroned further down Broadway.

Everyone seemed to have the same feeling about it, which is almost half the fight won from the start. Three months before opening, two signwriters were busy with the first poster on the marquee outside the theatre. 'Katharine Hepburn', it declared, 'in *Coco*'. One of them said to the other: 'We're giving a new actress a break.'

The show was estimated to cost a minimum of $750,000 – which meant that it was pretty well breaking every previous Broadway record. Beaton's wardrobe alone was costing $155,000 – to be worn by the leggiest chorus seen on Broadway in a generation, including one young lady who had come direct from the models' dressing room at the Chanel salon – and no one at all was saying how much Kate was getting for her own small part in the story.

Kate was very conscious of the fact that she could relate so well to the character she was playing. 'Everybody,' she told *The New York Times*, 'comes in from the country with a bundle of goodies – whatever they are – to sell. She came in and had something they liked, apparently.' The show was to prove much the same thing about Kate. It was not so much a box office sensation as a highly successful show and most people said that the most successful part of all was its star, and its choreographer Michael Bennett.

Coco seemed ideal for Kate, a nice in-between role for an actress who admitted she was too old for most of the parts being offered her and who didn't want to settle down to playing old women either. The original Mme Chanel may have been eighty-seven, but that was a matter of years. Neither she nor Kate were admitting to giving in to those years. But she was admitting to last-minute nerves, before the previews

[196]

started pumping all that adrenalin into her system. 'I must have been drunk to get into this,' she said, when she was told that the budget had been exceeded by at least $150,000. 'I feel about as big as a mouse and my one hope is that when I leave the theatre, I'll get run over by a truck.'

Time magazine would have been kinder had that actually happened. '*Coco*,' said the magazine, 'is more of a bore than a bomb [using the American term for a theatrical disaster]. Everyone who was anyone was there [it said of the first night], primed for some kind of theatrical night of nights. Dramatically, the champagne was flat, the hors d'oeuvres tasted of sawdust and the small talk on and offstage sagged into yawns. The show is one of those lavish reminders that the assembly line is not the fountain of inspiration, that known quantities gathered together do not necessarily produce the elusively unknown quantities of fine dramatic art or exciting entertainment . . . No wish is fulfilled. No dream comes true.'

The magazine's sister publication, *Life*, was a lot kinder. Its critic wrote: 'A lot of *Coco* is talent flapdoodle. Miss Hepburn makes Coco an amusing empress. In her surprising guise as a singer, she whacks out her songs with more clarity than melody and comes off best when she bunches down to a sort of barrelhouse chant that must go with Vachel Lindsay's poem "The Congo". Her peak of achievement is a wild victory dance after she is rescued from defeat by four New York buyers from "Orbachs, Bloomingdales, Best and Sacks." Hepburn puts into her dance the same gleam of mischief the same unlikely mixture of seduction and horseplay that sometimes shines from her eyes in a movie close-up. It beats casual elegance all to hell.'

And then came the most telling comment of all: 'Is Coco even Coco or is she really another truly rugged individualist known as Katharine Hepburn? As an actress, Hepburn has spent a lifetime filtering characters through the steely sieve of herself. She does not submit to roles; she rules them and everyone has grown terribly fond of her special brand of tyranny through personality . . . Her performance is a triumph of the will over intrinsic limitations. If she cannot dance, she kicks; if she cannot sing, she inflects the pattern of her speech to imply singing.'

[197]

The *Time* critic didn't even have a kind word to say for André Previn, usually regarded as the blue-eyed musical boy who couldn't do wrong. His music, said the magazine, 'misses and didn't even swing'.

Nevertheless the lines outside the Hellinger Theatre box office continued to grow and the people who had previously to content themselves with seeing Kate's films, or an exhibition of photographs tracing her career – as happened earlier that summer at the Museum of Modern Art – were delighted with what they were offered.

There were problems that only Kate Hepburn could either bring or quell. She wanted fresh air – so, in the midst of a New York winter, she opened all the stage doors during the rehearsals that go on even during a show's run. The Chanel girls didn't like that at all. So she bought them all woollen mufflers to stifle the bitter cold. When she found herself disturbed by the noise of workmen on a construction site opposite, she insisted that they stopped their activities during the show's twice-weekly matinees. They didn't argue with her any more than would a whole posse of Hollywood producers.

Sometimes, the scenery got stuck on one of the vast revolving stages. That didn't faze Kate either. She simply sat down behind the footlights and explained to the audience what was supposed to be going on while the stagehands were desperately trying to sort out the difficulty. When a vast mirror broke on stage, Kate called for a broom – and swept up all the mess while everyone else stood around gaping at her control of the situation. That, as someone doubtless pointed out, was showmanship. And it received a suitably warm round of applause from the audience.

Kate left the show seven and a half months later on 1 August 1970, after extending her run in it by two weeks, leaving the role to be taken over by the French star Danielle Darrieux. But Mlle Darrieux didn't take over the audience. Without Kate, it was also without its Coco. She had known what the audience felt about her – and said as much in her final curtain speech. No one would have expected hearts and flowers from a stolid New Englander. Her farewell sounded more like a threat. 'Well, you

[198]

love me,' she said. 'And I love you – and that's that.' You could read the dashes in her speech as she recited it.

17

Love among the Ruins

*I*F YOU COULD always be sure where you were with Katharine Hepburn, knowing her and the story of her life itself would be a lot less interesting. In fact, it was always difficult to work out whether she was going to be heroine or harridan.

For every story of eccentric behaviour there was one to counter it of supreme generosity. Whenever someone told about the funny things she did, there was another person on hand to tell a tale that just seemed outrageous. Often you could forgive even those outrageous episodes because you knew that what she did was precisely what you would have wished to do yourself.

Like when she was cycling near whatever served as her Hollywood home at the time. A motorist drove right in front of her, causing her to swerve as the cutting-up process continued in a long swoop. As she described it herself, she was 'blind with rage'. In the full and understandable belief that no mere car could match the power of a Hepburn in blind rage, she chased after the offending automobile. But her pedalling paid off. She caught up with him, jumped off her bike and banged on the man's side window. When the glass was rolled down, she glared. 'I just wanted to see what a pig looked like,' she said – and got back on the bike and rode away down hill. 'I got a kick out of that,' she said afterwards.

That was what she hoped her work always did for her audiences. Sometimes, she worked simply because she believed that certain plays or films had to be done properly and if she didn't take that responsibility on herself, who would do them? Such were her reasons for going in for Greek tragedy, for the first time since *The Warrior's Husband*. Except that *The Trojan Women*, which she made in Spain of all places – learning the local dialect in between her speeches – was the pure, undiluted, real thing.

She thought that it was something that just *had* to be done – even though she rightly predicted the film would lose a small fortune. Another reason she did it was Michael Cacoyannis, the director for whom she had an infinite respect. Other people had told her before to 'do the classics', but apart from her Shakespeare seasons, there had been all too few opportunities. Now when Cacoyannis invited her, she not only did not want to refuse: she enthusiastically accepted.

Also in the film were Irene Papas, Genevieve Bujold and Vanessa Redgrave. Kate knew her lines – she arrived on location after other members of the crew because of her extended run in *Coco* – and was fully armed with a scholar's knowledge of the play and the period in which it was set.

The ambiance of Spain appealed to her. She had ample opportunity to take her baths. She got to bed at seven most evenings and the sun was so bright and hot, the easiest thing in the world was to be up at five.

She was brilliant as the aged Hecuba. The years showed in her facial expression, in the way she held her hands, and wore her hair. But not in her reaction to others in the cast. When she heard and saw a performance she appreciated, she applauded wildly once the director had called 'Cut'.

She herself was required to grovel in her black dress on the dusty road. She did that with no more difficulty – in truth probably with a great deal more ease – than she wore the Chanel dresses at the Hellinger theatre. Off set, she would wear her usual uniform. 'I'm a bit square,' she admitted. 'Rather peculiar. But the squares carry the burden of the world.' That was why she didn't like the way the cinema was going – taking other branches of art along with it. 'Just porn,' she said at the time. 'Just porn.' Of course, *The Trojan Women* was nothing like that. But it was a film.

'I enjoy making films,' She told the *Los Angeles Times*,

'They're much easier. I feel *I* should pay *them*. On the stage, you're constantly proving yourself and there is the need of this tremendous effort. But I always come back to the theatre. I'm like a beggar in rags. Perhaps it's because I had such an immediate success in films but not in the theatre.'

Her aim now was to go back to the theatre, which she did – in a gruelling tour version of *Coco*, which opened its run at Hartford, her home town. There were the inevitable announcements that she would take the show to London. And, of course, everyone who knew anyone knew that she would make the film. There had to be a film, didn't there? And if this consummate film actress didn't make that film, then who would? The answer was no one. There was no film of *Coco*. Nor was there any London run.

It wasn't a totally happy tour either, soured by that opening at Hartford. It was in her own family house there that Kate was viciously attacked by the woman who had recently been her chauffeuse. It was 2.30 in the morning, which for Kate is normally almost well into the next day, when the woman jumped out at her from a closet.

Louella Gaines West, who had just been fired by Kate, was waiting for her in her bedroom – armed with a hammer, which she didn't actually use. But her weapon could have been even more deadly: her teeth. As Kate moved to resist the woman, her finger was bitten – the end was found lying on the floor. As she said afterwards: 'The human bite is very dangerous. Miraculously, I never had the slightest infection. I went from one hand specialist to another all over the country. The pain! But thank God, I didn't lose it. The show could have sunk.' As it was things didn't turn out quite so bad.

Fortunately, her doctor brother, Robert, was there and managed to rush her to hospital where the finger top was sewn on again. She continued the run of the play with the finger bandaged and in a splint. Meanwhile, West was found guilty of breaking and entering, assault and causing a breach of the peace. She had claimed that Kate owed her her salary.

By that time, Kate was working on *A Delicate Balance*, which really wasn't a very happy film for a lot of the people concerned.

[202]

The storyline established right from the beginning that Kate herself was in charge. She was the ageing head of a family living in Connecticut, which might have seemed the epitome of typecasting. But it wasn't her kind of affectionate, loving family. Instead, this matriarch presides over an atmosphere so threatening that the definition of 'family' needs to be rewritten.

All the action was filmed in one huge house in London, which was meant to double for the one in Connecticut. The filming took place in rooms downstairs. Upstairs were the dressing rooms, one shared by Paul Scofield and Joseph Cotten; another by Lee Remick, Kate Reid and Betsy Blair; a third used by Kate alone.

The story was of a couple (Kate and Scofield) whose daughter (Lee Remick) is expected home after a fourth broken-down marriage, which is perhaps not the worst family tragedy: Kate's sister (Kate Reid) is an alcoholic. There is also the problem of a couple who arrive unannounced and unwelcomed as houseguests who, like *The Man Who Came to Dinner*, won't go away.

Originally, Kate Reid's part was being played by Kim Stanley but, as things were to turn out, the role was a little too close to reality. The story was based on Edward Albee's play and Kate admitted that she didn't really understand it until the shooting had got at least half way, which was a very new thing for her indeed.

When Ely Landau, the producer – it was to be the first production for the American Film Theatre whose aim was to guarantee a showing of plays in film form in towns and cities that did not have live theatres – first approached her to take the role, she said: 'Oh, no. What's all this about? I'm a simple, nice person. I like to make Christmas wreaths, sweep floors. I don't *understand* all this complicated stuff! I'm rather like my sister who's a farmer and says that the most difficult thing she likes to attempt is carrying two pails of milk over a fence.'

But succumb she did – and later explained why: 'My God, that's a depressive play! I played it in order to be able to understand what it was all about.. It was only when I actually acted it out that I understood it. It's about self-protection. I think we are all *enormously* self-protected. I identified with those people who resented the intruders into their privacy, and I think that's what made me, after not wanting to do it at all, finally decide to go ahead. I'm a very private person.'

The executive producer on *A Delicate Balance* was Neil Hartley. He told me: 'She's an enormously talented and aware actress. She's always aware of who's on the set, where the light is, exactly where she should be. It's some sort of intuition that blends perfectly with the professionalism. It's as if she could see out of the back of her head. She always insisted on keeping a closed set. If anyone out of the ordinary was around, she knew it.'

Betsy Blair had known Kate since she herself was a teenage starlet and before she achieved her own fame as both a serious actress and sometime wife of Gene Kelly. 'I was closely influenced by her. She drove a small car so that was all I ever wanted to drive.' They sometimes were at the same lunch parties thrown by George Cukor – 'with Hepburn, Garbo, Ethel Barrymore and me. It was just George trying to be nice, but it was very thrilling for me to pretend that he invited me because he thought that one day I would be like them. Kate was the nearest to what I thought I might one day be. You could aspire to the things she did, as a doctor's daughter who was always very outspoken. I was a New Jersey schoolteacher's daughter. I couldn't aspire to be a Barrymore or a Garbo for heaven's sake.'

Her dreams were focussed on being a Hepburn of the future. Until *A Delicate Balance* in 1973, they hadn't been together since Betsy had left Hollywood some sixteen years earlier. The title seemed to convey as much about the way the film was made as the story itself. Their reunion came at director Tony Richardson's large Victorian house where rehearsals for *A Delicate Balance* were to take place. 'Kate was the last to arrive at Tony's first floor room – and I remember her literally running up the stairs carrying a little bunch of violets,' Betsy told me. She handed the flowers to all the women there.

She then gave everyone her phone number. Had there been some mysterious change in her makeup? What price privacy now? But there was a reason for it, which she believed highly logical. 'I think it's ridiculous not being able to contact anyone when you need them. So I'm giving you my phone number and in return I want each of yours. Only you're not to call me after 8 p.m. – ever. Because I go to bed at that time.'

Later, on the set, Betsy was sitting on the staircase, her legs outstretched as Kate stood by. 'You know,' she said in her most threatening New England voice, '*I* could never sit down in my costume – I'm always afraid there might be a long shot.' Which Betsy Blair found somewhat inhibiting. 'Suddenly I felt like a teenager being chastened again. I felt as if I should jump up and salute or something. Yet I wasn't a seventeen-year-old any more.' A few days later, she demonstrated her maturity. It was four o'clock in the afternoon and Kate was on set – yawning.

'I said, "Oh" and made a little joke, which I thought was getting back at what she had said to me. But she was very alert.

'She said, "I've been up since four or five o'clock."

'I asked her why. "Is it because you can't sleep?"

'"No," she replied. "It's that I have all these things to do in the morning. I get up and have a cold shower to wake up. And then a warm shower to loosen the muscles. Then I do my exercises. And I have another shower because I sweat when I do my exercises and then I roll my hair up.'

Any of the early risers among her close friends would have noticed the Hepburn curlers – little leather things with cotton wool inside. Once they were installed, Kate was back in bed for what she called 'my big breakfast' – 'Everything. Orange juice, coffee, scrambled eggs with chicken livers, salmon, toast, rolls, muffins, jam.' Then it was time to start work. Looking at the script. Going over the day's work. 'Then I have another shower. I do my makeup. By the time I come to the studio, I'm ready. So naturally by four o'clock in the afternoon, I may get a little tired.'

She had also had a reasonably large lunch – after which she had done some exercises for the back trouble she was experiencing – and then taken another bath. 'It made me think that even if for other reasons I might have made it, I could never have been a star. She had this wonderful gaiety and also a kind of integrity and self discipline.'

[205]

And there were always moments of encouragement for the other girls like Betsy herself and Lee Remick. For Lee there was a round of applause after one particularly difficult scene. For Betsy, a homily or two on what Spencer might have said in such a situation – 'and little hints; not offensively, just a general philosophy; how Spence would say you had to feel what was going on'.

In one scene, Betsy was expected to slap Lee's face. 'Tony Richardson said I could. She said I should. Properly. But I'd never slapped anyone in my life. I couldn't – and I didn't know how.'

Kate came up with the solution to the difficulty. 'Tony,' she said to the director, 'if you don't mind my pointing this out. It wouldn't be possible to slap someone's face from a sitting down position. She ought to be standing up.' At that one moment, Kate herself knew the answer to the difficulty that had been stumping both the director and his fairly experienced actress.

'She is just very impressive,' said Betsy.

But not impressive simply in the acting sense. The first time they had met at Richardson's house, after handing out the violets, Kate peered closely into Betsy Blair's face. Her eyes focussed on a small scar – the effect of removing a skin cancer. 'Who did that to you?' she probed in the way that nice people are not supposed to do. She noticed something that others were brought up to regard as none of their business.

Betsy told her: 'I had a bit of skin cancer,' she explained.

'Oh, I know,' she said. 'I know. But you must never let them cut it. Who's your doctor?'

Miss Blair told her. Kate, who collects the names of medical specialists the way small boys know the components of every local football team, was not impressed. 'These are the only doctors you should go to. One is in New York, one in Boston, the other in London. I know all about skin cancer. I have it, too. Every redhead who is foolish enough to play tennis in the sun gets it.'

Betsy took her advice and saw the London doctor. Later, Kate wrote to tell her that the New York doctor had retired and

[206]

gave her the name of another man to go to see. Afterwards, there were frequent notes either from Kate or from Phyllis Wilbourn. 'Kate was just incredibly kind.'

But there were other moments working on the film that occasionally made some people feel differently about her. There was, for instance, the Kim Stanley episode. Kim was an established, serious actress. She was, at the time, fifty-four years old and had a number of credits to her name, most notably *Seance on a Wet Afternoon*. Miss Stanley had a drink problem and it seemed to unnerve Kate to know that she did. She had it fully under control and at no time came to work with her problem evident.

Betsy Blair remembered: 'She hadn't worked for many years and was an alcoholic. She was getting herself back into condition and Tony had gone to Texas, where she was doing some drama therapy, to bring her to his house where he would take care of her, and work in the film. He knew that she was a great actress. It was very difficult. She was rather overweight and nervous. It was very hard because she was aggressive a bit with Paul Scofield – telling him when we were just reading that he had to look at her. She may have been drinking at ten o'clock in the evening, but she was perfectly sober on the set the following morning.'

That wasn't enough, however. Kate was unnerved by her presence. It hadn't been necessary for Paul Scofield to look at Kim when he read his lines – it was conventional at that stage of the work for actors simply to look at their scrips. Kate and Richardson went into a huddle. 'As Tony explained to me, "Without Hepburn there was no film." It was as if she felt the alcohol even if it wasn't there.' So Kim Stanley left.

'I felt,' Betsy Blair told me, 'we would all have been better had Kim Stanley remained. I was very upset at the time. I remember saying to my husband, "We should never idealise or idolise anyone. There's no way that anyone is so wonderful and so eccentric and so perfect . . ."' She confronted Tony Richardson, but it made no difference. 'Kate was also tough with Tony, but he is very tough himself. He adored her – and handled things very well. She would want to impose what she

[207]

thought was right. And if you're determined and important and difficult, and firm and interested . . . it is difficult to resist.'

Betsy said she had to get over her feelings and get on with work. 'It was only a four-week shoot, so I had to put them aside. I had my feelings afterwards. But it must be said that Kate never lost her temper. It was just that with her, it was the work that had to come first.'

Not, however, if it interfered with good deeds. For years Kate has, when in Connecticut, been driving over to a hospital to see a retired woman agent – the victim of a stroke. She never knew the woman very well during her healthy years, but now she feels that if she herself doesn't go to see her, no one else will. She also knows that if Katharine Hepburn goes to see her, it ensures that the woman will be well fed, washed and generally looked after. Years before, she had done the same thing for Ethel Barrymore in her final days.

Whether Jules Dassin, the American director who had lived for years in France and Greece, thought as kindly of Kate is, of course, a matter for conjecture in the nicest possible way. He sent Kate a play to read. Politely, she replied: 'Dear Mr Dassin. Thank you so much for sending me this fascinating play. I found it most interesting, but unfortunately . . .'

She didn't finish the letter. It wasn't honest of her she decided. So she started again: 'Dear Jules Dassin [more friendly and easing what was to come], Try as I will I cannot make head or tail of this confusing script and . . .'

Still not right. She started yet again: 'Mr Dassin [Straight to the point, no falsity], This is surely the most idiotic piece of claptrap . . .' Even Katharine Hepburn had to admit that was taking things much too far. So she started once more:

'Dear Mr Dassin. I am grateful to you for thinking of me in connection with your play. Alas, I am not available at this time . . .'

Now, lest anyone think that the kindness in her soul had intended Mr Dassin to be spared her previous sharpness, she folded the last letter, put it in an envelope – and then enclosed all the other started notes, too.

There were other people who were not so pleased with Kate.

For a time, they seemed to include John Ford, the director whose sleeve she had marked with blue ink all those years before.

In 1973, Ford was the first recipient of the American Film Institute's Life Achievement Award. Kate was not present at the Los Angeles ceremony at which even President Richard Nixon was a guest. The feeling was – and columnist Rex Reed had spelled it out – that it was Nixon's attendance there that prompted her own refusal of an invitation.

In a letter to the *Los Angeles Times*, Kate put her cards on the table. 'I did not attend [she wrote] because I had a good excuse – I was about to go to England to do a picture – because I am lazy and self-indulgent as far as these great public honourings are concerned and have no great belief in them. But I do respect the efforts of my compatriots to try to bring honour and importance and publicity to the profession. I do not agree that Mr Nixon's motive in attending the dinner was two-faced. I think that he was making an honest gesture toward the industry – that he is a movie fan – and that he was anxious and happy to honour Jack Ford.'

It was safer to be back in London. She spent the early morning hours day after day in the capital's parks – and in the Royal Hospital at Chelsea, home of the famous Chelsea Pensioners. She took her bicycle into their grounds – and almost succeeded in doing what the combined armies of the Kaiser and Hitler had been unable to do, forcing a number of old soldiers to run for their lives. She was asked politely to go away. A similar thing happened in most of the royal parks.

'I think I've been banned from every park in London,' she said. 'The only place I think I'm allowed to cycle in is the cemetery.'

She also took up skateboard riding. 'I learned,' she explained, 'just to irritate a nephew who thought I was ready for the grave. I thought, "Well, I'll show you, you great big ass." I'm a great ad for over-exercise.'

It was again part of her love affair with London, which during the early 1970s was being consummated by a whole succession of projects. It was there, too, that she made her television debut – in a made-for-American-TV version of Tennessee Williams's *Glass Menagerie*, which had starred in its original Broadway version one of Kate's greatest idols, Laurette Taylor. Later it was made as a film featuring Gertrude Lawrence and Jane Wyman. Kate revelled as the southern belle fallen on hard times. In one scene, highly reminiscent of Miss Haversham in *Great Expectations*, she wore the wedding dress she had herself worn in *The Philadelphia Story*. She rejoiced to know that it only needed a slight alteration to the hips.

Once more she stayed at the Connaught, which had by now got used to her trousers – although it was part of the same group as the rather more demanding Claridges. One thing she liked about that hotel, she was to tell British actor Leigh Lawson, was that it had an open fire – by which she could dry her still long, red hair after its daily wash.

The film had a limited theatre run as well as TV showings and was featured at the London Film Festival. Cecil Wilson wrote in the *Daily Mail*: 'It is incredible that this British-made film of Tennessee Williams's early play was completed in less than a month and it will be unforgivable if it is lost from our screens after tomorrow.'

The trouble was that the main circuits turned the film down as being uncommercial. Which was a pity. As Mr Wilson said: 'Miss Hepburn, forever prattling about her long-lost legion of "gentleman callers", blends shrewishness and pathos to just the right degree and her smother love goads the son to a shattering emotional experience.'

But not everything was going well. Around them, and for the first time in nearly forty years, a producer decided that there was no film *with* Hepburn, instead of the other way around. She was literally fired.

Kate had been contracted to play the elderly lady in Graham Greene's *Travels with My Aunt*, a sort of criminal *Auntie Mame*. Most accounts have it that she was given her marching orders by MGM, because she did what she had done in practically every play or film in which she had been involved – she proceeded to rewrite the script. That, the studio told her, was no longer how things were done in the 1970s. But it was

Hepburn's way and she insists till this day that she doesn't really know why she was sacked.

It would have been a reunion with the man who was always her closest friend among the dozens of directors with whom she worked, George Cukor. He said that if Kate went, he would go, too. But she refused to allow him to. Alec McCowen also volunteered to leave, but she talked him out of it as well. Her part was given instead to the very much younger Maggie Smith – and Kate has always said she thought Miss Smith did very well indeed.

The studio maintained that Kate had walked out of the film ten days before shooting was to begin. She denied it, said that she would never behave like that, and considered suing. 'The script was practically all mine. Cut to a hash.' She didn't sue because she decided, as she told a writer afterwards: 'That would be living backwards. And it is a bore, trying to prove that you've been misused or not paid or something. It would take two years. And trying to reform James Aubrey [then head of Metro] is not my responsibility.'

And then she added: 'Maybe I was tough with them. I don't think I was, because I thought I was Saint Katharine, to tell you the truth. (Now I know that I'm Saint Katharine because I was never paid a sou for eight months work, seven hours a day.) But I'd be curious to know why I was fired.'

She said that she read the book fifteen times before finally deciding that she herself could get some kind of a story out of it. The film's writers had been more optimistic, but all Kate would say was 'I'll read everything you write, but I'll not guarantee doing it.'

It was a time when everyone appeared to want to know Kate's views on practically everything. Having made her television debut and decided that it wasn't quite the demon she had always suspected it was, she agreed to be a guest on the Dick Cavett show. It took two complete programmes to cover the interview and is generally accepted as one of the best shows of its kind.

Others wanted the predictable answers – to questions on pornography, for instance. 'I find it offensive – and very sad,' she told the magazine *Box Office*. 'I find it sad that producers and actors are so willing to sell out for money.'

Nobody was asking her to do that in her next British-made TV film *Love among the Ruins*, which at the time must have been one of the most expensive and prestigious television plays ever. It was directed by George Cukor and co-starred Katharine Hepburn and Sir Laurence Olivier. It was Olivier's presence in the film that convinced her to do it. As he himself told me, it was the 'fruition of an ambition'. His only previous experience of sharing a scene with her was at the wedding with Vivien Leigh in Santa Barbara.

The story is set in Edwardian London and is the tale of a young girl who falls in love with a student who dreams of becoming a successful lawyer, but then marries a much older man who subsequently dies. Years pass and she is flattered by the attentions of a young man played by Leigh Lawson who falls in love with her. When his devotion is not returned, he sues for breach of promise. Her own defence is handled by an aging barrister – played by Olivier – of course, her original lover.

It was another one of those occasions when the beauty and experience of age has a resounding effect and influence on the sensibilities of youth. Leigh Lawson told me he found it 'quite amazing' to be working with the two stars, but particularly Hepburn. 'She had cast approval,' he recalled. They met at Tony Richardson's London house – Richardson was producing the play. 'I remember she drove up to the house wearing very old patched trousers and a black polo-necked sweater with holes in it. She also had a bike strapped on to the Rolls-Royce she used, and told me she used it for cycling on Wimbledon Common.'

She had a script on her lap as Lawson read for her. She joined in on cue – 'not reading her lines; she knew them off by heart.'

Olivier came in rather late. He immediately went up to Richardson and said, 'Thank you for writing such a very good part for me.' He gave Kate a peck on the cheek and shook hands with Leigh Lawson.

George Cukor who had been watching this, suddenly stood up and said: 'I hope we're not all going to be this fucking polite for the rest of the movie.'

'I could see,' Leigh Lawson told me, 'that they all had a profound respect for each other, in the way I imagine that Richardson and Gielgud and Olivier have for each other.' Again, Kate played her own director. 'She would decide what she wanted to do, and George would let her get on with it.'

And again she was very kind to the lesser actors. The film was shot on location in London and at Ealing studios, then a mere shadow of its former great self. When it was all over, she sent members of the crew letters saying how pleased she had been to work with them. The letters were written on the aircraft back to London. 'It was lovely to get it,' said Lawson. 'Except that I could hardly read it.'

In 1976, she had just as great a success on the New York stage in Enid Bagnold's *A Matter of Gravity*, a play in which her grandson was played by Christopher Reeve, later to make his name as the flying wonder comic-book hero in *Superman*. Writing in the newspaper *Newsday*, critic Allan Wallach said: 'As an aristocratic old woman stubbornly clinging to her magnificent English country home and her belief in tradition and family, Miss Hepburn is playing a part tailored to her talents and playing it beautifully. She is at her best when she stands leaning on a cane and delivering Bagnold's frequently witty lines with her familiar dry delivery. She's also impressive in her moments of emotion when her face becomes a mask of anguish after a quarrel with her adored grandson.'

But the real sensation of the play was Kate's later performances in what turned out to be a matter of extreme gravity. She had slipped on ice outside her New York home, seeing some guests into the street. After the excruciating pain of the fall, she tried to get up and found that she couldn't. She had, in fact, broken her hip. But she continued the run of the play, highly appropriately – she would not have been able to do it in *Coco* certainly – in a wheelchair. The audiences appeared to love her even more for it.

They even loved her when she wasn't officially in a play

[213]

herself. She went to see the then new Leonard Bernstein musical *Candide* – suffering from extreme pain caused by the fall. Halfway through, she could stand it no more. Eyeing enviously a couch on the stage, she moved out of her seat, climbed over the orchestra pit and walked to the couch herself – where she sat down with one of the other actors. It was Hepburn eccentricity carried to the point of unprofessionalism – whatever excuses she may have made at the time. She would never have tolerated anyone doing that in one of her plays.

It wasn't any more conventional, the time that she was making an outdoor shot for *Love among the Ruins* and spied John Wayne, walking through the West End. She left the camera team and ran towards him: 'Oh Mr Wayne,' she said. 'I'm Katharine Hepburn. I just want you to know how much I'm looking forward to working with you next month.'

Before 'the Duke' could have a chance of recovering what breath he had left, she had disappeared and rejoined her unit. The film in which she worked with him seemed highly reminiscent of *The African Queen*. Only *Rooster Cogburn*, a sequel to Wayne's *True Grit*, was set in America's Wild West. Wayne played the one-eyed discredited sheriff who was quicker on the draw in catching outlaws than any other star-wearing son-of-a-gun who had moseyed down the old corral. Kate was a missionary saved from a fate worse than death by Cogburn's care and consideration.

Hal Wallis told me that for Kate it was the culmination of an ambition. 'She obviously thoroughly enjoyed working with a man who was as strong and powerful as Duke was. I remembered the conversation we had had after *The Rainmaker* nearly twenty-five years earlier when I got the property of *Rooster Cogburn*. I thought that was made to measure for her. We talked about it here in Hollywood at length. She's a very constructive person who puts a great deal of input into a project. She isn't a method actress. She doesn't do anything by beats and counts. That's not her way – and *Rooster Cogburn* benefited by it.'

There had been the usual tussles with authority. The director this time was Stuart Millar who wanted them to play a court scene unsentimentally. Wayne was angry at that. 'You can only play a scene so many times before it means nothing,' he said. And Kate added: 'This is, I would say, impossible to play unsentimentally. However, we shall do what we can.'

Wayne told a writer at the time: 'She's the best. She knows everything that's going on, understands the slightest move by anybody.' It was a feeling shared by many. As Hal Wallis said: 'The idea of Wayne and Hepburn was quite magical. They got on fine. The only thing they disagreed on was politics.'

Wherever they were during the making of the film, Kate would lose no opportunity to go swimming. 'It was cold, bloody cold where we were making the film in Oregon but we were usually near a river or a lake,' Wallis remembered. 'But she would insist on diving in at the end of the day, and having her swim. Clothes on and all.' Less than that, of course, no one would expect. 'We had one of those fabulous caravan dressing rooms for her, but she would never use it. We put a makeup table and an umbrella under a tree. That's where she preferred to makeup. There was no nonsense with her.

'There was one scene in which she was supposed to be on a raft in a rushing rapid river and we had a double for her. But she would have no part of that. She insisted on doing it herself. "No," she said. "She doesn't stand the way I do. She doesn't walk like I do." It was really quite a tough scene and she'd just had the hip operation, but nothing would deter her in any way.' She bought her own kayak for twenty-two dollars and sailed it on the Rogue River.

She and Wayne hit it off beautifully. 'I think I thought he'd be high falutin and he probably thought I'd be stuffy. We were very candid with one another. There was nothing phony about it at all. It was totally honest. He's a funny man. And sharp and delicious,' she said.

Later she wrote about the experience of working with Wayne in America's best-selling magazine *TV Guide:* 'John Wayne is the hero of the Thirties and Forties and most of the Fifties. Before the creeps came creeping in. Before in the Sixties the male hero slid right down into the valley of the weak and the misunderstood. Before the women began dropping any pretense to virginity into the gutter. With a disregard for a truth which is indeed pathetic. And unisex was born. The hair grew long and the pride grew short. And we were off to the anti-hero and heroine.'

She liked his 'man's body'. As she explained: 'Good legs. No seat . . . Carrying his huge frame as though it were a feather. Light of tread. Springy. Dancing. Pretty feet.' She admitted 'leaning up against him' and 'as often as possible' because it was like leaning against a 'great building. He's a very, very good actor in the highbrow sense of the word.'

The feelings were mutual. 'I have never in my life worked with a woman who had the smell of drama as this woman has. She is so feminine. She's a man's woman,' he said. There would be no further opportunities for them to work together. Wayne was to die in 1979.

Kate's willingness to scare both the film company and the insurers over *Rooster Cogburn* was nothing new. She did it in her 1977 film *Olly Olly Oxen Free*, a title one might think was weird enough to guarantee either immortality or oblivion. In this case, the destination was very distinctly oblivion.

This story of a junkyard dealer who joins two small boys in their adventure in a balloon got into very few theatres and had barely more than a couple of TV airings. It wasn't because acting with children – to say nothing of the shaggy sheepdog with them – is always considered to be professional suicide for a mature actor or actress. Simply that it just wasn't commercial enough. It was more economical a prospect to let it gather dust on the shelf than print copies and farm them out to theatres that would remain empty.

That was sad because audiences – if only potential audiences – were denied the opportunity of watching Kate perform one of her most adventurous stunts. At the age of sixty-eight, she could be seen – for real – hanging from the anchor of the balloon, some 300 feet above the ground.

No one expected Katharine Hepburn to do the stunt herself and the assorted underwriters of a dozen insurance syndicates closed their eyes and held their collective breaths. But Kate insisted on doing it herself and not letting a professional stuntman get near a copy of the dress she wore in the picture. 'I decided that I just wanted to do it,' she told the *Ladies Home Journal*. 'You could tell by their great big feet if it were a man hanging from the basket.' As for Kate, her big success was in proving that *her* feet, eccentric though they may be, were always firmly on the ground. And she had more pastures to go to. Green ones.

18

The Corn is Green

*I*F YOU ASKED Katharine Hepburn what human –or perhaps even animal – quality she valued most, she would probably have said loyalty, and then added that dogs and cats have it to a supreme degree whereas a man could be awfully lax in that regard. That was why she had such a warm feeling for George Cukor and some of the other Hollywood people who had stayed with her since *A Bill of Divorcement* days – and who didn't give up on her even when tales were being spread about her noxious effect on the box office.

It is also why in 1970 she felt so let down by her old friend Garson Kanin, whose brilliant work *Tracy and Hepburn* had affectionately and with not the slightest trace of acidity broken the story of the romance between Kate and Spencer for the very first time. Once the word was out she was immensely disturbed that a man who had been so close had written of incidents which on their own had been unimportant, but together made up a picture of intimacy which she believed was nobody else's business. She didn't read it when it first was published because, she said, she was afraid it might affect their friendship. Later, when read it she did, she charged that Kanin, one of the most respected of American screenwriters, had either a photographic memory with complete recall or had been busy taking notes through the decades of their friendship. She did not suggest any of it was inaccurate.

There was no such reservation about George Cukor who was by now not just a veteran director with a reputation for working with women that was the envy of every other member of his craft. When Cukor had an idea for a story, he seemed to gravitate to Hepburn the way big-fight promoters chose candidates for their next bout in the ring. He said in a *Readers Digest* article in April 1974 that Kate had one particularly admirable quality: 'Whatever she does, she does openly. She is prepared to take consequences. She's very edgy. She can be nettlesome. She can be odd. She's no angel – no actress is. It's just that so many insensitive things have been said about her.'

They were all qualities that made her even more exciting to work with. After making the *Love among the Ruins* film, she was going to star in his picture *The Blue Bird*, in which she would appear as Light, the Fairy. But it didn't happen. There were script problems and the film, made in the Soviet Union, was to have Elizabeth Taylor in the role instead of her. But there were to be other opportunities on the horizon.

The one that presented itself in 1978 was by far the most interesting. But she had doubts here, too. Cukor was passing on a message from the Warner Brothers television division. They had in mind Kate's taking over a role that Bette Davis had had thirty-three years before – which, considering that the two women are very close in age (Bette was born the year before Kate) seemed quite remarkable. But the role was as ageless as the film that they had in mind, Emlyn Williams's story of the schoolmistress working in Wales, *The Corn is Green*.

Kate knew the story, of course. But she didn't want to play in it. 'Oh, George,' she said when the idea was first mooted. 'It's been done a hundred times – and all those illegitimate children! I should think not.' The story was of the teacher who works to allow her star pupil to take up a place at Oxford, even though when he believes he is the father of a local girl's baby, that seems a dream bound to fail.

But Kate read the script again and changed her mind. Perhaps it was that she saw it as a marvellous new opportunity that actresses of sixty-nine ought to jump at. Or simply that she would have a chance to cycle along the beautiful Welsh countryside. The fact is that she read the script and decided to jump at ideas as gamely as a challenging service on the tennis court.

'Yes,' she said, 'it's great. It's about falling backwards, about someone at the wheel of their own life instead of being dominated by excuses. The opening of the door of life.' As she said in a supremely revealing article in *TV Guide*: 'My! I laughed. And I cried and cried. Oh, indeed a wonderful part. Lovely for me. Such a relief. Alive. Not half dead.'

There was talk of making this version of the play in California. Typically, Kate would not hear of it. 'Must be done in Wales,' she said. Before long, a location had been found – with Kate joining in the reconnaissance, in the village of Isybyty-Ifan. She had scouted not merely for locations but for places to live and eventually found herself a slate farmhouse at Capel Garmon near Betws-y-Coed. The temptation was the lovely old fireplace – so convenient for drying her hair.

The studio work was done once again in London. And so was casting. Once more, she had the final say on this. The young boy, Morgan Evans was played by Ian Saynor, and Anna Massey was the prissy Miss Ronberry. There was also a colourful mixture of English character actors and actresses. Like Bill Fraser, who had first made his reputation playing a sergeant-major in an early British television series, *The Army Game*.

'We thought this was the end of her career,' said Fraser. 'She was showing the signs of frailty. But what a rod of iron, her will was – getting up at six, cycling on an old pushbike round the Welsh hills for an hour, then at seven, she'd have breakfast – a huge breakfast – and be on the set at eight. She was a lovely person to be with. She did a tremendous amount of good to Toyah Willcox, guiding her, telling her how to play her part.'

Toyah, since established in Britain as a highly successful pop singer, sometime TV chat show hostess and a stage actress – she starred in the play about a woman wrestling champion, *Trafford Tanzi* – played the girl at the centre of the problem, daughter of the cockney cook played by Patricia Hayes. Toyah is the first to recognise the debt she says she owes Kate. 'She would stand back to allow me the best camera angles. And she gave me tips about being more aware of the camera and making sure I didn't fidget too much. When we rehearsed the shots, she had little words with me, saying "Try this . . ." It was wonderful. I could be very open with her and call her simply "Hepburn", which got George Cukor very angry.'

Cukor insisted that this then nineteen-year-old girl, barely out of school, should call the star '*Miss* Hepburn'. Once he banned her from the studio for not doing so – although Toyah insists that Kate herself just laughed. Once, Kate got very upset with the director. 'She really scolded him,' Toyah remembered. '"She's only a child," she said repeatedly. And then she accused him of misdirecting me. She only ever had words with George. Never scolded any other member of the company. I reckon that was because they had such a strong bond, too. And George would take it. He wouldn't take it from anyone else. She was so wonderful when she lost her temper. She would say, "Oh George, why don't you shut up?"'

What most forcibly struck Patricia Hayes – a comedy actress until then known almost exclusively in Britain, although her appearances on the Benny Hill show had earned her a following in America, a country she has never visited -- was Kate's continuing habit of wearing the Tracy wardrobe, if now much more the worse for wear. They were his trousers she wore when they discussed the next day's work; his old white shirt. 'I noticed that the trousers were beautifully patched and darned in the seat and everywhere else.

'I was surprised that she talked about him the way she did. But she said, "Of course, I talk about him all the time." I told her that he was my great hero. In fact, I said that he had ruined my life – because I was always looking for someone like him.

'"No," she said, "You would never find anyone like him – because he was the only one of his kind."'

Kate was dressed much the same way when she held the initial auditions at the flat in London's Eaton Square which Cukor had taken. Kate got on the right foot with Miss Hayes the moment they met. 'You remind me of my mother,' she told Pat. But the English actress heard no more of the possibility of appearing in *The Corn is Green* until several weeks later – when Kate and Cukor saw her at London's Lyric Theatre. They had actually come to see Colin Blakely who had appeared in *Love among the Ruins*, and was now starring in *Filomena*. Pat had a supporting role in the play.

[221]

'There was a tap on my door – and Katharine Hepburn was standing there. "You are wonderful," she kept saying. "But what is that terrible thing you have on your head?"'

Miss Hayes told her it was a wig. 'Take it off!' Kate commanded – as only she could. 'Never wear it again! Refuse to wear it!' Three days later, Pat was told she had the part.

There was trouble over hair when Toyah Willcox auditioned for the daughter role.

'Would you mind taking off your hat?' Cukor asked her.

'I'm not wearing a hat,' she answered. 'This is my hair.' Since it was various shades of feather red, punk style, the mistake might seem understandable. Toyah had her confusions, too.

'I didn't know who George Cukor and Katharine Hepburn were – except that I recognised her the moment I saw her. They were remarkably polite – which people usually are not at times like that. They even made me a cup of tea. I was sat on a sofa next to her and then handed a copy of The Corn is Green and asked if I minded reading to her. I had been studying it from back to front and managed to make her laugh. At midnight that night, I had a phone call telling me I'd got the part.'

When she and Kate met for a second time, the two main topics of conversation were Toyah's hair and the band that she fronted. 'She kept asking me how loud we played!'

This version of The Corn is Green was much more real than the Bette Davis film, which was also produced by Warner Brothers. But although this was intended solely for the small screen, there was the stamp of large production to be seen everywhere – from the casting to the locations. The earlier version had been filmed entirely in Hollywood – and it showed.

Kate may have been a little old for the part of Miss Moffat but her dress style was almost identical to that of Miss Davis – although her blouses were always, as usual, done up high to the neck. Kate was the first to recognise that there would be comparisons. And, after all, they had always been considered something of rivals. As Kate said: 'Miss Davis has said that she envies me my bone structure. It's nature. I've simply always

[222]

believed in making the most of what one has.' It was what perhaps had really singled her out.

'And Katharine Hepburn was always the *star*,' said Pat Hayes, 'without ever losing the fact that she is a great actress. She had a bath put into her dressing room, which none of us other had . . . But you knew that despite this starring thing, she was a great actress. And always immensely truthful. Even about herself.'

Kate made up her mind to buy a property in Wales, although so far it is a dream that has not materialised. 'I love this weather,' she told Pat. 'I loathe the sunshine. Look what it's done to my skin. It's given me skin cancer!' She showed her worries – particularly on the days when her eyes were so bad that she couldn't face the cameras at all. There were times when the lower eyelid appeared to droop. 'These drugs,' she said to Pat with more than a tinge of sorrow, 'how long will they continue to work?'

The biggest handicap of all was also now manifesting itself more than ever. A neurological illness was causing her to shake her head, a state of affairs which would have persuaded almost anyone else to call it a day. To Kate it became another one of those challenges to surmount. She takes medication and she controls it bravely and earnestly, but it is there for all to see and she won't agree to curtail her career because of it.

Wales was good for Kate. It is a lot easier for her to cycle there than it subsequently was in suburban Wembley, where a number of the studio interior scenes were shot. In Wales, she had to use a vintage machine, circa 1898. She rode three feet – and crashed. 'I was disgusted,' she said afterwards. 'Am I losing my balance?' They decided to shoot the cycle scenes last – in case they caused her irreparable damage. The misty, dank atmosphere of Wales seemed to do her skin a world of good.

'She kept saying how pleased she was that her skin cancer seemed to have cleared up there,' Toyah recalled.

At that time, Toyah, too, was conscious of the presence of Spencer Tracy lurking in Kate's thoughts. 'Whatever the situation, she would find a way to relate to him,' she said. 'You could tell that she was still tremendously in love with him.'

[223]

In the scene where the Toyah character had to cry, Kate told her to be more hysterical, stronger. There was another scene which George decided should be done in one five-minute take. Toyah had one line to say right at the end as she was eating a large jam sandwich. It went perfectly – until Toyah choked on the bread. 'Cukor went mad at the way I ruined the scene.' Again, Kate laughed – and also applauded. 'She later said that I reminded her of herself at that age. "Toyah," she said, "You're a rebel." I expected someone very arrogant and starry. But she wasn't like that at all. She was so serene.'

The search for authenticity knew practically no bounds. One sequence, intended to be in a stately home's billiard room, was shot in Brocket Hall, the Hertfordshire house of wealthy landowner Lord Brocket. Needless to say, Kate found being there fascinating. Not just in the house itself, but also because the building in Ayot St Peter was close to Shaw's Corner, GBS's house at Ayot St Lawrence and the Shaws and the Hepburns were as potent a mixture in 1979 as ever they had been. Kate was drawn to the place as though it were some religious shrine.

But she was also drawn to Brocket Hall – and in the way she had for years been drawn to the unattended mansions of Beverly Hills. This time, however, with some rather more unfortunate results. The day that the company made their reckie – the location reconnaissance – the doors of the hall were barred and there was no one answering the bell. Kate was not to be put off by this little hiccup. She saw an open window and climbed in – without bothering to think that wealthy British landowners had burglar alarms.

Within five minutes, a fleet of police squad cars had arrived – asking some very awkward questions. Had not one of the officers immediately recognised the 'burglar' as Katharine Hepburn, she most certainly would have been arrested and made to cool her low heels – not the kind she wore when she wanted to intimidate Louis B. Mayer – in the local police cells.

The script called for scenes in a coal mine. Kate insisted that they should be shot in a real mine. 'Afterwards, she took off her period costume and went into the men's showers to clean up,' Bill Fraser remembered. 'After all, she was alone.'

When all the location work had been done, the studio scenes at Wembley were begun. One morning she arrived on the set at 8.30 to find all the lights out, the electricians standing by idle. 'What are you waiting for?' she asked them.

'The director hasn't turned up,' one of them replied.

'Well,' she answered. 'Don't you think someone ought to go to find Mr Cukor? He's eighty, you know. He may be dead.'

Cukor was not well at the time and Kate was constantly giving him her medical hints on his condition. But he was well enough to be a constant restraining influence on Kate. 'Particularly,' said Bill Fraser, 'when she occasionally went over the top, calming her down if he thought her acting had got a bit broad.' That in itself was somewhat unusual – since Kate was as busy as ever in directing the director.

She gave orders to other people, too, even off the set. It was while making *The Corn is Green* that Katharine Hepburn, film star, turned Katharine Hepburn, dressmaker. It happened when Pat Hayes had trodden on the hem of her long dress, loosening the stitches. She told a continuity girl who suggested that she ought to see someone from the wardrobe department.

Kate wouldn't hear of that. 'You don't want to do that,' she told the other actress. 'Phyllis. Go up to my room and get a needle and thread.' The ever-present Miss Wilbourn returned with the required items – and Pat thanked her for them and started to walk away.

'No,' said Kate. 'Come here. I'm going to do this for you.'

'And,' said Pat, 'she knelt at my feet and sewed up the hem for me. I can't imagine any other star doing that. She did it because she wanted to and that's a very wonderful quality. She's never had any children, but I could see there were still great maternal qualities in her.'

The wardrobe people had gone to great trouble to collect clothes that would fit perfectly into the period. The costumes of the extras were laid out on vast tressle tables in the village hall at Isybyty-Ifan. Kate watched this process as she did all the others. And it was while she was standing by the tables that a little girl poked her head through the window and called, 'Hey miss. What time does the jumble sale start?'

[225]

Kate's own clothes were of slightly better quality. At the end of the filming, she handed out blouses and skirts to other women in the company as souvenirs. 'I'll treasure the blouse she gave me for ever,' said Toyah.

The Corn is Green marked a reunion between Kate and Neil Hartley. The executive producer of *A Delicate Balance* was now producer of the TV film. Of her work at this time, he told me: 'She was particularly helpful on this film. Cukor was getting on at that point. She was extraordinarily generous as an actress and as a human being. She insisted on other actors having more lines, and that even in the shooting they be favoured as much as she. The whole things combined to bring out a great sense of performance in everyone in the cast. As we were doing it, I thought that Kate brought a great sense of magic to it. She made the school-mistress an unforgettable character. This curiously American character she had transferred perfectly to the role. I thought it was not only a great upgrading of television, but that it was an improvement on the original film.'

The Corn is Green tempted her back to work and there were other ears of corn to pick. Two of them by the same writer. 'When it comes to work,' she said in the autumn of 1981, 'I don't believe in talking and speculation. Why not just go ahead and do it? I get impatient with sensitive types who sit and reason everything out. They act like mummies, afraid that life is too hazardous for them. I've never been afraid to take a step and possibly fall on my face.'

With Ernest Thompson, however, she concluded that the risk was worth taking. Thompson had written a play about love in the last stages of old age, which had enchanted Kate when she saw it: *On Golden Pond*.

19

On Golden Pond

What enchanted Kate about *On Golden Pond* was that she knew it was a story that she would have loved to have made with Spencer, the one that would have taken the same couple from *Guess Who's Coming to Dinner* into their last experiences together; the final proof that their love had been right all along, and which finally presented the reality of a situation that said it all had to come to an end – and very soon.

She had been through just that fourteen years earlier. She could relate to it. More important, the stage play had proved that others in their position could relate too. So could couples who were much younger, for whom that story represented a loving but perhaps frightening glimpse into their own futures.

Kate was so taken with it all that she agreed not only to play in the screen version, but also to star in Thompson's next play *West Side Waltz* when filming was complete. What she had not bargained for was the effect *On Golden Pond* itself would have on her – and the relationship she would have with her co-star. For it was a film that began for most people concerned, not so much with uncertainty as with a degree of undisguised unease, bordering at times on sheer panic.

In the male lead as her husband, was Henry Fonda, whom everyone knew was merely having a respite from his own final illness. Not a comfortable state of affairs for an actress to contemplate, playing such an intimate role with a man who, though she greatly admired him, had never worked with her before.

Just as significant were the tensions that were also bound to arise with the woman who was playing the vitally important and equally strong supporting role. When that woman is in real life the daughter of the male star who has herself had a similarly difficult relationship with her father as the character she plays, the only thing that can be guaranteed is – tension.

When it is also considered that Jane Fonda is as spirited and individualistic as is Katharine Hepburn, if separated by a generation, the rivalry between them could be seen as a short trip to disaster; if, perhaps, exciting disaster. All this seemed to be in the wind when Mark Rydell began his initial discussions as director of the piece.

It was the story of a couple who, year after year, spend their summers in their country cottage in New England, a country that Kate, of course, knew so well. It is where the trees are vivid red in the autumn, where the loons squawk all day. For the first time for years, their daughter realises when she goes to the house on Golden Pond with her man friend and his son how the years of indifference she believed had been shown by her father were, after a long awakening, now as nought. They were precisely the feelings that Henry and Jane Fonda had actually had for each other.

The project had begun when Jane purchased the work as a vehicle for herself and her father. Both agreed that Kate was the one to play Henry's wife and all three, having studied his previous films, decided Rydell was the man they wanted to direct it. The film was very different from the original play. Rydell commissioned a new script. It was much more sentimental on stage, and also more humorous. On film a sexual dimension was added to the lives of the old couple, the concern of the man at his impotence was not covered up.

'I tried to sexualise it, which was not done in the original play and Kate adored that,' Rydell told me. 'She accused me of being eternally engaged in sex. I said that was part of my personality.'

The first talks were held at Rydell's Los Angeles home. He said he was prepared for an uphill trip. 'But I'm used to strong actors and have developed a kind of ability to be very tenacious and committed,' he told me. Just how tenacious was proved after the appointment for the first session was discussed. 'Kate wanted to start at 6.30 in the morning,' Rydell said. 'Finally we agreed she would come to my house at nine – which she felt was already midday. It was to be a three-day test period, I had to make it clear right at the beginning how I felt. People who are strong and with committed ideas are looking for leadership. If they feel you do have ideas, they will go along with them.'

The talks which began so hesitatingly ended with everyone having basically the same idea of how it would all turn out. They continued in a hospital room. Kate had fallen while playing tennis and severely damaged a shoulder. Three weeks before filming *On Golden Pond* was due to start, she was taken to hospital in New York for emergency surgery.

When Rydell called into her room, she was lying in bed, her arm supported by a hideous-looking traction device. The doctors warned that she couldn't possibly start work. In fact, they said that making the film at all would be too much for her. It could all have ended there and then – except that the medical men didn't know very much about Katharine Hepburn. Every day, Rydell would go to the hospital on 22nd Street and into the room overlooking the Hudson River and talk *On Golden Pond* with her, interrupted only by the doctors. When they worked on their patient, he waited in the hall outside. When they finished, the director and star talked more about the film.

'She was a feisty, tough and quite beautiful old woman, playing the teenager,' he told me. 'She refused to accept that she could no longer do all the things she had done when she was twenty. There is a light around her which it's impossible to escape.' Ruben Mamoulian had said much the same thing nearly fifty years before.

Eventually, the doctors conceded defeat and filming began at Squam Lake, New Hamsphire, one of the last remaining totally uncommercialised beauty spots in that part of the United States – like Golden Pond with its red trees and its squawking loons.

Kate and Henry Fonda were there that first day of shooting. When they came together, she made a four-word statement that deserves to go into the history books alongside Stanley's 'Dr Livingstone I presume' and Nelson's 'Kiss me, Hardy'.

She said simply, 'Well, it's about time.' Fonda and Hepburn were at last working together.

[229]

But the tensions were still there when the cameras first moved into action. As Mark Rydell remembered: 'For the first couple of days, she was talking about Spencer Tracy all the time. She would talk as though he were still there, and how *he* would have played the part. She said, "this would have been a great part for him."

'It made me very anxious for Henry. She was struggling to cover over the fact that she kept seeing the part as one Spencer should have had, and that it was *their* relationship on film that was about to be acted out. She would say how she loved to take care of Spencer. "I used to put him in a chair and bring his slippers," she told me. It was as though *they* were the ones in the film, not Kate and Henry.'

The really tough part was that both were in real life as conscious of their infirmities as were the characters they played: she with her obvious neurological problems; he with the now serious heart condition that would before long kill him. 'Yet,' said Rydell, 'I'd find her determination to work almost mulish. She would arrive at dawn and swim in the lake.

'It was an extraordinary experience all the way through – like some psycho drama. Everyone would rush on to the set every morning to watch these two greats of the industry who between them had a hundred years in the business.' The breakthrough came when Kate gave Henry a present: one of Spencer's old floppy hats. He wore it in the film. 'That's when we knew that they were going to get on well,' said Rydell. From that day on, a great love grew between them; an uncanny love similar in some ways to the one they portrayed on screen, if without the sexual dimension.

The friendship between director and star was plain to see. 'I told her,' Rydell recalled, 'how lucky she was to have a nice Jewish director to bring aroma to the roast of these two WASP stars. She loved that.'

Relations between Kate and Jane were more complicated. 'I was worried about it,' said Rydell. 'Here were these two immensely powerful women encircling each other like tigresses. Kate saw Jane as what she had been herself years before. Jane was concerned about Kate's authority and

[230]

strength. In fact, it took time for Kate to realise that Jane actually revered her. Then they began trusting each other and became firm friends.'

Jane said that she had taken the comparatively minor part in the film out of a feeling of logic. 'I wanted to play with my father and Katharine – it was a challenging thing to do. I was nervous that I wouldn't be good enough.'

And Henry said at the time: 'Jane's a young whipper-snapper, producing a movie to get a good part for her father. But all the time Katharine has been dying to play in it and Jane realises she's a pussycat about it. The part is offered and she grabs it – thank God.' They also managed to grab a feeling of good chemistry between them.

So much so that when Jane was doing a difficult scene with her father, Kate was hiding in the bushes out of camera range, watching anxiously. When the scene was completed, she came forward and cheered loudly.

'That's when a director is really blessed,' said Rydell. 'Kate is never casual or blasé. She meant it.'

Perhaps the hardest of all the roles was the one acted out totally away from the lights. It was the one occupied by Henry Fonda's wife Shirlee who when I spoke to her was still too moved to talk about it. But Mark Rydell said: 'Shirlee was very heroic and dignified. There was a sense of friendship between her and Kate although they never became firm friends.'

The partnership grabbed the public interest from the start. *Time* magazine paid it the supreme compliment by devoting a cover to the couple. 'At last Kate and Hank!' it said on the page heading its review of the film: 'In any season, *On Golden Pond* would be welcome . . . the film addresses itself seriously and intelligently without sermon or sociology to an inescapable human issue: in this case finding a decent ending for a life.'

The magazine's writer, Richard Schickel said 'If people were allowed to vote on such matters, the pair would probably be grandparents to an entire nation, since they are among the very few movie stars who have gone on working while four or five generations have grown up.'

When it was all over, Mark Rydell told me, he knew that

[231]

there was genuine love between the two stars. 'Oh, you could see it,' he said. 'You could see it.'

The film was a huge success. A dying Henry Fonda won an Oscar, his very first. Kate won her fourth Academy Award. No performer had ever done that before. The people of the world also knew that, at seventy-three, Katharine Hepburn was still among them.

20

Quality Street

KATE WALTZED INTO her next stage production knowing she was going to be a huge hit. She was. Not that Ernest Thompson's play was as good as *On Golden Pond* or even that Kate herself was quite as moving. But by now, she had become that institution she had worried about becoming – like the old Flatiron Building.

This play was a comedy, the audience was told, and on the whole both that audience and the critics were pleased to believe it. Particularly, they were able to appreciate the line in which Kate as a concert pianist, says she is subject to deteriorating health but reluctant to surrender her pride.

Kate's pride was all her own and no one would dare question that she was going to hold on to it. She had practised the piano for two hours a day ever since she signed the contract to do the play, although it was not her work that audiences heard. The music was on tape and dubbed, though not always successfully, to coincide with her finger movements at each performance.

The play toured the country but only ran on Broadway for four months. *Time* magazine said: 'The play takes it's own sweet three-quarter time to penetrate the twilight life of a Manhattan widow, but Hepburn triumphantly skirts sentimentality, displaying her radiance even as her character limps, hobbles and crawls toward accommodation with old age.'

It was set on the Upper West Side of New York in a once luxurious apartment hotel. Dorothy Louden played Kate's violinist neighbour. And as the critics noted, the audiences cheered. Sometimes, they did more than that. They snapped pictures of her – and Kate snapped back. More than once, she broke into the action to come to the footlights and tell an erring photographer what she thought of him, or as things turned out, her.

In Boston, she shouted at a girl who had taken a picture: 'You up there, get out of the theatre. Beat it! I'll pay twice the cost of your ticket to get you out.' And then she told the audience: 'That person clicking that camera is a pig.' The customers burst into applause as a weeping young woman was escorted out.

In New York, she stopped the play to berate a man who was resting his feet on the apron of the stage. Everyone was with her and what she said was still of interest. They were still, for instance, asking her views on abortion. 'It seems incredible to me,' she told *Family Circle* magazine in January 1982, 'that there is such a hoopla about abortion. It would seem to be a simple necessity in the case of rape, possible death of the mother, where an under age girl has become pregnant with no possible way of caring for the baby after it is born . . . I cannot understand the new view that the sanctity of life begins at conception. We are living in a world that is over-populated. We should be considering every possible means of taking better care of those children already here.'

But she said she regretted promiscuity. 'Obviously,' she went on, using one of those phrases that proved she had words for things that others only thought, 'so dear as we hold ourselves, so dear are we.' Then no less effectively, the sensitivity of the words changes. 'And this is especially true of the ladies. I think that we should pull ourselves together and face facts. If we roll around with any old fool, we finally become cheap housing. And it is true of the men, too. They become sad old things.'

From there it was only one short hop into the old question of birth control. Family planning was once more being discussed in Congress and she wanted to give it her backing just as her mother would have wanted her to do. 'Normally,' she said, 'I don't get involved in public controversy. But reproductive freedom is a basic public issue and one I feel very strongly about for personal reasons.'

Another time she wrote: 'The female body is undraped, the

[234]

four-letter words are rampant and, worse, nobody bats an eye. I'm wondering if some censorship is such a crime.'

Mostly, however, if she wanted to talk about anything, and her public statements were still looked on by her as infringements of her privacy, she wanted to talk about her work. And, if people caught her in a right mood, about her home. Whenever she could, she would escape to the old family house at Fenwick – and sleep in the room she had slept in as a child. 'With the fireplaces going, I'm living in the same place and nothing really has changed. I go back there and see someone on the street and they say, "Well, Kathy, so nice to see you." My family is still the greatest part of me. The respect kids have for me I got from my mother and father. No doubt about it.'

But in case too many people had the idea to go and visit her there, she has a sign outside that says in huge yellow-on-red letters: PLEASE GO AWAY. Underneath it, in smaller type is the warning KEEP OUT.

She admitted that she was in a business that was essentially 'egocentric'. 'It's a very embarrassing profession,' she said. Another time, she said disarmingly that acting is 'the most minor of gifts. And not a very high-class way to earn a living. After all, Shirley Temple could do it at four.' As for herself, she said, 'I was discovered before I knew what the hell I was doing. I knew I could make people laugh or cry, but I'm blessed if I knew how I was doing it. It's only in the last years that I feel I know a little bit of what I'm doing.'

That was why she didn't hold herself back when she thought people were unduly standing on ceremony. All that business about discouraging fans had nothing to do with inbred conceit. She simply didn't think her affairs were anyone else's business. When one guest arrived unexpectedly, she said: 'Hello, you're a novelist. Do you want coffee? I bet you don't sleep at night.' She gave him coffee and then looked at him slightly disturbed: 'If you're finished, mop the terrace or something. Try to be useful.' That was part of her lifestyle, too. Being useful.

But there were people who still thought there was the smell of sour apples about her. 'I am not a devotee of that cult of nostalgia wherein practically anyone who was a Hollywood star in the Thirties receives instant apotheosis,' wrote Helen Lawrenson in the *Los Angeles Herald Examiner*.

Miss Lawrenson had written one of the best known articles ever to appear in *Esquire* magazine, 'Latins Are Lousy Lovers', so it was something to take note of. 'To my mind, the most egregious example is probably Katharine Hepburn, to whom everyone now refers as a great actress, incomparable and sacrosanct, with at least one writer going overboard as to call her "our greatest living actress". This is twaddle. A personality? Yes. An actress? No. When she was awarded the Oscar for best actress in 1967 and again in 1968, I figured it must have been for longevity.'

There were other people who thought differently about her. She was, it seemed, all set to play Rose Kennedy in an ABC TV mini-series about the matriarch of what was still considered to be America's most interesting political family. But then, in December 1982, she was involved in a serious car crash. Her vehicle skidded out of control on a snowy, icy Connecticut road and practically cost her a foot. As it was, an ankle was broken and for the best part of 1983 she was on crutches. Her devoted friend Phyllis broke a wrist. But she was still expected to answer every time Kate interrupted the quiet dignity of the clinic with the shout, 'Phyllis!'

Only a month earlier, Kate had gone back to New York for treatment to her shoulder injury. Although once the plaster cast was removed, she could resume swimming, it was hard for her to realise that at seventy-four she wasn't able to get straight back to work. Worse than that, four months after the accident, she wasn't well enough to attend the funeral of George Cukor. She had long given up the house she and Spencer shared on his estate, but she still felt very close to him. Now another link in the chain with the past was broken.

She was asked her own feelings on death. 'It's the big sleep,' she said. And she didn't fear it. 'One shouldn't waste time thinking about things one cannot change,' she said.

Meanwhile, she still liked to be busy – although she has said, 'I find time I can be lonely a blessing.' Which still strikes a lot of people as very strange for a woman who for half a century has been a public figure. On television, she told Morley Safer: 'I'm like one of those long-distance runners who just keeps a-goin'. And they think, "Well, she's not bad. But she's been runnin' for a hell of a long time!"'

And when she could run a bit at home, polishing the furniture or scrubbing the floors – despite Phyllis's protestations – she was happiest of all. That was one of the pleasures of which she was robbed by her accident.

She is a great believer in women knowing their place. Now that may sound as though she is betraying all that she and her mother had once stood for. Not at all, she says. Simply that it's ridiculous to compete in a man's world on a man's terms. She has never forgotten the woman electrician working on a film set who couldn't manage to lift some of the heavy equipment. 'Now, don't you feel like an ass?' she asked her. 'Yes,' said the woman, 'I do.'

No one has ever dared call Katharine Hepburn that. But she is not satisfied. 'When I look back on what I was given by way of inheritance – the milieu into which I was born with wildly brilliant parents, I can only say I should have done fifty times more than I have done.' But she also said once, 'It drives me crazy to be mediocre. Just drives me insane. And I'm willing to do anything to try to be really good. I'm very aware when I'm good and I like to be very, very good. I think perfection is the only standard for people whatever they are doing.

'The older you get, the more intelligent you get, so the more aware you are of where you're rotten. Life kills us all one by one. But until it does, you crawl along one way or another.'

Everybody, she said, had to realise that life was going to be difficult. 'Dreadful things are going to happen. What you do is move along. Get on and be tough. Not in the sense of being mean to others, but tough with yourself and make a deadly effort not to be defeated.'

She had done her best to remind herself of that philosophy. On the fireplace of her New England home is the inscription, 'Listen to the song of life.' She has been listening to it for nearly seventy-five years. But she says, 'When I close the book, I'll never think I've been an actress.' Others, of course, will.

[237]

And she has gone on to prove it. In late 1983, she was doing so again – in *The Ultimate Solution of Grace Quigley* – a film she was making with Nick Nolte. It was a black comedy – but nothing in the script matched her reaction to his late arrival on the set one day. Burt Lancaster, Peter O'Toole and a host of others could have told him what to expect.

'I hear you've been drunk in every gutter in town,' she told him. To which Nolte responded, 'She's just a cranky old broad who's a lot of fun.'

There could be a reason for that. Spencer Tracy used to tell her, 'Whatever you do, kid, always serve it with a little dressing.' But then he also, in a broad New York accent in the film *Pat and Mike*, said, 'Not much meat on her, but what there is . . . is choice.'

That's Katharine Hepburn – choice. And with a little dressing.

Filmography

A BILL OF DIVORCEMENT (RKO) 1932
With John Barrymore, Billie Burke and David Manners. Produced by David O. Selznick. Directed by George Cukor

CHRISTOPHER STRONG (RKO) 1933
With Colin Clive, Billie Burke and Helen Chandler. Produced by Pandro S. Berman. Directed by Dorothy Arzner

MORNING GLORY(RKO) 1933 (Her first Oscar winner)
With Doublas Fairbanks, Jnr, Adolphe Menjou, Mary Duncan and C. Aubrey Smith. Produced by Pandro S. Berman. Directed by Lowell Sherman.

LITTLE WOMEN (RKO) 1933
With Paul Lukas, Joan Bennett, Edna May Oliver, Douglass Montgomery. Produced by Kenneth MacGowan. Directed by George Cukor.

SPITFIRE (RKO) 1934
With Robert Young, Ralph Bellamy, and Martha Sleeper. Produced by Pandro S. Berman. Directed by John Cromwell

BREAK OF HEARTS (RKO) 1935
With Charles Boyer, Jean Hersholt and John Beal. Produced by Pandro S. Berman. Directed by John Cromwell.

THE LITTLE MINISTER (RKO) 1935
With John Beal, Alan Hale, Donald Crisp. Produced by Pandro S. Berman. Directed by Richard Wallace

ALICE ADAMS (RKO) 1935 (Oscar nomination)
With Fred MacMurray, Evelyn Venable, Fred Stone. Produced by
Pandro S. Berman. Directed by George Stevens

SYLVIA SCARLETT (RKO) 1935
With Cary Grant, Edmund Gwenn, Brian Aherne. Produced by
Pandro S. Berman. Directed by George Cukor

MARY OF SCOTLAND (RKO) 1936
With Fredric March, Donald Crisp, Florence Eldridge. Produced by
Pandro S. Berman. Directed by John Ford

A WOMAN REBELS (RKO) 1936
With Herbert Marshall, Elizabeth Allan, Donald Crisp. Produced by
Pandro S. Berman. Directed by Mark Sandrich

QUALITY STREET (RKO) 1937
With Franchot Tone, Fay Bainter, Eric Blore. Produced by Pandro S.
Berman. Directed by George Stevens

STAGE DOOR (RKO) 1937
With Ginger Rogers, Eve Arden, Adolphe Menjou, Lucille Ball,
Andrea Leeds. Produced by Pandro S. Berman. Directed by Gregory
La Cava

BRINGING UP BABY (RKO) 1938
With Cary Grant, May Robson, Charles Ruggles. Produced and
directed by Howard Hawks

HOLIDAY (Columbia) 1938
With Cary Grant, Doris Nolan, Edward Everett Horton. Produced by
Everett Riskin. Directed by George Cukor

THE PHILADELPHIA STORY (MGM) 1940 (Oscar nomination)
With Cary Grant, James Stewart, Roland Young, Ruth Hussey.
Produced by Joseph L. Mankiewicz. Directed by George Cukor

WOMAN OF THE YEAR (MGM) 1942)
(The first Tracy–Hepburn picture. Oscar nomination)
With Spencer Tracy, Fay Bainter, William Bendix. Produced by
Joseph L. Mankiewicz. Directed by George Stevens

KEEPER OF THE FLAME (MGM) 1942
With Spencer Tracy, Richard Whorf, Stephen McNally. Produced by
Victor Saville. Directed by George Cukor

STAGE DOOR CANTEEN (Sol Lesser) 1943
One of dozens of stars doing their bit for the war effort – others
included Harpo Marx, Yehudi Menuhin, Merle Oberon, Johnny
Weismuller etc. Produced by Barnett Briskin. Directed by Frank
Borzage

DRAGON SEED (MGM) 1944
With Walter Huston, Aline MacMahan, Akim Tamiroff. Produced by
Pandro S. Berman. Directed by Jack Conway and Harold S. Bucquet

WITHOUT LOVE (MGM) 1945
With Spencer Tracy, Keenan Wynn, Lucille Ball, Patricia Morrison.
Produced by Lawrence Weingarten. Directed by Harold S. Bucquet

UNDERCURRENT (MGM) 1946
With Robert Taylor, Robert Mitchum, Marjorie Main, Edmund Gwenn.
Produced by Pandro S. Berman. Directed by Vincente Minnelli

SEA OF GRASS (MGM) 1947
With Spencer Tracy, Melvyn Douglas, Robert Walker, Ruth Nelson.
Produced by Pandro S. Berman. Directed by Elia Kazan

SONG OF LOVE (MGM) 1947
With Paul Henreid, Robert Walker, Henry Daniell, Leo G. Carroll.
Produced and directed by Clarence Brown.

STATE OF THE UNION (FRANK CAPRA – MGM) 1948
With Spencer Tracy, Adolphe Menjou, Van Johnson, Lewis Stone.
Produced and directed by Frank Capra

ADAM'S RIB (MGM) 1949
With Spencer Tracy, David Wayne, Tom Ewell, Judy Holliday.
Produced by Lawrence Weingarten. Directed by George Cukor

THE AFRICAN QUEEN (IDF–Romulus) 1951 (Oscar nomination)
With Humphrey Bogart, Robert Morley, Peter Bull. Produced by Sam
Spiegel. Directed by John Huston

PAT AND MIKE (MGM) 1952
With Spencer Tracy, Aldo Ray, Jim Backus. Produced by Lawrence
Weingarten. Directed by George Cukor

SUMMERTIME (SUMMER MADNESS in Britain) (Alexander Korda)
1955 (Oscar nomination)
With Rossano Brazzi, Isa Miranda, Darren McGavin, Andre Morell.
Produced by Alexander Korda. Directed by David Lean

THE RAINMAKER (Paramount and Hal B. Wallis) 1956 (Oscar
nomination)
With Burt Lancaster, Wendell Corey, Lloyd Bridges. Produced by
Paul Nathan. Directed by Joseph Anthony

THE IRON PETTICOAT (Remus–Harry Saltzman) 1956
With Bob Hope, James Robertson Justice, Robert Helpmann, David
Kossoff. Produced by Betty E. Box. Directed by Ralph Thomas

DESK SET (HIS OTHER WOMAN in Britain) (TCF) 1957
With Spencer Tracy, Joan Blondell, Gig Young. Produced by Henry
Ephron. Directed by Walter Lang

SUDDENLY LAST SUMMER (Columbia/Horizon) 1959 (Oscar
nomination)
With Elizabeth Taylor, Montgomery Clift, Albert Decker. Produced
by Sam Spiegel. Directed by Joseph L. Mankiewicz

LONG DAY'S JOURNEY INTO NIGHT (Ely Landau) 1962
With Sir Ralph Richardson, Jason Robards Jnr, Dean Stockwell.
Produced by Ely Landau. Directed by Sidney Lumet

GUESS WHO'S COMING TO DINNER (Columbia/Stanley Kramer)
1967
(Oscar winner. The last Tracy–Hepburn picture).
With Spencer Tracy, Katharine Houghton, Sidney Poitier. Produced
and directed by Stanley Kramer

THE LION IN WINTER (Avco Embassy) 1968 (Oscar winner)
With Peter O'Toole, Jane Merrow, Anthony Hopkins, Nigel Stock.
Produced by Martin Poll. Directed by Anthony Harvey

[242]

THE MADWOMAN OF CHAILLOT (Warner Brothers/Common-wealth United) 1969
With Danny Kaye, Yul Brynner, Charles Boyer, Edith Evans, Claude Dauphin, Paul Henreid. Produced by Ely Landau. Directed by John Huston and Bryan Forbes

THE TROJAN WOMAN (Josef Shaftel) 1971
With Vanessa Redgrave, Genevieve Bujold, Irene Papas. Produced (with Anis Nohra) and directed by Michael Cacoyannis

A DELICATE BALANCE (American Express/Ely Landau/Cinevision) 1975
With Paul Scofield, Lee Remick, Betsy Blair, Kate Reid. Produced by Ely Landau and Neil Hartley. Directed by Tony Richardson

THE GLASS MENAGERIE (Talent Associates/Norton Simon) 1973 (Her TV debut)
With Sam Waterson, Joanna Miles, Michael Moriarty. Produced by David Susskind. Directed by Anthony Harvey

ROOSTER COGBURN (Universal) 1975
With John Wayne, Anthony Zerbe, Richard Jordan. Produced by Paul Nathan for Hal B. Wallis. Directed by Stuart Millar

LOVE AMONG THE RUINS (ABC) 1975 (Emmy winner)
With Laurence Olivier, Colin Blakely, Leigh Lawson. Produced by Allan Davis. Directed by George Cukor

THE CORN IS GREEN (Warner TV film) 1978
With Patricia Hayes, Ian Saynor, Toyah Wilcox. Produced by Neil Hartley. Directed by George Cukor

OLLY OLLY OXEN FREE (Rico-Lion) 1978
With Kevin McKenzie, Dennis Dimster, Peter Kilman. Produced and directed by Richard A. Colla

ON GOLDEN POND (ITC/IPC) 1981 (Oscar winner)
With Henry Fonda, Jane Fonda, Dabney Colman, Doug McKeon. Produced by Bruce Gilbert. Directed by Mark Rydell

Plays
THE CZARINA 1927
THE BIG POND 1927
DEATH TAKES A HOLIDAY 1928
THE MAN WHO CAME BACK 1928
A MONTH IN THE COUNTRY 1928
THE ADMIRABLE CRICHTON 1928
ART AND MRS BOTTLE 1929
A ROMANTIC YOUNG LADY 1929
THE MALE ANIMAL 1930
THE WARRIOR'S HUSBAND 1931
THE LAKE 1934
JANE EYRE 1937
WITHOUT LOVE 1942
AS YOU LIKE IT 1951
THE MILLIONAIRESS 1952 (London)
MEASURE FOR MEASURE 1955 (Australia)
THE TAMING OF THE SHREW 1955 (Australia)
THE MERCHANT OF VENICE 1955 (Australia)
THE MERCHANT OF VENICE 1957 (Stratford, Connecticut)
MUCH ADO ABOUT NOTHING 1957
TWELFTH NIGHT 1960
ANTONY AND CLEOPATRA 1960
COCO 1970
A MATTER OF GRAVITY 1976
WEST SIDE WALTZ 1981

Index

[245]

[249]

[250]